USING HISTORY

USING HISTORY

JEREMY BLACK

A MEMBER OF THE HODDER HEADLINE GROUP

First published in Great Britain in 2005 by
Hodder Education, a member of the Hodder Headline Group,
338 Euston Road, London NW1 3BH

www.hoddereducation.com

Distributed in the United States of America by
Oxford University Press Inc.
198 Madison Avenue, New York, NY10016

Hodder Headline's policy is to use papers that are natural, renewable and
recyclable products and made from wood grown in sustainable forests.
The logging and manufacturing processes are expected to conform to the
environmental regulations of the country of origin.

The advice and information in this book are believed to be true and
accurate at the date of going to press, but neither the author nor the publisher
can accept any legal responsibility or liability for any errors or omissions.

British Library Cataloguing in Publication Data
A catalogue record for this book is available from the British Library

Library of Congress Cataloging-in-Publication Data
A catalog record for this book is available from the Library of Congress

ISBN-10: 0-340-88893-8
ISBN-13: 978-0-340-88893-3

1 2 3 4 5 6 7 8 9 10

Typeset in 10/12 New Baskerville by Servis Filmsetting Ltd, Manchester
Printed and bound in Great Britain by the Bath Press Ltd, Bath

What do you think about this book? Or any other Hodder
Education title? Please send your comments to the feedback
section on www.hoddereducation.com.

For Don Yerxa

With thanks for his encouragement

Contents

Preface

This is a book about the uses that are made of history in the public domain, and the focus is deliberately not on academic historiography. My starting point is the view that there are essentially two types of history – history as questions and history as answers – and that many academics tend to focus on the former and underplay the role of the latter, despite the fact that it is particularly important to the public use of history. Instead, I wish to emphasize that history is important for the uses to which it is put outside the academy as well as in it. Two underlying themes are, first, the way governments, leaders and societies use history and, second, the gap between how professional academics view history and, on the other hand, broader public attitudes toward the past, with a largely self-referential academic culture frequently having little to do with a popular interest in history that often ties into current preoccupations.

In thinking about and writing this book I have benefited from the opportunity to read and speak to many other scholars, but also, valuably, to travel widely and to discuss the topic with many non-academics. In particular, a visit to Estonia, Latvia and Lithuania in 1994, and a lecture trip to Australia, New Zealand and China in 2004 were especially fruitful. To listen to debate about what should be displayed in the National Museum of Australia, and to consider the juxtaposition on King George Terrace in front of Old Parliament House in Canberra between official remembrance, such as the statue of George V, and the Aborigine 'Embassy', a prominent show of Aborigine anger and rejection of the Australian state, is to be made sharply aware of the controversial nature of the past in a country addressing the role of 'black armband' history.

I also learned much from teaching the MA course on Historical Explanation and Interpretation at Exeter. The comments of four readers on the synopsis and of three readers on the final text proved most helpful, and Michael Strang, the commissioning editor, has proved an important support. Barbara Massam proved an exemplary copy-editor and Susan Dunsmore helped greatly in the checking of the proofs. I have benefited from the comments of Kristofer Allerfeldt,

Paul Fideler, Bill Gibson, Will Hay, Peter Hoffenberg, Rana Mitter, Nick Smart and Don Yerxa on an earlier draft. Simon Barton, Pradeep Barua, Oliver Baudert, Michael Bennett, Richard Butterwick, James Chapman, John Gascoigne, Robert Gildea, David Graff, Bob Higham, Harald Kleinschmidt, Wayne Lee, Stewart Lone, James Mark, Josh Stein and Martin Thomas provided advice on particular points. None is responsible for any errors in what follows. I owe an especial debt to the friendship and encouragement of Don Yerxa, a fine scholar, good company, and a valued friend. His major role as co-editor of the newsletter *Historically Speaking* is an important contribution to the discipline.

1

Introduction

To travel round the world is to be reminded of the very public presence of history, of the past as issue and identity, and yet that presence is sometimes underrated in the academic and pedagogic writing on history as a subject. Works on historiography and historical method focus instead on a standard cast of writers and topics, mainly those of the USA and Western Europe. This cast has been expanded in recent years, not least (although not only) by those embracing postmodernism, an approach and subject, however, that leave most non-academics (and indeed some of them) confused or uninterested. Furthermore, whether the focus is on traditional or on novel perspectives, the general (but not invariable) emphasis remains that of history as seen in, and from, the USA and Western Europe, despite the fact that since 1945 over 120 new states have been created, each of which has defined a new public usage of history.[1]

In the West, the gap between academic and public history, symbolized by the differing responses to the postmodernist perspective, tells us something about the academic profession, not least its focus, and its concern about itself both as audience and as setter of goals and standards. The gap between academe and public history, defined as the use of history by states and civil society, also reflects a benign characteristic of the profession: in particular, on the one hand, the contrast between the questioning ethos and methods that are central to the modern notion of scholarship, and, on the other, a public use of history in which the emphasis is rather on answers, with public myths providing ways to make sense of the past.

At one level, this is a gross oversimplification, not least because in both teaching and research academics also seek to offer answers, while those scholars who see history 'as the construction of a usable past' to help offer prescriptive strategies for the present[2] are not totally removed from the use of the past by politicians. Nevertheless, a cultural distinction can be noted between the humane scepticism that is seen as normative across much of the profession as goal and/or method, with a judicious definition of terms and with answers arising after careful questioning, and the more didactic justification and simple approach that can be seen in the public use of history, including by historians. This public use of history focuses on history as answers and as assertion, and it is the subject of this book. There is an emphasis on how state action has played a critical role in shaping group identities, power relationships and political legitimation. If 'using' and 'confronting' the past therefore serve as the metaphors that best characterize the approach to history in this book, it is also important to note that 'learning from the past', often presented as the goal of public history, can have a positive aspect. This in part reflects the ways in which historians seek to stake out a more independent role as a source of 'lessons' that may cut across the prevailing fault-lines of politics and offer something genuinely fresh.

In the space available – and the book has been deliberately kept short in order to encourage students to read it,[3] and to conform to the requirements of the publisher – only so much can be covered. Furthermore, it is certainly impossible for one individual to address the issue as fully as is required on the global scale, but the main themes are clearly outlined. Rather than seeing academics as the drivers of historical assessments, the central claim is that changes in the public usage of history are crucial to the general understanding of the past, and that these developments stem largely from current political shifts and pressures. This is a consequence of the extent to which the role of public history goes beyond individual interest and fulfilment, or the quest for knowledge. Instead, issues of national identity are centrally involved.

In turn, the understanding of this public usage of history in large part is a product of broader patterns of social experience, such as shifts in collective memory, and of social change, for example the rise of literacy. This reflects the extent to which the public at issue is both official and unofficial. The latter was referred to in the preface to the commercially-successful humorous account of English history *1066 and All That* (1930), in which the authors, Walter Sellar and Julian Yeatman, noted the range of the circles in which ideas of history circulated, while in the book mocking received wisdom, not least with their puns and ironic complacency:

> This is the only Memorable History of England, because all the History that you can remember is in this book, which is the result of years of research in golf-clubs, gun-rooms, green-rooms, etc. . . . The Editors . . . take this opportunity of acknowledging their inestimable debt to the

mass of educated men and women of their race whose historical intuitions and opinions this work enshrines.

History, indeed, is remembered, and thus recreated, in many unofficial forums, and the social span of Sellar and Yeatman's list needs to be greatly expanded.

Historians themselves are not separate from the impact of political changes on the understanding of history. This was made abundantly clear in China in the last third of the twentieth century, a period that was a rollercoaster ride for intellectuals. Historians were attacked from 1966 in the Cultural Revolution for being insufficiently committed to Maoist doctrine and, for example, a major scholar Wu Han, then described as a traitor, died in prison in 1969. Chinese historians were treated more gently from 1979, as the reaction against Maoism gathered pace, and there was then an active search for cooperation with Western scholarship. The repression that followed the crushing of pro-reform demonstrations in 1989 affected historical expression, however, with a revived emphasis on the Marxist approach, but that abated as China increasingly entered into the Western-dominated international order from the 1990s, and this remains the case at present and for the foreseeable future. Nevertheless, the interests of the state remain very important in the Chinese conception and expression of history and in 2004 a book on the anti-intellectual 'Anti-Rightist' campaign of 1957–8 was banned by the Communist Party's Propaganda Department.

Western academics are also directly affected by the historical process. Over the last century, conscription ensured that many served in the armed forces or in the war effort and this was a powerful direction of their lives at the behest of the state. In the Second World War, many British historians served in branches of the Intelligence services. Furthermore, the ideological conflicts of the century involved and affected intellectuals such as historians. As a result in particular of virulent Nazi anti-Semitism in the 1930s and early 1940s, this was especially true of Jewish historians. Many, for example the influential French *Annales* scholar Marc Bloch, were killed: Bloch, a patriot who joined the French Resistance to German occupation, was captured and shot by the Germans.[4] Other Jews who were already historians, such as Ernst Kantorowicz, or who subsequently became so, for example Geoffrey Elton, fled from areas under Nazi control. The intellectual legacy of this flight was a profound one, as these refugees helped in particular to strengthen and colour Anglo-American historical scholarship.[5] The widespread impact of the period on historians and historical research was also particularly harsh in occupied countries. The Germans slaughtered much of the Polish intelligentsia, but even in conquered states that were treated less brutally there was still hardship and disruption. In Belgium and the Netherlands institutions closed included Leiden University and the Free University in Brussels, while academic historians imprisoned for resistance included Johan Huizinga and Léon Halkin. Conversely, the historian H.J. Elias, who had been the head of the collaborationist Vlaamsch National Verbond in Belgium, was sentenced to death in 1946, although subsequently granted clemency.

It was not only Jews and Europeans who felt it vital or expedient to leave their native countries. As an undergraduate at Cambridge in the 1970s, I heard lectures not only by Elton but also by Walter Ullmann, a Catholic who had left Austria in 1938 because of his opposition to the Nazi takeover, and by Moses Finley, a left-wing American classicist dismissed from Rutgers University for political reasons in 1952 who had moved to England in 1954. The persecution of historians continues in some countries. In 2004, Uladzimier Mikhniuk was prevented from taking up the post of director of the Institute of History of the Belarus Academy of Sciences to which he had been appointed because he clashed with the politicized control over academic affairs exercised by the Higher Attestation Commission, and he died suddenly soon after.

In more peaceful contexts, many historians feel it appropriate to take a public role in politics not least through acting, or seeking to act, as a collective memory. In the USA in 1998, 'Historians in Defense of the Constitution' took a full-page signed advertisement in the *New York Times* of 30 October to proclaim that

> As historians as well as citizens, we deplore the present drive to impeach the President [Bill Clinton]. We believe that this drive, if successful, will have the most serious implications for our constitutional order.
>
> Under our Constitution, impeachment of the President is a grave and momentous step. The Framers [of the Constitution] explicitly reserved that step for high crimes and misdemeanors in the exercise of executive power. Impeachment for anything else would, according to James Madison [one of the Founding Fathers], leave the President to serve 'during pleasure of the Senate,' thereby mangling the system of checks and balances that is our chief safeguard against abuses of public power.
>
> Although we do not condone President Clinton's private behavior or his subsequent attempts to deceive, the current charges against him depart from what the Framers saw as grounds for impeachment. The vote of the House of Representatives to conduct an open-ended inquiry creates a novel, all-purpose search for any offense by which to remove a President from office.
>
> The theory of impeachment underlying these efforts is unprecedented

in our history. The new processes are extremely ominous for the future
of our political institutions. If carried forward, they will leave the
Presidency permanently disfigured and diminished, at the mercy as never
before of the caprices of any Congress. The Presidency, historically the
center of leadership during our great national ordeals, will be crippled in
meeting the inevitable challenges of the future.

We face a choice between preserving or undermining our Constitution.
Do we want to establish a precedent for the future harassment of
Presidents and to tie up our government with a protracted national
agony of search and accusation? Or do we want to protect the
Constitution and get back to the public business?

We urge you, whether you are a Republican, a Democrat, or an
Independent, to oppose the dangerous new theory of impeachment, and
to demand the restoration of the normal operations of our federal
government.

The attempt to impeach President Clinton also prompted historical references to earlier cases of impeachment in the USA (Andrew Johnson) and abroad (Warren Hastings), underlining the links between law, history and politics. The full-page advertisement in the *New York Times*, which was seen at the time as a partisan move rather than as expressing the wisdom of the historical profession, was part of a process in which liberal opinions were advocated by groups of prominent American historians. Thus, in 1982, the American Historical Association (AHA) passed a resolution criticizing President Ronald Reagan's rearmament policy and, instead, pressed the case for a nuclear freeze. The expression of such opinions alienated some historians who left the AHA and helped lead in reaction to the formation of The Historical Society (see p. 126). A leading member of the latter, Marc Trachtenberg, used the nuclear freeze issue to argue 'Even more ludicrous was the very idea of a professional organization adopting a particular historical interpretation by majority vote, and doing so for obvious political reasons.'[6]

Across the world, public history, in the sense of the public use of history, has itself been a factor in accounting for historical developments: the past serves as a point of reference, helping not only as an apparent explanation of events but also as a way to frame policies. Thus, in Britain, history informed debate during the Crimean War with Russia (1854–6), while the appeasement of the dictators, particularly Hitler, by Britain and France in the 1930s served subsequently for policymakers as a way to explain crises and was used as a spur and call to action, especially during the Suez Crisis of 1956 and in the run-up to the Iraq War of 2003.[7] President Nasser of Egypt's nationalization of the Suez Canal was treated as if the act of a Fascist dictator of the 1930s, who should not be appeased, and President Hussein of Iraq was cast in the same light in 1991 and 2003. The irony of the 'Munich lesson' was that Neville Chamberlain, the British prime minister, thought he was learning from the mistake of 1914 when a cataclysmic war had been launched as a result of the inability to negotiate the settlement of a crisis in Eastern Europe.

The range of history on offer and the 'lessons' that could be drawn indeed vary. In the early 1960s, President John F. Kennedy made reference to appeasement, but also saw the outbreak of the First World War in 1914 as a warning about how a nuclear war with the Soviet Union that was sought by neither side could still break out, in part due to a failure of communication. He read Barbara Tuchman's *The Guns of August* (1962), a Pulitzer Prize-winning account by a non-academic about 1914, and was so impressed that he gave copies to Harold Macmillan, the British prime minister, and to the American envoy in Paris.[8] President George W. Bush, Saddam's nemesis, kept a bust of Winston Churchill in his office in the White House, both inspiration and ostensible point of reference for his own campaign against Iraq. When Bush or Tony Blair, the British prime minister, offered Churchillian echoes, it was presumably not the Churchill of failure at Gallipoli (1915) and unsuccessful foreign intervention in the Russian Civil War (1919–20) that they had in mind, but rather the prophetic critic of appeasement in the 1930s.

The apparent military aspects of past lessons were abundantly presented during the build-up to the attack on Iraq in 2003, as the merits of expeditionary warfare were widely canvassed and as historians and others using historical examples took public positions. Thus, in *The Times* of 29 July 2002, retired British Field Marshal Lord Bramall drew prescient attention to the contrast between achieving military objectives and securing outcomes, citing:

> [a] remark by a notably 'hawkish' General Gerald Templar who when, during the Suez crisis [1956], Britain was planning a massive invasion of Egypt through Alexandria, said something to the effect of: 'Of course we can get to Cairo but what I want to know is, what the bloody hell do we do when we get there?'.

The appeasement of the 1930s was a key issue in locating the public debate, being extensively used by supporters of action against Iraq in order to justify the policy. In turn, critics had to contest the analogy. In a letter in the *Daily Telegraph* on 29 January 2003, the historian Correlli Barnett, who opposed the invasion of Iraq, included the following:

> I am sorry that Sir John Keegan joined those who rubbish as an
> 'appeaser' anyone who believes that an American-led war on Iraq would
> be unjustified and potentially disastrous in its wider political conse-
> quences . . . I am on record as a harsh critic of [Neville] Chamberlain's
> attempt to 'appease' Hitler in the 1930s and as a convinced supporter of
> the campaign to re-take the Falkland Islands [in 1982].

The same issue contained a letter from Nigel Nicolson criticizing Keegan's facile analogy and declaring 'the true comparison is with the Suez crisis of 1956 and the Cold War'.

In the run-up to the war with Iraq in 2003, ahistorical (inappropri-ate) comparisons were indeed offered with alacrity by public figures and media pundits: history served as a box from which words and images could be pulled for citation. The direct applicability of past examples, however, is unclear. For instance, in 1798 the uprising in Cairo against the policies of the French occupying force was quickly suppressed by the ruthless use of artillery, as was the uprising against the French in Damascus in 1926, but the relevance of either to American policy in Baghdad in 2003–5 was uncertain. This was because, to be understood, each instance needs to be considered in its context, which makes comparison difficult. Furthermore, although the use of 'lessons from the past' in 2003, in the shape of both comment pieces and correspondence, was extensive, as it had also been over American-led intervention in Afghanistan in 2001, it is far from clear that it had any influence on policy in either the USA or Britain and, instead, the indications are that there was no such influ-ence.

Another aspect of the public use of history is related to the process described as the invention of tradition. At present, there is a scholarly emphasis on the extent to which 'all communities are to some extent imaginary' and, more particularly, on the definition of the nation as 'an imagined political community', in other words, one invented thanks to a shared set of beliefs.[9] This has proved a profitable way to examine the historical consciousness of particular groups and nations, and is an important way to consider the topic of public history. States, in this approach, were created as political entities, this creation owed much to the formulation and dissemination of new images, and pres-entations of history were important to this process.[10] Identities and images, however, were qualified by the multiplicity of views that circu-lated: political communities are the product of more than one imagi-nation. As a result, those propounding particular views of the nation and its identity sought to offer a distinctive national history that culmi-nated in, and thus supported, these views and not those of their rivals.

The definition and depiction of public history were aspects of power and, in part, means to gain it.

The invention of tradition approach appears to have been politically influential, at least in Britain with the Blair government that took power in 1997. Many of its policies reflected a sense that the past could, indeed should, be readily discarded, and that the future could be easily shaped without reference to historical continuity, that indeed the latter was anachronistic and the product of past invention. This was seen, for example, with constitutional changes to the House of Lords and to the governance of Scotland and Wales, and a rejection of the past was strongly asserted in support of attempts to lessen sectarian divisions in Northern Ireland. 'New Labour' sought to 'repackage' national identity with soundbites such as 'New Britain' and 'A Young Country'. As David Willetts, a Conservative MP, pointed out in 2004, the Blair government had drawn on the ideas of a number of historians who emphasized the extent to which nations were imagined communities. He named Linda Colley, David Cannadine, Eric Hobsbawn and Perry Anderson.[11] A similar sense of national malleability is displayed by proponents of greater integration within the European Union.

The public usage of history is a matter not only of the role of the state but also of popular history, the use of history by civil society. The two can come together, but can also be divergent, indicating the danger of defining public history, i.e. non-academic history, in a rigid fashion. Furthermore, aside from variations in the public usage of history around the world, there also have been important chronological shifts, and these will be discussed during the book, especially in Chapter 4. Public history must include state-sponsored activity, such as school curricula and textbooks, museums and heritage, all of which offer different accounts of history[12] and affect popular awareness of the past. 'Heritage' highlights the problem of definition, as what is understood by the term varies around the world. The state's role in funding means that 'heritage' generally reflects an establishment view, but the extent to which this is popular is far from constant.[13] Heritage as both concept and industry has been criticized, as in Bill Woodrow's sculpture *English Heritage – Humpty Fucking Dumpty* (1987), and is often castigated on the left as misleading, snobbish and/or nostalgic, although the popularity of this critique appears to be limited.

The intimate but varied relationship between public history, politics and heritage helps explain why the first frequently has a close relationship with myth-making. It is important, however, also to do justice to those ventures in public history dedicated to undoing the effects of myth. The various Truth and Reconciliation Commissions, for example in Chile and South Africa, are crucial here. In South Africa, where such a process has been important, the net effect from the 1990s has been to respond to the end of the white-minority apartheid regime in 1994 by creating a new public history that overturns the earlier Afrikaner nationalist version, with its emphasis not only on the minority white community but also on only a portion of it. The Afrikaner version had presented the Great Trek of the Boers (whites of Dutch descent) of the 1830s, away from British rule in Cape Colony and towards independence in the Orange Free State and the Transvaal, as a response to British duplicity, and as an exemplary founding myth. The history, like the geography, of the native Africans was ignored or minimized. Their lands had been brutally seized by the Boers, but this was justified because they were dismissed as lesser people who were unable to look after their own and whose inferior role was due to their descent from Noah's cursed son Ham.

This was a biblical view of history, an apparently divinely-sanctioned account of ethnography based on a particular moment in time, that had support from many fundamentalist Christians around the world. It was only in South Africa, however, that such a view was so clearly articulated as a public historical myth, being employed there in school textbooks, although biblical views also played a role elsewhere, for example the view of Northern Ireland's Protestants as a 'lost tribe of Israel' or the presentation of the Pilgrim Fathers in New England. Part of the apartheid mythology of South Africa, the empty land theory, created particular problems for archaeologists who were expected to interpret discoveries, such as the ruins of Great Zimbabwe – the remains of a technologically-advanced society – not as the products of Africans but as those of Arab traders or Indians. Apartheid historical views were criticized by more liberal English-speaking white South Africans and also by Marxists, especially from the 1960s, but with only limited effect until the entire debate was transformed from 1994 as black majority rule was introduced.[14]

In considering public history, it is not generally easy, or indeed helpful, to distinguish between history and memory: the public use of history is frequently a matter of collective memory and its uses. A voluminous literature has emerged in recent years on the topic of collective memory, and it is clear that collective memory is influenced by politics (and indeed by films and other aspects of national myths) and vice versa. While the stress on collective memory and oral history[15] is welcome, it represents a democratic view of the public usage of the past that is apt to underrate the importance of state action and direction. In part for this reason, the emphasis here is on the latter, rather than on collective memory. A geographical dimension is also at issue, as the role of state action and direction provides a ready approach to the subject around the world, whereas the current scholarly treatment of collective memory is more patchy.

This then is a short introduction to an area of history to which, despite an important scholarly contribution, many historians (academics and students) pay little attention but which, nevertheless, is significant. In setting out to consider the content of public history worldwide, and to analyse its modes of dissemination, the book both ranges widely over historical examples from around the world and also has contemporary relevance. The latter will not change in the future, as group identity and political validation are both generally vested in a historical perception. This is either in terms of a representation of the authority, and authorization of a presentation, of the present in terms of the past, or as a rejection of abuses and hardships really or supposedly demonstrated in both. Sometimes the two are combined, with new governments grounding their legitimacy in terms of a rejection of an unwelcome past, for example colonial rule. Whatever the process of validation, the key image is its usage of the past.

In this, the agency of usage is hidden because that would lessen the validation represented by the citation of history. This contrasts with the Western academic ethos in which the agency of scholarship (and its ethos, methods and priorities) is explicit. This difference echoes in many parts of this book, but it is important to note that the dissemination of public myths of the past, and their relationship with the present, can be seen in the West as well as elsewhere.

Several questions arise when considering the relationship between academic and public histories. First, whether an overarching narrative, a grand organizing principle, is necessary for the writing of readable history accessible to those not professionally engaged in the study of history. Second, how far is academic history at some point a reaction against public history? Issues of veracity also arise. Did rulers and politicians, and those who wrote at their behest or to influence them, consciously and deliberately say things that they knew were not true? Did they in that sense invent the past? Or is it rather that they passionately believed that what they said was true, even though their beliefs were based not on any rigorous study of sources but rather on what they had absorbed as they grew up from their parents, their families, their friends, their church, their community, their locality, and in a looser sense the world around them? The role of experience is also important. Do people who live through dramatic events feel that their experiences give them a special knowledge and understanding, and that therefore what they say when recalling them is the plain unvarnished truth? Do certain historical events and issues become public bones of contention because the events and issues with which they deal are still living concerns for those who raise them? This leads to the question whether history has to be divided between that which is immediately relevant to current public debate and policy, and that which has no such contemporary resonances. Following on from that, there are the issues of what makes a historical event or development into something that matters greatly to politicians, commentators and people generally, and what that implies for the study and understanding of historical events that do not feature in 'public history'. From the perspective of Britain, there is the question of whether there is an English 'exceptionalism' here, with fewer events in English history the stuff of current political debate in England than in, say, Ireland or Italy. This may help explain the strength and depth of scholarly empirical historical research in England over the past century, although such work cannot be divorced from its wider context.

Notes

1   See, for example, D. Cannadine (ed.), *What is History Now?* (London, 2002); P. Burke (ed.), *History and Historians in the Twentieth Century* (London, 2002); J.L. Gaddis, *The Landscape of History. How Historians Map the Past* (Oxford, 2003).

2   W. Palmer, *Engagement with the Past. The Lives and Works of the World War II Generation of Historians* (Lexington, Ky., 2001), p. 303.

3   This remark greatly irked one reviewer of the proposal but is a reflection of my experience of teaching, and of my determination to try to be practical.

4   N.Z. Davis, 'Censorship, Silence and Resistance: The *Annales* during the German Occupation of France', *Rivista di Storiografia Moderna*, 14 (1993), 161–81; C. Fink, *Mark Bloch: A Life in History* (Cambridge, 1989).

5   C. Hoffmann, 'The Contribution of German-Speaking Jewish Immigrants to British Historiography', in W.E. Mosse (ed.), *Second Chance: Two Centuries of German-Speaking Jews in the United Kingdom* (Tübingen, 1991), pp. 153–76; P. Alter (ed.), *Out of the Third Reich: Refugee Historians in Post-War Britain* (London, 1998).

6   M. Trachtenberg, 'The Origins of the Historical Society: A Personal View', *Historically Speaking*, 4 (June 2003), 48.

7   E.R. May, *'Lessons' of the Past: The Use and Misuse of History in American Foreign Policy* (Oxford, 1973); J. Record, *Making War, Thinking History: Munich, Vietnam and Presidential Uses of Force from Korea to Kosovo* (Annapolis, Md., 2002).

8   A. D'Agostino, 'The Revisionist Tradition in European Diplomatic History', *Journal of the Historical Society*, 4 (2004), 258.

9   C. Herrup, 'Introduction', *Journal of British Studies*, 31 (1992), 307.

10 E. Hobsbawm, *Nations and Nationalism since 1780: Programme, Myth, Reality* (Cambridge, 1990); M. Pittock, *The Invention of Scotland: The Stuart Myth and the Scottish Identity, 1638 to the Present* (London, 1991); M. Todorova, *Imagining the Balkans* (Oxford, 1997); G. Cubitt (ed.), *Imagining Nations* (Manchester, 1998).

11   David Willetts, presentation on 'Culture and Identity' to Agora think-tank, London, 21 October 2004. For criticism of Cannadine, Colley and 'the Left', M. Gove, 'Killing the State on the battlefield of ideas', *The Times*, 7 Nov. 2000. For a similar criticism of Israeli scholars, Y. Hazony, *The Jewish State: The Struggle for Israel's Soul* (New York, 2000).

12   P. Philipps, *History Teaching, Nationhood and the State: A Study in Education Politics* (London, 2000); D. Lindamann and K. War, *History Lessons: How Textbooks from around the World Portray U.S. History* (New York, 2004).

13   R. Hewison, *The Heritage Industry* (London, 1987); D. Lowenthal, *Possessed by the Past: The Heritage Crusade and the Spoils of History* (London, 1996); R. Foster, *The Irish Story: Telling Tales and Making It Up in Ireland* (Oxford, 2002). On the public usage of history, G. Ricuperati, 'Uso pubblico della storia. Sull'utilità e sull'abuso di un concetto banalizzato', *Rivista Storica Italiana* (2001), 703–45, and M. Vaudagna, 'Gli usi pubblici della storia', *Contemporanea*, 2 (2002), 327–64.

14   F.A. Var Jaarsveld, *The Afrikaner's Interpretation of South African History* (Cape Town, 1964); H.M. Wright, *The Burden of the Present: Liberal–Radical Controversy over Southern African History* (Cape Town, 1977); M. Hall, 'Pots and Politics: Ceramic Interpretations in South Africa', *World Archaeology*, 15 (1983), 262–73; P.J. Stickler, 'Invisible Towns: A Case Study in the Cartography of South Africa', *Geographical Journal*, 22 (1990), 329–33; S. Terreblanche, *A History of Inequality in South Africa, 1652–2002* (Pietermaritzburg, 2002), p. 3.

15   P. Thompson, *Voice of the Past: Oral History* (3rd edn, Oxford, 2000).

2

The state

The family and the state

The most immediate focus of history is the family. It comprises the prime source of historical awareness and collective memory, and not simply for family history. It is no accident that genealogical research is the fastest growing branch of historical scholarship across much of the West, leading for example to the greatest number of visits to British county record offices. Modern American and British census data are also most commonly scrutinized for this reason. In 2001, when the immigrant records of Ellis Island (the immigration handling station in New York harbour, now a museum) went online, they took 50 million hits on the first day, and when the British National Archives put the 1901 census online the pressure on the system was so intense that it crashed. To researchers in this field, one of the most important institutions is the Church of the Latter Day Saints (the Mormon Church), thanks to its International Genealogical Index, one of the most extensive and expensive historical projects of recent decades.

Such research provides a valued sense of continuity, not least in the face of disruption. In Australia, for example, there is an emphasis on tracing roots, both in the experience of immigration and in the traumatic process of familial loss and collective identity presented by participation in both world wars. This can be seen in many of the visitors to the National Archives and the Australian War Memorial, and in the exhibits they offer. A very different, and far more controversial, context for the tracing of Australian roots is that of the quest by Aboriginal children taken from their parents in order to 'improve' them by placing them in white society.

The interest in tracing roots is true even of countries where immigration generally involved a rejection of a background deemed unhelpful, if not hostile, as with the USA, and where some immigrants were convicts, as in Australia and the USA during their time as colonies. Roots can also be malleable. In his speech to the Republican National Convention in 2004, Governor Arnold Schwarzenegger of California claimed to have remembered Soviet tanks from his Austrian childhood, although there were none in the part of the country where he grew up: it was not conquered by the Soviets in 1945 and was not part of the Soviet occupation zone. The image, however, served his purpose of offering himself and others an uplifting account of his personal history as a refugee reborn in a free America. Alongside family history, interest in the vernacular architecture and manners of societies from which ancestors came, an interest that prompts television reality shows, is another aspect of this drive for strengthening or grounding an image of the past. Across the world, this interest in the family links directly to the popularity of oral history and also acts as a focus for work on local history.

The search for roots is not only characteristic of the established and successful, and not only a continuation of the age-old practice of asserting lineage, with the British television series of 2004 *Who do you think you are?* tracing the family trees of celebrities. Such a search for roots, instead, is common across society, and indeed is part of the process of assertion by minority or marginal communities and individuals. Thus, the link between African-Americans and Africa was fostered by interest in roots and pathways, most prominently by Alex Haley's popular book *Roots* (1967), although sometimes there is a lack of awareness about tensions within African society and, even more, about rival ethnic groups. In Britain in 2003, lottery money from the New Opportunities Fund funded a website that brought together archival sources on immigrant history, a step greeted by Sam Walker, director of the Black Cultural Archives, as helping to dispel the myth that black people were absent from British history. An interesting sign of changing social mores in Britain is that most people do not now seem to mind if they discover that their ancestors were unmarried parents or illegitimate, and in some cases criminal. This is very different from the traditional interest in lineage.

The dynamics and nature of collective memory within families vary, not least depending on whether the prime form of social organization is the nuclear or the extended family, but, whichever the case, it is from parents and other older family members that most people learn about themselves. They do so within a narrative pattern in which their received identity springs in large part from their role in this story. Oral historical research indicates that the relationship between the kind of memory preserved in families, and that which functions on the public or political level, varies greatly. In some societies, families tend largely to remember the births, deaths and marriages of members of the family, and if they do remember public events, they tend only to be coronations, royal marriages and such like, rather than changes of government and, still less, political policies. In these cases, the extent to which the state affects, let alone arbitrates between, these different forms of personal and collective memory varies, but it often plays little role in this memorialization. There are still, however, public events that take place independently of direct state action but which make a profound impression, at least in the short term, for example, in Britain the death of Diana, Princess of Wales in 1997. Elsewhere, for example in China, the often traumatic impact of governmental changes and policies ensures a different recollection at the level of individuals and families, as well as an attempt by the state to control the process of recollection. Abnormal and, even more, catastrophic events in the public sphere mark private memories.

More than personal and familial identity is involved at the family level. Notions and issues of collective awareness are also transmitted within the family context, and it is this context that determines the participation of most people in the groupings that help dictate communal roles: religion, ethnicity and gender assumptions. At the same time, these groupings can themselves create tensions, with familial conventions and hierarchies challenged by gender issues or by inter-ethnic unions or religious conversions. The first has been a prime topic of research by historians interested in the role of women, an expanding field of scholarship in recent decades,[1] and many have criticized families as systems of patriarchal control. The extent, however, to which the challenges to familial conventions occur varies by society and it is necessary, in particular, to be cautious about reading from the example of practices in North America and Western Europe. In addition to the role of families, it is important to note the extent to which 'community' and 'cultural' cohorts and consciousnesses challenge interest in the history of the state.

The role of the family in providing the means and content of history is underrated in standard historiographical approaches, but it emerges as a background to the attempt to shape history by the state. This is because the modern state acts as the public equivalent of the family, for example in the provision of protection, justice and, frequently, social welfare. The state does so in particular in its role as educator, a function in which, at least formally, it has largely replaced both families and communal bodies, especially religious institutions. There are societies where formal education is of limited scope, for example the war-torn Congo, or where it is under the control of other, particularly religious, bodies or where the latter play a major role, for example Pakistan. Elsewhere, however, the state is the principal educator and, as such, the main shaper of the institutional awareness of history and, therefore, an important shaper of popular views, although, in turn, these views affect the nature and content of institutional provision.

Moulding views of the past

That, however, is not the limit of the state's role, both direct and indirect. Important other functions arise from the state's role as controller, or at least overseer, of the media as well as from the state's role as the prime organizer of public symbolism. The former will be considered in the next chapter, but the latter vies with education in its importance. Whether in designating public holidays or organizing memorial celebrations, or in naming streets, squares, buildings, schools and warships after historical figures, and thus designating both public time and public space, government is important for its role in moulding and sustaining public memories and thus in shaping the recognition of sites of memory.[2] At a very different level, archaeology across the world depends greatly on state support. Governmental permission is required in order to organize digs and to move artefacts.

The emphasis on commemorative anniversaries offers contrasting exemplary viewpoints on national histories. For example, the authoritarian conservative Salazar regime in Portugal, which governed from 1932 to 1974, focused on the celebration of the foundation of Portugal as well as on great events in the age of discoveries, such as the life of Henry the Navigator, and on the restoration of Portuguese independence from rule by the King of Spain in 1640. The dramatic Monument to the Discoveries was erected in Lisbon in 1960. Israel, a democratic but embattled state, marks the calendar with a series of commemorative dates, including Independence Day, as well as memorial days for fallen soldiers and for the Holocaust, that match the contrasting, if not rival, commemoration of the Jewish religious calendar. The Israeli state thus uses the calendar to make inclusive (for Jews, but not non-Jewish Israelis) points that underline the Jewish origins of the state, but also its secular character. In Germany, the unification of East and West was marked by an annual holiday, Unity Day, although that could not be on 9 November, the date on which the Berlin Wall fell in 1989, as that had also been the date of major anti-Semitic pogroms in 1938. Instead, 3 October was chosen.

This process is not new. In England, war with Spain from 1585 to 1604 fostered national consciousness and, as popular allegiance to Protestantism grew, new national days of celebration recalling England's recent Protestant history became popular. Church bells were rung every 17 November to celebrate the accession of Elizabeth I in

1558, and thus the end of Catholic rule under her predecessor and half-sister Mary. Gunpowder Plot (or Guy Fawkes after the leading conspirator) bonfires were to follow each 5 November from 1605, marking the failure of a Catholic attempt to blow up Parliament.[3]

Dates, however, could also be contentious. These celebrations were not welcome to English Catholics as they seemed to suggest that Catholics were all disloyal. To take, in contrast, an anti-establishment commemoration which was opposed by the agencies of central government: the celebration in England during the eighteenth century of the anniversary of the restoration of the Stuart dynasty in 1660 in the person of Charles II, which had marked the end of a republican interregnum, was, correctly, seen as a call for legitimism and a second restoration: that of the exiled Stuart claimant to the throne, in this case at the expense of the Hanoverian dynasty which ruled from 1714.[4] Local celebrations could also be contentious. In Taunton, 11 May, the anniversary of the raising of the siege of 1645 during the English Civil War, seen as a great providential salvation against the Royalists, was celebrated way into the eighteenth century: sermons were preached into the 1720s and an annual celebration took place into the 1770s. Politically, they were a Dissenter radical expression of opposition to the Tory corporation.

In the modern world, alongside annual anniversaries has come the cult of the centenary, bicentenary and so on, a process driven by both state and media concerns, although with more recent anniversaries, such as those for the Second World War, it is important not to underrate popular interest. An important form of commemoration is provided by that of the dead.[5] The very costly Iran–Iraq War of 1980–8 is commemorated in Iran by the Sacred Defence Preservation Foundation, which seeks to sustain support for the Islamic Revolution and has erected a large number of war memorials across Iran. Furthermore, coffins of the dead, whose bodies continue to be unearthed near the Iraqi border, are paraded around Iran in order to provide opportunities for public displays of support.

In Australia, memorialization is different but also potent. The layout of the national capital, Canberra, focuses attention not only on Capital Hill, the site of Parliament House, but also on past heroism: the vista of Anzac Parade leading to the Australian War Memorial. Along the Parade there are a host of war memorials, creating a sense of national unity and commitment through burdens borne, and this culminates in the memorial with the emphasis on the heavy sacrifice of 102,000 lives, particularly in the two world wars but also in more recent conflicts. Under the Howard government in the early 2000s, much money was spent on redeveloping the memorial. To critics, this was of a piece with the commitment of that government to a military posture, including the contentious dispatch of forces to Iraq in 2003.

With a different level of political commitment, political purpose as well as national identification are also served by the annual celebration of the unsuccessful Warsaw rising of 1944 against German occupation. This both marks a major episode of mass heroism and suffering and also contributes powerfully to the fixing of blame that is so potent in Polish national memorialization. Alongside the odium heaped on the Nazi regime comes criticism of the Allies for not doing more to help, especially of the Soviet forces which had advanced to near Warsaw. The memorialization thus contributes to the anti-Communist, and anti-Russian, character of Polish historical consciousness, and also places an emphasis on the 'Polish' uprising of 1944, rather than that by the Polish Jews of the Warsaw ghetto the previous year.

Another annual celebration became an issue of controversy on 12 October 2004, when an effort was made by the new Socialist government to make more inclusive Spain's National Day, the day on which Columbus sighted the New World. The annual celebrations include a military parade attended by the king and the prime minister, but in 2004 they were accompanied by Angel Salamanca, a veteran of the large Fascist volunteer force sent by General Franco, the right-wing Spanish dictator, to he'p the Germans on the Eastern Front in the Second World War, and also by Luis Royo, who had fought for the Republicans against Franco's right-wing Nationalists in the Spanish Civil War (1936–9), as well as with the French forces in the Second World War (as did many other Republican exiles). The defence minister, José Bono, declared that this was seen as offering 'a symbol of peace and harmony forever'. This was rejected by some of the left, angry at the inclusion of the Fascist veteran, Gaspar Llamazares, the head of the United Left, boycotting the event, which he termed 'an injustice, a historic falsitude by seeking an equivalence between liberty and fascism'. Bono argued: 'Those resentments have to be eradicated . . . if you left out all the Spaniards you may not agree with: the [medieval] Reconquistas, the [nineteenth-century] Carlists, the Fascists . . . You wouldn't have many people left. It's all Spain.' A different form of memorialization, in the form of creating traditions, was also at issue because, in response to the 11 September 2001 terrorist attacks on New York and Washington, a party of American marines took part in the 2001, 2002 and 2003 parades (held under the conservative Aznar government), but this invitation was not extended for that in 2004, leading to considerable anger on the part of the American ambassador.

The new Socialist government elected in 2004 also proposed to challenge the Francoist memorialization in the Valley of the Fallen. After the Civil War, Franco spent two decades and about £200 million on building the basilica in which he was buried in 1975, as well as a monastery and a towering crucifix. The vast edifice, visible 30 miles away, was designed as a monument to the Nationalist dead in the Civil War, Franco declaring 'The stones that are to be erected must have the grandeur of the monuments of old, which defy time and forgetfulness.' However, some of the ex-Republicans used as forced labour for the building died, and this attracted the attention of politicians in 2004 seeking to commemorate the suffering under Franco. One senator, Jaume Bosch, pressed for 'a monument that not only remembers the dictatorship in a one-sided way, but also denounces it. For millions of Spaniards, this place continues to be an insult to our democracy.'

The naming of public spaces after historical moments and figures is an attempt to disseminate official memory, if not to assert control, and it is furthered by the commissioning of statues to define, if not dominate, such spaces. This rhetoric of public monuments is not a new process. Erected in 1843, Nelson's Column dominated much of London prior to the age of the skyscraper, serving as a secular counterpoint to St Paul's Cathedral. Hitler regarded the column as the 'symbol of British naval might and world domination', and planned to take it as war booty to his capital, Berlin. In Hawai'i in the mid-nineteenth century, a statue of Kamehameha I, the unifier of the archipelago from the 1790s to the 1810s, was produced, with the former king depicted in Roman style. This was an assertion of the legitimacy and grandeur of the Hawaiian dynasty in the face of Western pressure. After the Turkish army conquered much of Cyprus in 1974, numerous statues of Kemal Atatürk, modern Turkey's founding father, were erected in order to assert the link with Turkey. Similarly, pictures and photographs of him are much in evidence.

A sense that government ought to be involved in memorialization is apparent in democracies of varied character (as well as in autocracies). Indeed, it is increasingly the case as heritage is seen as a justifiable activity of government and an appropriate call on the national purse. To take mid-March to late May 2002, history-related bills in the US Congress sought to attract national financial support for the memorialization of aspects of nearly two centuries of American history. On 15 March 2002, the Port Chicago Naval Magazine National Memorial Study Act was introduced into the House of Representatives. It pressed for a study to ascertain whether the magazine should be a part of the National Park Service, which has proved a key way to shape American historical consciousness.[6] A Pacific coast munitions depot, the magazine, already designated a National Memorial, was the site of an explosion that caused the largest loss of life in the USA during the Second

World War. On 18 April, the Civil War Sesquicentennial Commission Act of 2002 was introduced in the Senate. Arguing that the Civil War was a 'defining experience in the development of the United States', the bill proposed a 26-member commission, including nine selected by the president 'with experience in history', to introduce and implement programmes to increase understanding of the Civil War's significance. Appropriately, the bill had sponsors from states in the former Union and the former Confederacy. On 8 and 9 May, legislation was introduced to designate Fort Presque Isle National Historic Site, and Forts Gaines and Morgan respectively as parts of the National Park Service.

On 21 May 2002, a bill introduced into the House proposed to create the 225th Anniversary of the American Revolution Commemorative Program within the National Park Service. This, understandably, was not intended to propose a Loyalist, pro-British approach: the theme was to be 'Lighting Freedom's Flame'. There was also legislation for a feasibility study to establish the Southern Campaign of the Revolution Heritage Area in South Carolina. The following month, in hearings on a bill to approve a study to identify sites and resources to commemorate and interpret the Cold War, the chairman of the Silent Heroes of the Cold War National Memorial Committee, Steve Ririe, pressed for a national memorial and museum to 'honour all those who lost their lives during the longest and most dangerous conflict our country ever faced'. The sensitivity of memorialization in the USA led in the 1990s and 2000s to major efforts to remove Confederate symbols from the public sphere with bitter debates over state flags and memorials.

At a less heated level, and one intended in accordance with the values of the age to emphasize the role of ordinary individuals, in 2004 the British Royal Mail marked the 150th anniversary of Britain's participation in the Crimean War by printing stamps featuring ordinary soldiers, their images deriving from photographs taken in 1856 on their return from the war. The Royal Mail publicity claimed 'Thanks to these six men, the memory of the 22,182 who died in the Crimea will live forever . . . There are a number of different ways you can preserve a part of our nation's history', the 'you' and 'our' underlining the role of the individual in sustaining the national heritage, in this case by purchasing particular stamps. In 1999, the Royal Mail celebrated the Millennium with 48 stamps grouped in 'Tales': Inventors', Travellers', Patients', Settlers', Workers', Entertainers', Citizens', Scientists', Farmers', Soldiers', Christians' and Artists'. As was pointed out by critics, this meant that the traditional pantheon of past rulers and military commanders was not commemorated.

If an emphasis on the role of government and politicians in moulding public views of the past can suggest a somewhat passive stance on the part of the population, that would be misleading because, in practice, a range of factors, especially religion and ethnicity, create different demands for memorialization. Furthermore, these demands frequently compete, and are sometimes mutually hostile, with public myth shaped by this interaction. Thus, alongside the theory and practice of often authoritarian direction, the role of the state frequently emerges most prominently as the arbiter between very different popular views. This process became more prominent during the twentieth century as societies became more educated and articulate, not least with far higher rates of literacy than hitherto. Moreover, especially from 1945 and, in the case of the Soviet Union and Eastern Europe, 1989, democratic practices and ideas spread across the world while, within democracies, the effects of democratization have been to increase demands that the popular voice should be heard. Thus, the state acts within a context of competing voices (including, at the extreme in Eastern Europe, the resurgence of neo-fascism), ensuring that the historical consciousness government propagates can be contentious.

In serving as public arbiters, states also seek to affirm particular views of the past as authoritative. This is not simply a matter of totalitarian societies. Indeed, a good example can be seen in a major democracy, Japan. There, the brutal conduct of the military during the Second World War was actively contested subsequently in public memorialization, with nationalist commentators determined to prevent critical comment by scholars and others. The *cause célèbre* were high school textbooks dealing with Japanese conduct in China. Cases brought in the Tokyo District Court in 1965, 1967 and 1984 opposed the Japanese Ministry of Education and the historian Ienaga Saburo, whose descriptions of the Nanjing Massacre in 1937 and of biological warfare experiments in China by the Japanese army in his projected high school textbook *Shin Nihon shi* (*New History of Japan*) had attracted the attention of the ministry's censors. The ministry won cases in 1989 and 1993 but, in 1997, Ienaga narrowly won a decision from the Supreme Court.[7]

The Nanjing Massacre of 1937 was fiercely contested within Japan, with discord over both the numbers of civilians killed (the figure was in fact very large[8]) and the extent to which massacre was an integral aspect of Japanese warmaking in China. In both government and in public in Japan, there is a widespread reluctance to note what happened during the Second World War, and a determination to accept nothing that will compromise the creation of a patriotic citizenry, proud of their past. This tendency is accentuated by conservative activists. The *New History of Japan* (2001) produced by the Society for the Creation of New History Textbooks adopted a crudely apologist, if not jingoistic, account that led to formal protests from both China and South Korea, while visits by Japanese prime ministers to the Yasukuni war shrine also led to controversy.[9]

Conservative activists sought to put a favourable gloss on the Second World War. This involved emphasizing the role of Japan in challenging and gravely weakening the colonial rule of Western powers and thus, by bringing forward their demise, being on the side of progress. Such a process was presented as occurring both directly and indirectly. In the former case, it was seen in Western colonies conquered by the Japanese, such as Indonesia and Burma, in each of which Western rule, after being revived thanks to Allied success at the close of the war, had ended by 1950. It was also discerned indirectly, as in China, where Western economic and political interests were largely destroyed during the Japanese attack. Definitions, dates and nomenclature play a role in the controversy, as they also do in so many others. The conflict is not known as the Second World War in Japan: critical left-wing historians referred to the Fifteen Years War of 1931–45, beginning with the invasion of Manchuria, and conservatives to the Great East Asia War of 1937–45 that began when large-scale war with China commenced. A more neutral viewpoint refers to the Pacific War of 1941–5, although much of the rationale for the attack on the USA, Britain and the Dutch in 1941 stemmed from the intractable nature of the ongoing Japanese intervention in China.

The attempted elision, indeed suppression, of unwanted views of the past goes very far in modern Japan, but is taken much further in authoritarian societies and can indeed be an aspect of anti-societal warfare. Thus, the genocidal Nazi assault on the Jews before and during the Second World War also involved an attempt to destroy artefacts of their culture and their historical consciousness, particularly sacred books and buildings. Looking back centuries for a parallel, the prominent British Jewish scholar Cecil Roth compared the Nazis with the Spanish Inquisition, on which he finished a book in September 1937. In his preface, he wrote 'The Spanish Inquisition was until yesterday an antiquarian diversion. The events of the past few years, and above all of the past few months, have converted it into a dreadful warning.' Roth made direct comparisons between the Nazis and the Spanish Inquisition over censorship and the obsession with racial purity,[10] and followed up his criticism by publishing *The Jewish Contribution to Civilisation* (1938). The assault on the Jews was particularly vicious and comprehensive, but was not unique. In trying to make occupied societies, such as Poland and Ukraine, ductile, both Nazis and Communists sought not only to enforce their own historical consciousness but also to weaken native views and the native capacity to retain a sense of distinctive history. This process involved the killing of intellectuals, including historians, the destruction of historic buildings and the seizure and removal, or destruction, of archival holdings, each on a large scale.[11] This 'cultural cleansing', a deliberate assault on communal memory, was also seen in the Balkan conflicts of the 1990s, with the attacks on the city of Dubrovnik, the destruction of the iconic bridge at Mostar and the shelling of the National Library at Sarajevo.[12]

The consequences of authoritarianism have an important after-effect for democratic societies as they struggle to provide an account of the recent past that reduces political tension while also assuaging the grief and anger of those who suffered under the earlier regime. This was seen in Argentina from 1982, Brazil from 1985, Chile from 1990, and South Africa from 1994. The circumstances of the fall of the authoritarian regime were crucial in each case. Where, as in Brazil, such a regime was not overthrown nor subsequently discredited, it was particularly difficult to obtain closure. Indeed, in Brazil the regime gave itself an amnesty in 1979, the military who had ran the government from 1964 to 1985 never apologized, and subsequent politicians were reluctant to tackle them, instead closing access to archives that might throw light on past killings and other abuses. The opening of the archives in the 1990s led to the disclosure of contentious material that indicated that senior military figures had been responsible for torture, and then to their rapid closure.

It was not only in Japan and other formerly authoritarian regimes that public authorities in democracies found themselves in a controversial position over the presentation of history. The exhibition in Washington DC planned for 1995 by the Smithsonian Institution's National Air and Space Museum designed to centre on the *Enola Gay*, the plane that dropped the atomic bomb on Hiroshima a half-century earlier, was popularly berated as unpatriotic although, in practice, the critical script that accompanied the plane reflected the state of scholarly research. In the event, due to popular pressure, not least extensive coverage in the *Washington Post*, a belated and curtailed display was offered.[13] This dispute was related to the more general one of war guilt between the USA and Japan,[14] an issue that can be charted through changing and often controversial nuances in public memorialization, for example at the impressive USS *Arizona* Memorial dedicated at Pearl Harbor in 1962.[15] Attempts have been made to make the memorial less critical of Japan's role in beginning the war in the Pacific. As an instance of continued sensitivity, a historian writing about Japanese-Americans who fought for the Japanese has received threats as his scholarship challenges the established public view about the wartime loyalty of Hawai'i's Japanese-Americans.[16] Despite questionable American interpretations, governmental distortion of the record is far worse in Japan than in the USA, and it would be inappropriate to suggest any equivalence.

The Smithsonian continued to be a source of contention after 1995. The *Enola Gay* was displayed in the Steven F. Udvar-Hazy Center, the annexe of the National Air and Space Museum that opened at Washington Dulles International Airport on 15 December 2003. The opening day saw a protest that focused on the *Enola Gay*, with the complaint that the accompanying information did not discuss the effects of the bomb. The protesters included atomic-bomb survivors from Japan, and a container of red paint (symbolizing blood) was thrown at the plane, denting it. The complaint of the protestors accorded with the views of some historians, but the museum director, John Dailey, an ex-general, defended the Smithsonian's policy: 'we're going to present the aircraft primarily in terms of its technical capabilities and leave the interpretation as to how it was used to the visitor'. More generally, this approach makes it possible to avoid reference in displays to the emotive issues of context, but is criticized on that head by those who expect exhibits to match their sectional views, as well as by critics who argue that any failure to provide adequate contextualization makes it difficult to understand what is displayed.

The continued sensitivity of the Second World War was shown in 2004 when Italian television addressed the brutal treatment by advancing Yugoslav forces of Italian civilians in Istria in 1945. This was an episode of ethnic cleansing that had hitherto escaped the public eye, not least because the victim culture approach to the Second World War was less pronounced in Italy than in Germany (see pp. 111–12) and, thanks to the atomic bomb, Japan. In Britain, there was anger that the Heritage Lottery Fund pledged £1 million to a Women at War memorial, but refused to contribute to a Battle of Britain memorial.

Controversies over the presentation of history are most apparent in democracies. Israel is an embattled democracy in which the active role of the state in education has ensured a need to respond to bitter divisions over national identity and interests. The established account after independence in 1948 was the secular and socialist one of the Labour governments, but in 1977 the conservative Likud Party gained power and its leader, Menachem Begin, demanded that the treatment of history by the education system reflect the more conservative and religious attitudes of his party. Fresh controversy was caused by left-wing historians who argued in the 1980s that Israel had played a role, particularly through massacres, in encouraging the Arab population to flee in 1948, and thus bore a partial responsibility for the major Arab refugee problem and for the destabilization this brought to the Middle

East. This approach was anathema to the nationalist right, and led to controversy in 1991: as in Japan, a school textbook proved the crucial issue. The controversy continues.[17]

The role of the state is considered in a historical context in Chapter 4, and, for more recent decades, in the subsequent chapters. Repeatedly, the role of government and politics emerges as crucial in the presentation of history. The extent to which this can be regarded as public education, propaganda or indoctrination varies, and the analytical problems this poses are serious.

Notes

1   See, for example, *Gender and History* (1989–), the *Journal of Women's History* (1989–), and *Women's History Review* (1992–). Important books include, S. Rowbotham, *Hidden from History: 300 Years of Women's Oppression and the Fight Against It* (London, 1973); R. Bridenthal and C. Koonz (eds), *Becoming Visible: Women in European History* (Boston, 1977); S.J. Kleinberg (ed.), *Retrieving Women's History: Changing Perceptions of the Role of Women in Politics and Society* (London, 1988); D. Riley, *'Am I that Name?' Feminism and the Category of 'Women' in History* (London, 1988); B.G. Smith, *The Gender of History: Men, Women and Historical Practice* (Cambridge, Mass., 1996); R. Shoemaker and M. Vincent (eds), *Gender and History in Western Europe* (London, 1998); J.W. Scott, *Gender and the Politics of History* (2nd edn, New York, 1999); P.N. Stearns, *Gender in World History* (London, 2000); M.E. Wiesner-Hanks, *Gender in History* (Oxford, 2001); J. Alberti, *Gender and the Historian* (Harlow, 2002).

2   P. Nora (ed.), *Les Lieux de Mémoire* (7 vols, Paris, 1984–92), on which see N. Wood, 'Memory's Remains: *Les Lieux de Mémoire*', *History and Memory*, 6 (1994), 123–47.

3   D. Cressy, *Bonfires and Bells: National Memory and the Protestant Calendar in Elizabethan and Stuart England* (London, 1989).

4   P.K. Monod, *Jacobitism and the English People 1688–1788* (Cambridge, 1989).

5   G.K. Piehler, *Remembering War the American Way* (Washington, DC, 1995).

6   J. Bodnar, *Remaking America: Public Memory, Commemoration, and Patriotism in the Twentieth Century* (Princeton, NJ, 1992), pp. 169–205.

7   H. Teruhisa, *Educational Thought and Ideology in Modern Japan: State Authority and Intellectual Freedom* (Tokyo, 1988).

8   I. Chang, *The Rape of Nanking: The Forgotten Holocaust of World War II* (London, 1997); K. Honda, *The Nanjing Massacre: A Japanese Journalist Confronts Japan's National Shame* (Armonk, NY, 1999).

9   R.B. Jeans, 'Victims or Victimizers? Museums, Textbooks, and the War Debate in Contemporary Japan', *Journal of Military History*, 69 (2005), 149–95.

10 C. Roth, *The Spanish Inquisition* (New York, 1996 reprint), preface, pp. 194, 199.

11 P. Grimsted, *Trophies of War and Empire: The Archival Heritage of Ukraine, World*

War II, and the International Politics of Restitution (Cambridge, Mass., 2001), pp. 196–209.

12 R. Bevan, *The Destruction of Memory: Architecture and Cultural Warfare* (London, 2004).

13 P. Nobile (ed.), *Judgment at the Smithsonian* (New York, 1995); K. Bird and L. Lifschultz (eds), *Hiroshima's Shadow: Writings on the Denial of History and the Smithsonian Controversy* (Stony Creek, Conn., 1997); E.T. Linenthal and T. Engelhardt (eds), *History Wars: The Enola Gay and Other Battles for the American Past* (New York, 1996); R.P. Newman, *Enola Gay and the Court of History* (New York, 2004).

14 E.S. Rosenberg, *A Date Which Will Live: Pearl Harbor in American Memory* (Durham, NC, 2003).

15 E.T. Linenthal, *Sacred Ground: Americans and Their Battlefields* (Urbana, Ill., 1991), pp. 175–212.

16 J.J. Stephan, *Hawaii Under the Rising Sun: Japan's Plans for Conquest After Pearl Harbor* (Honolulu, HI, 2003).

17 B. Morris, *Righteous Victims: A History of the Zionist-Arab Conflict, 1881–2001* (New York, 2001). For a critique of these revisionists, E. Karsh, *Fabricating Israeli History: The 'New Historians'* (2nd edn, London, 2000).

3

The private sector

The chain that joins historical works, novels and films: they are the products of a society whose memory is a collective pastiche, formed as much by one component as another and in a pattern almost impossible to discern, much less control.

Neil York, *Fiction as Fact: 'The Horse Soldiers' and Popular Memory* (Kent, OH, 2001), p. 126.

The impact of the state on public history is a powerful one, but is by no means uncontested. Particular importance also attaches to the visual media, publishing, religion, and to autonomous institutional pressures. As with the role of the state, however, discussion of each should not lead to underplaying the role of familial and communal networks, nor their ability to mould the pressures to which they were subject or by which they were affected. Reference to familial and communal networks, however, can serve to underrate the role of individual choice, although a focus on the latter might, in turn, minimize the extent to which such choices are moulded by structures and by group experiences. Wherever the emphasis is placed, some individuals prove resistant to pressure to reconsider their beliefs, including their individual history. Thus, personal memory serves as one of the most conservative elements of the historical world, conservative not in the sense that it does not change, because it frequently does, but rather in that it can be consciously resistant to public (and private) direction and challenge. Personal memory can be partial and contradictory, is generally self-validating and so often repeats the memories of others that its formulaic element is clear; but, nevertheless, personal memory is asserted with vigour and conviction.

The visual media

The moulding of personal memory became more insistent in the twentieth century, as it saw hitherto unprecedented expansion in the possibilities for the distant transmission of ideas and reports, a process that was largely driven by technology and prosperity and governed by commercial considerations but in which governments also played a major role. In the early decades of the twentieth century the technology in question was a matter of radio and film, but in the second half of the century television became the prime form, followed by the development of the Internet. This was not only a matter of changes in the West. In addition, the spread of television in the developing world was such that by 1986 there were 26 million television sets in Brazil, 10.5 million in India and 6.6 million in Indonesia. Such figures, however, especially the very low per capita rates of the latter two, were put in perspective by the 195 million televisions in the USA in 1986, or by the fact that, by 1994, 99 per cent of British households had a television. Nevertheless, although the per capita rate of television ownership varied, and remained particularly low in Sub-Saharan Africa and South-East Asia, the growth of telecommunications created a very different context to the earlier situation for the spread of ideas, however much this was constrained by state licensing of television channels. Much of Third World television viewing is, or has been, a communal activity, with television sets in public buildings such as village halls, whereas in the West it tends to be much more domestic, with the exception of sports broadcasts in pubs and sports bars.

There was opposition to television from those who felt threatened. Extreme supporters of apartheid in South Africa tried to prevent the introduction of the 'devil's box', while television was banned by the Taleban regime in Afghanistan as part of the process by which Islamic fundamentalists sought to stop or limit the spread of information about Western life. Certain fundamentalist interpretations of Islam frown upon any visual representation of the human face.

Television is a medium not a message: it could as readily be used by autocratic as by democratic regimes, and is an adjunct of the state across much of the world, particularly in Russia and in the Third World. Television was also a new media through which public history was created, sustained and reflected, and through which commercial interests could seek to profit from popular interest in the past. Due in part to state interest but also, in many countries, to cultural norms, television's historical coverage is generally in support of the established national account of the past, and the British habit of criticizing this account is relatively uncommon. Public control of television can also lead to greater international sensitivity to televised accounts of the past, as with complaints from the former Yugoslavia in 2004 about Italian television coverage of atrocities against Italian civilians committed by advancing Yugoslav forces in 1945 as Istria was subject to what was later termed 'ethnic cleansing'.

One feature of contemporary television is the emergence of dedicated history channels on cable and satellite, which have done much to popularize a certain type of history. Britain in 2004 had two, the History Channel and UK TV History. The History Channel, sometimes known as the Hitler Channel because of its focus on the Second World War, had 125 million subscribers worldwide, including 83 million in the USA. As well as repeats of 'classic' documentaries, such as *The World at War* and *People's Century*, these channels show a range of programmes using archive footage and on-camera interview material, with a particular emphasis on military history and the Second World War. They also use – controversially for purists – historical reconstructions and re-enactments of, for example, Boudica's rising against the Romans and the Anglo-Zulu War of 1878–9. These channels succeed in popularizing history for the interested general viewer.

Cinema was and is largely dominated by the West, particularly the USA,[1] ensuring that images of the world, including its history, were refracted through American lenses. 'American lenses', however, makes the situation sound more coherent and consistent than was, and is, the case. Thus, for example, the view of America's past provided by D.W. Griffith's epic silent film *The Birth of a Nation* (1915), with its sympathetic portrayal of the Ku Klux Klan, was not held by all, and became marginal as attitudes shifted or changed. On seeing the film in the White House, President Woodrow Wilson, a sympathetic Southerner, testified to the power of cinema when he said that it was 'like writing history with lightning'. Despite differences in interpretation, cinema generally provided an account in accordance with mainstream views. At the same time, film added a distinctive perspective, as seen by the presentation by Hollywood of the conquest and settlement of the American West in visually attractive as well as positive and heroic terms in films such as *Stagecoach* (1939), *Angel and the Badman* (1947), *Red River* (1948) and *She Wore a Yellow Ribbon* (1949), in all of which John Wayne was portrayed as an exemplary leader of men.

The largely dominant role in cinema of the USA was shown by its ability to portray not only its own history but also those of other countries, both factual and imaginative. This was seen with the Hollywood 'British' films of the inter-war years, such as *Lives of a Bengal Lancer* (1935), *The Charge of the Light Brigade* (1936), *The Adventures of Robin Hood* (1938), and *Gunga Din* (1939), and with 'French' equivalents such as *Beau Geste* (1939). There were both economic and cultural reasons for this process. Usually, a major Hollywood film could expect to recoup its costs in the domestic North American market, but it would be dependent on overseas markets for the vast majority of its profits. In the 1930s, the British market accounted for approximately 50 per cent of all Hollywood foreign revenues, and the share rose to 80 per cent during the Second World War when most of continental Europe was closed to American films. As a result, the studios turned increasingly to 'British' subjects (historical subjects and classic novels) that would appeal to the British as well as the American market. The cultural reason was in part a latent Anglophilia in Hollywood, particularly with Louis B. Mayer of MGM. The degree to which in the 1930s there were very few major Westerns (as opposed to B-movies) was also important, as the Northwest Frontier (of India) adventure epic (which includes *The Charge of the Light Brigade* in which an Indian guilty of atrocities against the British takes refuge with the Russians and is killed in the charge) to an extent took the place of the Western for a while. The Western, however, came back with a cycle of major A-films in 1939–40, coinciding with the disappearance of the Northwest Frontier film, which was quiescent during the war due to the US Office of War Information's disapproval of British imperialism.[2]

The inter-war market for empire among the British public was seen with films such as *The Drum* (1938) and *The Four Feathers* (1939), the latter based on A.E.W. Mason's novel of 1902, a presentation of imperial endeavour in Sudan as a definition of manliness and heroism. Sensitivity to local opinion, however, affected the distribution of films about the history of India, then the leading British colony. In 1938, *The Relief of Lucknow*, a proposed film dealing with an iconic episode in the Indian Mutiny of 1857–9 (on its nomenclature see p. 152), was banned by the India Office, as were later moves to film stories from the mutiny, and in 1939 the American film *Gunga Din* was prohibited following opposition to its showing by Indian newspapers. This led to the issue of guidelines by the India Office that banned films based on episodes in the history of British India, adaptations of the stories of Rudyard Kipling, a narrator of empire, and films that presented Indians as villains.[3]

Other cultures produced film (and television), but with far less impact in the West. This was true of the Soviet Union and also of India, the world's most active alternative to the USA in the film industry in the last three decades of the twentieth century. Bollywood, the Indian film capital in and near Mumbai (Bombay), was consciously named by Western critics as an alternative to Hollywood and, by the late 1990s, was producing more than 800 films a year. The vast majority were not historical in the sense of trying to provide an account of actual episodes from the past, although an ahistorical mythic character played a part in many Indian films. The ethos of Indian films accorded with those of many societies, especially in Asia and the Middle East. The norms, and even the tunes, of Bollywood musicals were very influential in the film musicals of not only South Asia, but also East and South-East Asia, and even Latin America. The influence, however, is almost entirely in the Third World, unlike Japanese or Hong Kong films. Some Indian films engaged with recent history and political factors played a role in their content: in 1999, the governing Bharatiya Janata Party, a Hindu sectarian movement, sought via the Ministry of Information and Broadcasting to have the role played by Hindu extremists in Gandhi's assassination greatly downplayed; a move that led to a public furore.

In some Third World countries, indigenous cinema offered readings of the past. In left-wing states, political cinema tended to focus on the history of revolutionary struggle, not least because the industry was nationalized. This was true of Cuba and Algeria, and led to accounts of struggle such as, from Cuba, Humberto Solas's film *Lucia* (1968). Although made by Italians, an Algerian production company partly financed Gillo Pontecorvo's *The Battle of Algiers* (1965), an account of the Algerian war that was sympathetic to the Communists and hostile to the French.[4] *Camp Thiaroye* (1987), an Algerian film about the brutal French suppression of dissidence by Senegalese soldiers in 1944, was banned, as inaccurate, in France and was unwelcome in Senegal whose government was close to France.

In China, over 40 films a year were produced annually in the 1970s. Films offered an exemplary account of the past, *The Great Battle of Taierzhuang* (1986) for example focusing very positively on a victory over the Japanese in 1938 during the generally disastrous Sino-Japanese War. After privatization, however, the number of new films fell to about five annually in the 1990s, not least because policing by the Film Bureau restricted initiatives. Commercial opportunities and a measure of liberalism subsequently led to expansion, so that by 2004 the annual figure for new films was about 100. Many were on themes from Chinese history, presented in an exemplary fashion, and in 2004 the Chinese government took steps to encourage the use of Chinese historical figures rather than American imports in computer games.

Due to global dominance by the USA, the films shown across much of the world challenged indigenous accounts of history. The cinema also matched television, especially where government regulation was weak – in Europe and North America – in providing a focus for public history that could be different from those of state-directed projects such as public education and celebrations. This focus was particularly different because, although the nature of public culture in the USA created self-regulating codes and expectations to which the media responded, especially when enforced by the Production Code Administration established in 1934, the regulatory regime did not extend to a programme of governmental direction of contents. This was a reflection not only of American public culture but also of the establishment of cinema before the partial militarization of parts of this culture from 1941. Nevertheless, Western governments were able to influence the content of films, sometimes by legal means. In Italy, there were restrictions on the coverage of military history. In 1953, military law was used to prosecute with success two film critics (both former soldiers) for vilification of the armed forces after a screenplay based on events in Greece during the Second World War was published. The following year, the distinguished film-maker Luchino Visconti was led by the threat of prosecution to alter his film *Senso* which referred to Italy's defeat at the hands of Austria at Custoza in 1866.

The insistent quality of the media is such that it accurately depicts the past for a large section of the viewing public around the world, however much at one level they know they are watching 'stories'. As a result, the ancient world is that of such films as *Ben-Hur* (1959), *Spartacus* (1960), *Cleopatra* (1963), *Gladiator* (2000), *Troy* (2004) or *Alexander the Great* (2004), the European Middle Ages that of *Robin Hood* (1922), *El Cid* (1961), *Camelot* (1967), *The Lion in Winter* (1968) or *The Name of the Rose* (1986), and so on.[5] In creating such public impressions, works that were intended as largely fictional could be as influential as counterparts seeking to be more factual. The latter indeed were not free from serious errors of fact and interpretation that reflected the precedence of production values. Thus, *Braveheart* (1995), Hollywood's account of William Wallace (made before God discovered the film's star, Mel Gibson), included not only a large series of factual errors (the English were not hanging Scots in Scotland during the reign of Alexander III of Scotland, Wallace never captured the city of York, and so on), but also a more central flaw: the anachronistically nationalist perception that all Scots should have been united against Edward I of England, and that those that did not were traitors. The film also served the ahistorical purpose in the 1990s of vindicating modern Scottish nationalism, thus strengthening the impact of the earlier work of the Scottish writer John Prebble on the Jacobite rising of 1745–6, his book *Culloden* (1961) which led to Peter Watkins's film *Culloden* (1964).

Braveheart is but one instance of a wider problem with cinema, that films about the past are really as much about the present,[6] but the perspective of academic critics is to miss the point as, however much film-makers might draw attention to their academic advisers, as those responsible for *Alexander the Great* did in 2004, the market that is sought is not that of scholars. Nor, much more seriously, are the values the same. To return to the point made in Chapter 1, film and television present history as answers, necessarily so as the amount of time available for verbal elucidation is limited. Film and television also present history as narrative, preferably with a beginning, a middle, and an end, rather than as a social process. One of the complaints that professional historians repeatedly level against historical films is that they focus too much on individuals (kings, queens, statesmen, generals, etc.) and leave out the wider social context of the past. Some films, however, have some nice incidental points of social observation, for example Richard Lester's *The Three Musketeers* (1973) and *The Four Musketeers* (1974), with D'Artagnan concealing his inability to read. One of the few historical feature films ever to receive an endorsement from the historical profession was Kevin Brownlow and Andrew Mollo's *Winstanley* (1975), a low-budget, independent British film about Gerard Winstanley, the leader of the radical mid-seventeenth-century English Diggers. This film, however, had only a very limited release through film clubs. It was recommended by the Marxist historian Christopher Hill in *Past and Present* (December 1975) and is quite difficult to find now as it did not attract the video market.

The interaction of filmic values and audience reactions also encourages stereotypical responses, especially in terms of goodies and baddies. Furthermore, the set cast of characters, demeanours, accents, and, indeed, facial characteristics helps to guide the audiences. Thus, for long it was possible to tell the baddies in Hollywood films as they were unshaven and, often, dark. Today, they tend to speak with an English accent. Once encoded as evil, that depiction then automatically places characters that employ it. History is thus structured because it is possible to adopt this identification across time. It serves to pigeonhole characters in the present, but also fulfils a comparable function for their predecessors. The common identification of the villain in a modern Hollywood historical film is of a snobbish cruelty, outwith the communal energy of the heroes and their supporters. Thus, the use of the English accent as indicator serves to locate traitors within and enemies without.

If, with the exception of the genre of *film noir* (which has conventions of its own), film therefore seeks moral clarity, this lends itself to a public history that is happy with a clear distinction between heroes and villains. The principal constraint comes from the desire to sell to the international market, an increasingly important issue as non-Western markets, such as India and China, have become more prominent. This factor opposes Hollywood to the public history and ideology of nation states, a process demonstrated when, for example, Malaysia, an Islamic state opposed to Israel, refused to permit the showing of Steven Spielberg's *Schindler's List* (1993), a film that depicted an episode from the Nazi persecution of the Jews, an act that to critics was an aspect of the more widespread practice of 'Holocaust denial' or, at least, diminution.

Selling films to the international market creates problems when searching history for villains to depict, as modern societies are frequently unhappy about critical portrayals of their predecessors. Thus, for the depiction of British naval pluck and prowess in the Napoleonic period in the Hollywood film *Master and Commander: The Far Side of the World* (2003), it was preferable that the villains be the French, rather than the Americans of the War of 1812, who were indeed Britain's opponents in one of the novels on which the film is based. Heroes are also transformed, with an American submarine playing a crucial role in grabbing a German naval code in the commercially successful but repeatedly inaccurate film *U-571* (2003), rather than the British submarine, HMS *Bulldog*, really responsible.[7] This was merely the latest in a line of 'the Americans won the war' films.[8] The most controversial was *Objective: Burma!* (1945), which Warner Brothers withdrew from distribution in Britain following a hysterical reaction in the press to the suggestion that the actor Errol Flynn and a platoon of American soldiers won the war in Burma. This was an unfair reaction to a good work that illustrated the hardships of war in the jungle, and made it clear that it is a patrol film and not an account of the entire Burma campaign. More generally, the Second World War was (and still is) presented very differently in historical films made by the combatants, encouraging a sense of very disparate struggles with extremely contested memories.[9] The role of Filipino collaboration with Japanese conquerors was ignored in the popular Filipino film *The Ravagers* (1964) in which the focus was on guerrillas joining with American commandos against the Japanese.

The desire to meet audience expectations ensures that the depiction of the past in television and film provides an important guide to public history in the shape of the public's view of history, or at least to the perception of this. The particular characteristics of this depiction were very much those of American public culture, especially in the democratic ethos attributed to good characters. Indeed, there is something very Jeffersonian in the repeated account in numerous historical contexts of sturdy farmers moved to fight for their liberties, as in the account of the War of American Independence against British rule (1775–83) in *The Patriot* (2000). The film in fact was made by Roland Emmerich, a German director, whose inaccurate vision of the British army, and attribution to them of atrocities they never committed such as burning people in a locked church, was coloured by German public memory of the SS, who indeed committed such atrocities, including at Oradour in France in 1944. The vision of sturdy German peasants fighting against East European hordes, another Nazi staple, was possibly also present in the background of the director's mind, while the view of the British may have been coloured by the prominence of the Holocaust-related public memory of the SS in American culture. The help of the Smithsonian Institution in providing advice on historical detail was publicized but the wider historical meaning was lost to the conventions of one-sided adventure drama. The impact of the Second World War on Hollywood has been particularly strong, and is not only seen with war films. Thus, in Steven Spielberg's *Indiana Jones and the Last Crusade* (1989), a highly indicative title, the Nazis and their allies were depicted as an aspect of total evil opposed to an eventually victorious trans-historical cosmic good that is furthered by the brave faith of the individualistic American hero.

Two more, frequently ahistorical, factors in Hollywood films are proto-feminism – many of the female characters are plucky and independent-minded – and a concern for national self-determination. In short, Hollywood history looks to the values of liberal nationalism seen in the nineteenth century, rather than the authoritarian nationalism that became particularly pronounced in Germany in the late nineteenth century. The latter was not an acceptable model for the democratizing historical myth propagated by Hollywood.

This underlines the extent to which, although a critical stance can be adopted towards the ahistorical ethos and much of the practice of Hollywood history, its essential liberal model over the past 50 years – tolerant, pluralist and directed against injustice and tyranny – is more desirable than many of the alternatives on offer. The contrast with autocratic societies is readily apparent because, in permitting the expression of only a small range of opinion, they rarely give even that margin to their presentation of history. Nevertheless, Hollywood also has to note the conservative nature of much American public opinion. In 2004, the depiction in *Alexander* (the Great) of the protagonist as bisexual led to considerable criticism, especially from evangelical Christians, and this may have played a role in its failure at the box office. In another respect, the film was very much in accord with the norms of American cinema: a blonde (dyed in this case) bloodily conquers much of the darker-hued world in order to extend civilization.

Film is one of the media in which the depiction of the past retains its role in the cross-currents of public debate. Events, such as the sinking of the liner *Titanic* in 1912, were, and are, not only made to speak to the concerns of contemporary politics, society and culture, but also took a role in subsequent debates, in this case over race, gender, class and politics. In particular, in the case of the *Titanic*, there were criticisms of the conduct of particular groups during the calamity. For example, some writers presented the lower-class passengers as panicking and acting badly, while others wrote the same of the first-class passengers, or of particular ethnic groups such as the Chinese. While claiming to find trans-historical truths in the disaster, commentators in fact grounded them historically in their own circumstances and purposes. The 1960 Broadway musical *The Unsinkable Molly Brown*, filmed in 1964, used the disaster to underline themes of American resilience and exceptionalism, but in 1965 the singer Bob Dylan included the sinking in a satirical indictment of modern America that challenged notions of consensus and benign progress. The story has also served the interests of German Second World War propaganda (*Titanic*, 1943), American Cold War propaganda (*Titanic*, 1953), British end-of-empire nostalgia (*A Night to Remember*, 1958), and Hollywood globalization (*Titanic*, 1997).[10] Similarly *Kingdom of Heaven* (2005), a film about Saladin's defeat of the forces of the Crusader kingdom of Jerusalem at Hattin in 1187, was criticized by British and French historians for present-mindedness, especially in its depiction of the Templars.

The tension in political values can be seen in the post-war American depiction of the Vietnam War with the presentation of the war as without positive meaning in the films *Apocalypse Now* (1979), *Platoon* (1986) and *Full Metal Jacket* (1987) contrasting with a more pro-American message in *Rambo: First Blood Part II* (1985).[11] Politics and filmic history also overlapped not only with the use of archive material in documentaries and contemporary history films, but also with the superimposing of fictional characters into archive footage, so that the fictionalization of public history is apparently validated. In *Forrest Gump* (1994) the protagonist shakes hands with Presidents Kennedy and Johnson,[12] and Woody Allen's *Zelig* (1983) is another example of a film placing a fictional character into archive film.

Film and television tend to take things out of their original context and label them in simplistic terms, then jump to simplistic conclusions. The process by which any film or programme is produced is overlooked by viewers and sometimes by critics: the blurring of the reality is as much a dramatic technique as it is deliberate deception. Filmmakers are apt to argue that they are portraying a deeper 'truth', although the search for profit, and thus impact, tend to be the dominant factors.[13] Oliver Stone, director of *JFK* (1991), in which he pushed the idea of a conspiracy behind the assassination of Kennedy, defended his treatment of *Alexander*.

Stone acknowledges that the film conflates events, battles and characters, but he strenuously denies distorting history. 'What do I care
anyway?' he says. 'I've been falsely accused on many occasions, and
have made people think again about JFK and Nixon. . .'. Stone admits
that he has committed the usual mistake of attributing contemporary
psychological drives and attitudes to his pagan, pre-Freudian characters.[14]

Television and cinema indeed have the ability to collapse history by
making 'them' seem like 'us', an ahistorical approach that contrasts
with academic ethos and practice but one that serves the cause of
accessibility. This can be seen in recreations of the past in reality television, for example *1900 House* (1999), a British Channel 4 television
series in which a modern family lived in a house restored as it would
have been in 1900. Initially designed as a programme about domestic
technology,[15] the project was humanized by involving a real family, but
then the response of moderns to the past, captured on video-diary
cameras, could not but offer an account of 1900 that focused on the
family and their dynamics. The same was true of the 2002 British re-
creation of a family's experience of Second World War life on the
Home Front, although personal reflections made the consequences of
rationing vivid.

A similar immediacy is captured on screen when actors talk in asides
to the cameras but, again, they tend to reveal ideas of the present day,
especially on romance and social hierarchy, rather than those of the
period they are depicting. The popular approach to the past, and to
heritage in particular, frequently wants it quaintly different but also all
too accessible, literally so as issues such as road links and parking are
emphasized in discussing historic houses and other sites that can be
visited.

The encouragement of popular engagement with the past provided
by re-enactment was taken further by television polls of national greatness, as in Britain in 2002 and the Netherlands in 2004. These registered popular assumptions: one of the top ten Dutch people was Anne
Frank, a Jewish schoolgirl diarist killed by the Nazis, while the British
list was singularly short of imperial heroes. If the winner, Winston
Churchill, was the greatest, as well as the last, of the imperial heroes, he
was presented, as were Elizabeth I and Horatio Nelson who also made
the top ten, as defenders of an endangered country/people/culture,
rather than as an exponent of empire. In a clear sign of presentism
Elizabeth I herself gained far fewer votes than Diana, Princess of Wales.

The role of cinema and television in shaping historical understanding is being followed by those of the digital media: CD-Rom and the

Internet. The media combine to affect collective memories and thus oral evidence.[16]

Publishing

The private sector of public history is not restricted to television, film and other media. A host of non-governmental institutions and practices is also important. The world of publishing for example, is not the automatic product of public taste but, instead, helps mould the latter. At the same time, as an aspect of a more general two-way interaction, the very essence of competitive capitalism is that it seeks to maintain and expand market share by producing what is perceived to be the product sought by the consumers. The type of history thus encouraged varies by publisher, but there is a general emphasis on readily accessible stories, which ensures that 'trade houses' seeking a large market have little time for academic history, especially theoretical and postmodern approaches. The emphasis, instead, is neither on complexity in interpretation, nor on the views of groups judged minority, marginal or anachronistic, but rather on a teleological account that is unproblematic in its analysis. Publishers focus on national markets and their approach encourages a 'vitalist' narrative account in which nations or peoples are the key groups, have a common purpose, and act like living bodies. This organic interpretation of the people and state is one that essentially developed in the nineteenth century, and still remains crucial across the varied manifestations of public history.

The growth in publishing history books for a popular market in the West towards the close of the twentieth century – in Britain consistently from the late 1970s[17] – reflects a range of interest also seen in the major expansion of television history. Indeed, in Britain, history in the early 2000s was referred to (somewhat misleadingly) as the 'new gardening' and the 'new rock and roll'. The autonomous character of publishers and their institutional continuity need to be borne in mind when considering the forces that affect the historical 'products' generally available, but this autonomous character is, in turn, affected by commercial pressures stemming from the nature of society and the resulting cultural preferences, and from the general character of a society's political culture.

Museums

Another form of autonomy is provided by museums. Many are under state control, and institutions such as the Beijing War of Resistance Museum record shifts in government attitudes.[18] Equally, a large number of museums are not under state control, especially in countries where the role of government has been, and is, limited and instead there is often a mix of public and private funds and control. This is particularly true of the USA, where many museums arose from the associational nature of society and the strength of voluntarism. In other words, behind the 'public' character of, say, museums on the history of individual localities frequently lay the vision, energy and funds of private groups and individuals. The tableaux and descriptions presented by museums were, and are, seen by large numbers. A staple of historical education for the young, they are also much visited by older members of the community, and are therefore a prime source of historical knowledge and opinion. Many exhibitions are exemplary in intention and in particular support founding accounts or myths. For example, in Texas it is difficult in museum displays to find views sympathetic to Mexican rule prior to independence.

Changes in the contents of museums are instructive as instances of shifting fashions in public history. The Virginia Historical Society in Richmond offered a potent memorialization of the Confederacy. The French mural artist Charles Hoffbauer was commissioned in 1914 to paint a series of Civil War murals that, after wartime interruption, were finally unveiled in 1921. They helped ensure that, reflecting the public culture of the time with its emphasis on the reconciliation of North and South but also providing a heroic account of the South that excluded incomers and African-Americans, the Confederacy took a central role in the presentation of Virginia's history offered by the Society. In the 1990s, however, this was qualified with a much greater allowance within the long-term exhibition 'The Story of Virginia, an American Experience' for the Native-American and African-American experience in Virginia. In 2004, the Museum of History for the State of North Carolina in Raleigh replaced a major display on the Civil War, which had earlier been adapted to draw attention to the role of black soldiers, by one on Civil Rights, a change that led to numerous complaints. More generally, from the 1960s there has been increased criticism of ante-bellum (pre-Civil War) Southern history and culture, a shift linked to the ending of racial segregation.

The foundation of museums is a continuing process, with controversy surrounding not only objectives and proposed contents but also funding. In the 2000s, efforts to establish a Cold War Museum in Lorton, Virginia, were associated with a pro-American view of the struggle. Also in the USA, the opening of successive presidential libraries led to discussion about what was left out in the accounts of the presidency in the accompanying displays. In the William J. Clinton Presidential Library and Museum opened in November 2004, and costing $165 million (£88.7 million), there was scant mention of his controversial relationship with Monica Lewinsky. The Republican attack on him over this issue was presented in the display text as partisan and not in moral or constitutional terms: 'The impeachment battle was not about the constitution or rule of law, but was instead a quest for power that the President's opponents could not win at the ballot box.'

In Britain, the allocation of Heritage Lottery Fund money to museums in the late 1990s and early 2000s apparently reflected the priorities of the Blair government. The self-conscious modernizers of Blair's 'New Labour' project were unhappy with much about the nation's past. This seems to have been linked to the difficulties that the new Museum of the British Empire at Bristol encountered in obtaining government funds, while none were forthcoming for the projected Museum of National History in London, and attempts to include a history section in the Millennium Dome were rebuffed. The sensitivity to Britain's past was also shown in the furore over exhibitions at the National Maritime Museum and in the ill-advised removal of 'racist' paintings in the Foreign Office.

Particular exhibitions provide a basis for controversy, not only over what to show but also over how to show it. An emphasis on regional history, as with the Wittelsbach exhibitions in Bavaria in 1978, can be seen as subverting national identity, in this case that of Germany. There is also the issue of whether museums should be 'living' or static: offering, for example, re-enactments, dioramas or machines. This offers an overlap with historical theme parks, such as Beamish in England and the Famine Theme Park in west Limerick in Ireland, which have become common in recent decades. The contentiousness of what is shown therefore operates at a number of levels. The display of historic sites provides comparable issues, although they also offer greater opportunities for commemoration and popular engagement. These sites can also be the cause of contested memories, as shown by the former concentration camp at Auschwitz.[19] The interrelationship of ways of recalling the past was demonstrated by the film *Alamo* (2004), which brought a conjunction of film and historic place. This is also related to the branding of the past in the marketing of national images that has much to do with the selling of particular products such as holidays or theme restaurants.

Religion

One of the most significant non-governmental spheres for the creation and presentation of historical views, and one that it is all too easy to forget when writing about history, is religion. The extent to which religion can be allocated to the private sector varies, however, and this is itself part of the public history of societies. In the West, the state role of religion is limited, not least in higher education, although public attitudes are less clear-cut. For example, there is a tension between histories written by Christian academics, which tend today (but not in the past) to avoid any explicit reference to God or divine intervention, and attitudes widely held among the devout public in which such references are frequently made. In modern Islamic societies, in contrast, religious and political authorities are almost inseparable, most notably in Iran under the revolutionary regime that took power in 1979.

The approach to the past on the part of most religions is very different from that of secular societies, because of the former's belief in the timelessness both of God and of the revelations of the prophet. Religions have an eschatological dimension that links present, past and future, and religion is a key element in social memory. Religions also require particular forms of public history, for example the recording of saintly acts by the Catholic Church in order to justify sainthood. The pace of this has increased under the current pope, John Paul II, who has beatified people at a greater rate than his predecessors. Many of his choices have been contentious, involving as they did a clearly partisan reading of twentieth-century history. For example, nuns and priests killed by the Republicans during the Spanish Civil War (1936–9) were beatified. So, in 2004, was the last Habsburg emperor, Karl, despite a mixed record during the First World War that included support for the use of mustard gas. John Paul II allegedly wishes to canonize Pius XII, the wartime pope, whose position on the Holocaust is controversial as it is claimed that he could have done more to criticize the Nazis.

Despite Vatican activism, there has been a decline in the role of the Churches in the teaching of human history in the West. In marked contrast to the past, Western clerics no longer play a key role in writing Western history or, indeed, in discussing it publicly, although there is a professional organization of Christian historians, the Conference on Faith and History founded in 1967, devoted to the question of how Christian faith affects historical scholarship.[20]

Religious world-views, nevertheless, include by their very nature a strong historical component. These become more pronounced with religious assertiveness, although the relationship is a complex one. In the modern Christian world, this assertiveness is especially pronounced in the USA, Eastern Europe and Africa. Changes within American Protestantism have encouraged a 'fundamentalist' Christianity that focuses on a direct relationship between God and worshipper, largely in terms of the personal religious history of the latter, without much, if any, role for the sacrament or interest in Church history. As a consequence, congregations are knowledgeable in Scripture but lack a historical sensibility. This emphasis reflects a shift in support and energy from long-established and more liberal denominations – Episcopalians, Methodists and Presbyterians – while 'born-again' conservative churches, particularly the Southern Baptists and the Assemblies of God, have become more prominent.

The resulting political commitment focused on current concerns: Christian conservatism in the USA led first to the 'Moral Majority' movement, and then to the Christian Coalition. This also, however, drew on a historical imagination that made sense of the recent past as a moral crisis stemming from 1960s' liberalism, a key element in America's 'culture wars' (see pp. 124–32). The historical application of this Christianity scarcely matched academic methods. For example, an emphasis on the role of a strong Israel as a prelude to the Second Coming of Christ played a part in influencing the public attitudes of 'born-again' Americans to the Middle East crisis of the 2000s, ensuring that many evangelical Protestants supported not only Israeli security but also settlements in occupied territories.

The election as president of Bill Clinton in 1992 and, even more, his re-election in 1996 were blows to the political cause of American evangelicalism and the movement failed to achieve many of its goals, but it also contributed to, and reflected, a sense that the expression of religious conviction was normative in public life. In the 2000 presidential election, both candidates vied to assert their born-again piety. In a debate in the Republican primary contest in 1999, when asked the political philosopher who had most influenced him, the winning candidate, George W. Bush, replied 'Christ – because he changed my heart.' Christian awakenings indeed play an important role in American culture.[21] President Bush also presented religion as the issue when, on his visit to Africa in 2003, he went to the major slave-trading post at Goree, a choice of destination designed to send a message about his concern for African-Americans. Bush declared that 'Christian men and women became blind to the clearest commands of their faith . . . Enslaved Africans discovered a suffering Saviour and found he was more like themselves than their masters.'

The rise in the West of 'alternative' religions was related to born-again Christianity in the stress on the individual, but was a very different form of religious commitment, although some cults straddled both 'new' and 'established' categories. In Europe and North America, 'alternative' religions proved better able than many Churches to capture the enthusiasm of those who wished to believe amidst a material world where faith had become just another commodity. The popularity of cults was also a reflection of the atomization of a society that now placed a premium on individualism and on personal response. Such a society was peculiarly unsuited to the coherence and historical basis of doctrine, liturgy, practice and organization that was characteristic of the established Churches. Alongside New Age and apocalyptic cults, the latter of which had a distinctive perception of history, came the popularity of astrology. All of these offered world-views with their own history and teleology, as did the marked late-twentieth-century Western revival of interest in paganism, for example in Druids and shamans.[22]

If one of the major themes of the last century has been consumerism, with its consequences for public history especially prominent in the case of the media, another has been the persistence and, in many circumstances, resurgence of religious beliefs and ways of interpreting the world, including its history. The first led to a commodification of Western culture and, to a considerable degree, to an at least partial Westernization of popular culture, including attitudes towards time and change, around the world; the second reflected the resilience of diverse cultures that might adopt modern technology, but not some other aspects of modernization. The historicist imagination of these cultures is underrated in modern discussions of history.

Furthermore, over the last century religion remained a political bat-tleground, especially as authoritarian states, particularly, but not only, the Communist ones, sought to challenge rival ideologies and sources of identity. This led to an assault on institutions and practices that included an attempt to destroy the living history they represented. In Turkey, Kemal Atatürk, president from his foundation of the republic in 1923 until his death in 1938, pushed through what he presented as a secular Muslim cultural revolution that abolished what he saw as reac-tionary, for example religious courts. In Tibet, the Chinese, especially after the 1959 revolt, attacked institutional aspects of Buddhism, parti-cularly monasteries, which were seen as expressions of Tibetan identity.

Between and within religions, struggles for converts and influence involve claims for authority and integrity that are historicist in the sense that they search for historical roots and parallels within contexts that put an emphasis on historical legitimacy. This is seen in debates over theology, liturgy and organization within churches, for example among Christians over the validity of female ministry. In clashes between and within religions there is frequent reference to past rights and griev-ances, especially where religion serves as a prime focus for identity. In India, the Hindu nationalist Bharatiya Janata Party (BJP) was respon-sible for a long campaign that in 1992 led to the very controversial destruction of the Babri Masjid mosque at Ayodhya in order to reclaim as a Hindu site what is the supposed birthplace of the god Ram. As a more pointed instance of the adaptability, as well as reiteration of historic rivalries, Indian and Pakistani missiles are named after legendary figures from the years of Hindu-Muslim rivalry in South Asia.

Historic sites of worship and religious resonance were contested in many countries. In the Balkan conflicts in the 1990s, churches and mosques proved important targets for destruction. In Afghanistan in 2001, the fundamentalist Muslims of the Taleban regime destroyed the giant statue of Buddha at Bamian, completing a process begun by predecessors who had removed the statue's face. The assault on its Baha'i minority by the Islamic Republic of Iran, whose mullahs regarded the Baha'is as heretics and apostates, led to the demolition of the House of the Báb in Shiraz, the centre for Baha'i pilgrimage, and also to the destruction of the graves of Baha'i heroes and saints. In 2004, the house of Mirza Abbas Nuri, whose son Baha'ullah founded the Baha'i faith, was destroyed although it was a key example of Iranian architecture. More generally, historical claims are pressed hard as an aspect of the struggle over sacred spaces, for example between Christians, Muslims and Jews over those in Jerusalem.

As far as the Islamic world is concerned, the distinctions between Sunnis and Shias are fortified by an acute awareness of historical wrongs, however distant. This is sustained by commemorations, for example *Ashoura*, which record Shia suffering at the hands of Sunnis. Religious heroes are also provided by a scrutiny of the past. Thus, in India, modern Hindus make much of Shivaji Bhonsle (1627–80), the Maratha leader who successfully resisted the (Muslim) Mughal Emperor Aurangzeb. This is an important aspect of the Hindu nationalism pushed hard by those concerned to reject the secular tradition of the Congress Party, offering a concrete historical example to parallel the emphasis on the god Ram as a Hindu warrior. This sectarian interpretation of India's past rejects signs of assimilation in the past between Hindus and Muslims.

The historical dimension of conflict is not the sole theme in relations between confessions. In 2004, Pope John Paul II employed a powerful historical symbolism to try to improve relations with the Russian Orthodox Church. He gave the icon of the Madonna of Kazan to a delegation to take to Russia. Made in the thirteenth century, the icon was believed to have helped Russia to victory against foreign invaders and was an object of veneration in Russia until stolen in the 1920s. As a reminder of the multiple value of historical images, the Madonna is seen by John Paul II as representing the Virgin Mary's prediction to children at Fatima that Russia would revert to Christianity after the Russian Revolution. The ownership of the icon reflected this double identity, as it had been purchased in 1970 by an American Catholic organization and lent to the shrine at Fatima before being given to the Pope. Ironically, the present icon is probably an eighteenth-century copy. The Pope also wished to retrace Abraham's steps from Mesopotamia (Iraq) to Canaan (Israel and Palestine) and, in the process, give witness to the prophetic connections from Abraham through Christ to Muhammad, although this plan was thwarted by poor health.

The interacting roles of religious identity and historical reference were indicated in 2004 in the debate over the desirability of Turkish accession to the European Union (EU), which challenged concepts of Europe focused, at least in part, on Christian identity. In September 2004, Fritz Bolkestein, an EU commissioner, compared the large-scale immigration into continental Europe from Turkey that he predicted would follow membership with past political challenges from the Ottoman Empire, the state out of which modern Turkey emerged. Quoting the historian Bernard Lewis, who had suggested that, by the end of the century, Europe would be predominantly Muslim, Bolkestein added 'If he turns out to be right, the liberation of Vienna in 1683 will have been in vain.' This was a deliberately emotive historical reference, as the defeat of the Ottoman siege of the fortress-city was (and is) seen as a turning point in the struggle against Islam in Europe, and also because his point of reference was a military episode.

The public histories of religious groups attract insufficient attention, but their importance was highlighted by concern about Islamic fundamentalism in the early 2000s. This drew attention to a world-view grounded in a historical perspective of religious struggle. Furthermore, new events were understood in terms of this perspective. Thus, to fundamentalists the inroads of infidels, for example Soviet forces in Afghanistan in 1979–88 and American troops in Iraq from 2003, were seen as counterparts to earlier assaults especially, although not only, those of the Crusades and also the medieval Christian conquest of al-Andalus – Moorish Spain. Both the latter were referred to by al-Qaeda, whose leader, Osama bin-Laden, marshalled ancient and recent history, referring not only to historical 'wrongs' but also to signs from recent events. He appears to believe that the Soviet defeat in Afghanistan shows that the Americans can be defeated.

A historical perspective was not restricted to Islamic fundamentalists. When in early 2003 the far more secular Saddam Hussein, president of Iraq, wished to conjure up nationalist support against American pressure, he referred to the Mongol storming of Baghdad in 1258, which was followed by a massive slaughter of the population. The Mongols were not Muslims. President George W. Bush's reference to a 'crusade' against terror was held to be a provocative remark to Muslims, apparently linking the struggle to holy warfare in which Christians had taken the initiative and conquered part of the Islamic world. The Muslim attempt to create an acceptable pedigree had earlier led both Saddam and his rival, Hafez Assad, dictator of Syria, to develop the reputation of Saladin, who had defeated the Crusaders in 1187, regaining Jerusalem. Large portraits and statues of Saladin were commissioned by both men. With Jerusalem then under the rule of Israel, the comparison was readily obvious to contemporaries. Saddam made much of the fact that, like Saladin, he was born in Tikrit.

Nor was this perception of the present in terms of a long-term struggle restricted to Muslims. Indeed, the strongly-grounded historical perspective, especially the sense of ancestral wrongs, seen from both Muslims and Hindus in South Asia or Catholics and Protestants in Northern Ireland,[23] perplexes Western commentators more used to public histories that focus on recent decades. They mistakenly assume that the weight of the past should not vary across the world in this fashion. More generally, the strength of religious consciousness, and the role of religion in society, can reflect the failure of both nation states and secularism. The Western experience is the topic of Chapter 6, but, in Chapter 8, its limited purchase across the world is considered.

Notes

1   Among the large number of works in this area, the following ones published since 1990 are worthy of note: M.C. Carnes (ed.), *Past Imperfect: History According to the Movies* (New York, 1995); R.A. Rosenstone, *Revisioning History: Film and the Construction of a New Past* (Princeton, NJ, 1995); V. Sobchack, *The Persistence of History: Cinema, Television and the Modern Event* (London, 1996); R. Burgoyne, *Film Nation: Hollywood Looks at U.S. History* (Minneapolis, 1997); J. Kilpatrick, *Celluloid Indians: Native Americans and Film* (Lincoln, Nebr., 1999).

2   H.M. Glancy, *When Hollywood Loved Britain: The Hollywood 'British' Film 1939–45* (Manchester, 1999).

3   P. Chowdhry, *Colonial India and the Making of Empire Cinema: Image, Ideology and Identity* (Manchester, 2000).

4   J. Chapman, *Cinemas of the World: Film and Society from 1895 to the Present* (London, 2003).

5   For twentieth-century examples, S. Jenkins, 'History Is Not Bunk, but Most Historians Are', *The Times*, 5 July 2002.

6   J. Chapman, *Past and Present: National Identity and the British Historical Film* (London, 2005); F.J. Wetta and M.A. Novelli, '"Now a Major Motion Picture": War Films and Hollywood's New Patriotism', *Journal of Military History*, 67 (2003), 861–82.

7   T. Mulligan, 'Film Review: U-571', *Headquarters Gazette*, 11, no. 3 (Summer 2000), 8–9.

8   L.H. Suid, *Sailing on the Silver Screen: Hollywood and the U.S. Navy* (Annapolis, Md., 1996) and *Guts and Glory: The Making of the American Military Image in Film* (Lawrence, Kan., 2002).

9   G. Hurd (ed.), *National Fictions: World War II on Film and Television* (London, 1984).

10   S. Biel, *Down with the Old Canoe: A Cultural History of the Titanic Disaster* (New York, 1997), and J. Richards, *A Night to Remember: The Definitive Titanic Film* (London, 2003). For another example, L.C. Gardner, *The Case That Never Dies: The Lindbergh Kidnapping* (North Brunswick, NJ, 2004).

11   Chapman, *Cinemas*, pp. 147–8.

12   S. Radstone, 'Screening Trauma: *Forrest Gump*, Film and Memory', in S. Radstone (ed.), *Memory and Methodology* (Oxford, 2000), p. 79.

13   For a defence of historical film-making that appears in a perceptive collection, K.M. Coleman, 'The Pedant Goes to Hollywood: The Role of the Academic Consultant', in M.M. Winkler (ed.), *Gladiator: Film and History* (Oxford, 2004). See also R.B. Toplin, *Reel History: In Defense of Hollywood* (Lawrence, Kan., 2002).

14   *Sunday Times* review section, 5 Dec. 2004, p. 5.

15   M. McCrum and M. Sturgis, *1900 House* (London, 1999), p. 6.

16   R. Perks and A. Thomson (eds), *The Oral History Reader* (London, 1998), p. 301.

17   P. Mandler, *History and National Life* (London, 2002), pp. 100–1.

18   R. Mitter, 'Behind the Scenes at the Museum: Nationalism, History, and Memory at the Beijing War of Resistance Museum, 1987–1997', *China Quarterly*, 161 (2000), 279–93.

19   A. Charlesworth, 'Contesting Places of Memory: The Case of Auschwitz', *Environment and Planning, D: Society and Space*, 12 (1994), 579–93.

20   G. Marsden, *The Outrageous Idea of Christian Scholarship* (Oxford, 1997); A. Walls, *The Cross-Cultural Process in Christian History: Studies in the Transmission and Appropriation of Faith* (London, 2002).

21   G. Marsden, *Fundamentalism in American Culture* (Oxford, 1982); G. Wills, *Under God* (New York, 1990).

22   R. Hutton, *Stations of the Sun* (Oxford, 1996) and *The Triumph of the Moon* (Oxford, 1999).

23   B.J. Graham, 'No Place of the Mind: Contested Protestant Representations of Ulster', *Ecumene*, 1 (1994), 257–81.

4

The public use of the past: a brief history

The manner in which states mould the image of the past, indeed create public history, varies greatly through time and space and it is dangerous to reify this process as that suggests a false coherence. For example, to write of twentieth-century European approaches to history is to encompass Nazi Germany, the Communist Soviet Union and also, in contrast (and not as an equivalence), liberal stances, although the latter themselves were far from uniform. Public history today includes the leadership cult of North Korea, as well as the 'culture wars' of the USA, in which government interference exists but to a very different extent to the situation in China, let alone North Korea. Nevertheless, allowing for this extraordinary variety, it is still important to try to shape a history of the role of states, not least because it is necessary for explaining the present position.

To go back in time, the development of history, in the modern sense of a narrative and analysis of change in human society (as opposed to an account of divine intervention), rested in part on an understanding of the significance of time. In particular, in order to create the past as a subject it was necessary to understand its separation from the present. For societies that put an emphasis on cyclical theories of time – on a return, in the future, to the present, and on a desire to recreate the past – this was not a separation that had particular weight, and those theories were especially apt for peoples who focused on the rhythms of the seasons that dominated agriculture, fishing and forestry, which indeed were the systems that determined livelihoods in pre-industrial time.[1]

Furthermore, the interaction of human and sacred space did not encourage a sense of development through time. This interaction involved events – the works of divine Providence, the actions of prophets, or the malign doings of diabolical forces and their earthly intermediaries such as witches, but news of these told, and retold, familiar tales and superstitions as part of a religious world-view that linked past, present and future. Limited literacy also led to an emphasis on community agencies – families, kindred, localities, and religious and economic groups (such as guilds) – for the assessment and transmission of news. Memory represented the key approach to the past.

The development of a different situation around the world was far from simultaneous and, in some areas such as New Guinea, is still incomplete. These regions attract relatively little interest from historians being instead generally the preserve of anthropologists, although the approach of the latter has been incorporated by historians interested in oral history. Traditional forms of historical consciousness, especially the notion of the past, particularly ancestors, as still present,[2] may appear redundant, not least in terms of the scholarly understanding of the past, but they have value as indicators of still widespread public attitudes, not only outside the West but also within it. This is particularly the case in terms of religious views, specifically the role of providentialism. The popularity of astrology is also instructive as it provides a clear indication of widespread belief in other-worldly factors in explaining events (or providing histories), as well as of the strength of cyclical interpretative tendencies. In addition, there is frequently, both within and outside the West, an often conscious overlap of history and fiction that does not accord with the established Western academic understanding of history. The latter is a benign phrase; a harsher one in terms of its resonance would be doctrine, which captures the often didactic nature of this understanding.

The key elements in the creation of a new historical consciousness that can be seen in Western societies from the sixteenth century were an often reluctant and incomplete new awareness of change through time as a transforming, rather than a cyclical, process,[3] and the rise of what has been termed the 'public sphere'. In the latter, traditional communal ways of mediating between individuals or localities and the external world were increasingly joined by more uniform ways to mould thought and opinion. Two were of particular importance: the culture of print and the role of government. These were linked, in that the ends of government benefited from a favourable press.

Thus, in England, John Foxe's *Acts and Monuments of Matters Most Special and Memorable Happening in the Church with an Universal History of the Same* (1563), popularly known as the *Book of Martyrs*, was an extremely influential account of religious history that propagated an image of Catholic cruelty and Protestant bravery that was judged to be of value to the government of Elizabeth I (r. 1558–1603) as it sought to define and defend its notions of identity, and therefore loyalty. Foxe provided an account of England as a kingdom that had been in the forefront of the advance towards Christian truth and depicted the Catholic alternative to Elizabeth as wicked. After an order of Convocation (the clerical parliament of the established Church) of 1571, cathedral churches acquired copies and many parish churches chose to do likewise. Foxe's *Book of Martyrs* was to have a resonance into the twentieth century and was crucial to the Protestant martyrology that was important to the national role of the Church of England, but is now clearly part of a world that has been lost.[4]

The culture of print created a new way to disseminate impressions of the past, but was not itself responsible for these impressions. Instead, the moulding of national identities was important. The development of senses of political identity owed much to long-lasting conflicts, such as those between the kings of England and France in the thirteenth and, even more, fourteenth and fifteenth centuries. The English acquired or strengthened their identity by fighting the French, and vice versa, and these conflicts provided a ready national history to match that of royal and aristocratic dynasties.[5] In the Low Countries, a verse account of the battle of Worrington of 1288 served as an epic for Brabant. In Scotland, the wars of independence against England (1296–1357) helped develop a sense of national consciousness that was historically grounded.[6] John Barbour's poem the *Brus*, composed in Scots in 1375, was an anti-English national epic centring on Robert the Bruce and the 'freedom' of Scotland. Other late-medieval histories of Scotland – the *Chronicle of the Scottish People* by John Fordun (1380s), the *Orgynale Cronikil* by Andrew Wyntoun (1410s) and the *Scotichronicon* by Walter Bower (1440s) – were produced to show that Scotland was a distinct state with its own history. Although this was not the sole factor, its identity was defined by these writers in terms of opposition to England. The idea of Germanness took shape after the tenth-century Saxon emperors began to take armies into Italy and legends about earlier migrant bands of soldiers, for example Trojans, played an important role in accounts of particular German 'descent groups'.[7]

In England, Shakespeare's plays, from the late sixteenth century, were to provide a vivid account of national history and one that served political interests as an aspect of a wider historical culture that encouraged a sense of distinctive national development.[8] A German equivalent was the work of Ulrich von Hutten, a supporter of Martin Luther, whose *Arminius* (1519) depicted its hero, victor over the legions of Augustus Caesar at the Teutoburger Wald in 9 CE, as a defender of Germany against the tyranny of Rome.[9] Art served the same end, as with the commissioning in 1660 of Rembrandt to paint the *Conspiracy of Claudius Civilis* for Amsterdam's new town hall. Civilis had led resistance to the Romans in 69 CE and his role was recorded by the Roman historian Tacitus.

Revisiting the Classical world

The Classical inheritance in European culture was also important in the creation of a distinctive historical imagination. It provided a general frame of reference, specific comparisons and the example of praiseworthy histories and historians. The resonance was not restricted to intellectuals. Thus, the relationship between empire, Enlightenment and the Classics is indicated by the response of Thomas Ashe Lee, a British officer, to the Jacobite rebels of Highland Scotland. Writing in 1746 after the British victory at Culloden, he referred to the British troops 'dispersed through the several parts of this heathenish country, converting them to Christianity, and propagating a new light among them. Some few of them bring in their arms, others skulk in the woods and mountains, but we take care to leave them no sustenance, unless they can browse like their goats.' Seeing the Highlanders, who were in fact Christians, as barbarians, Lee sought a historical comparison with the campaign by reading Julius Caesar's *Gallic Wars*.[10]

Such a locating of the present with reference to the Classical past (mainly Roman in the eighteenth century, but much more Greek in the nineteenth) was commonplace in Anglophone Britain, a society whose reverence of, and reference to, the past were focused on the Classical world.[11] Although the cultural context was very different, there is an instructive parallel with modern American commentators searching for historical parallels for their current international position, especially in the Middle East, by looking back to previous empires, particularly that of Britain. The parallel with eighteenth-century Britain is instructive, as it also was coming to terms with a global imperial presence. Comparisons with Classical Rome then seemed obvious because the focus on the Classical past was scarcely novel in European culture. Instead, it had a venerable heritage. Britain was not alone in this historical resonance. History painting, a public, demonstrative and declamatory art, proclaiming noble and elevated ideals, and depicting the actions of, mostly Classical, heroes at moments of moral or historical significance,[12] remained at the top of the French academic hierarchy of subjects.

Aside from providing an acceptable pedigree and cultural context for political systems, civic virtues and cultural preferences, the Classical legacy was also valuable in large part because it was so fluid and open to interpretation that did not fall foul of authority: a marked contrast to that of Christianity where questionable interpretation could lead to charges of heresy. Joseph Addison's frequently-staged play *Cato* (1713), with its plot of republican Roman self-sacrifice, based on a real individual, was applauded for different facets across the British political spectrum. The *Whitehall Journal*, a pro-government London newspaper, in its issue of 6 November 1722 criticized opposition writers in vain: 'The state of the Roman Empire, under all its varieties . . . they are all promiscuously made use of by these authors, to influence and illustrate politics . . . by no force of wit . . . can those words in any one Roman sense be applied to our English constitution.'

In practice, such references were more than suitable for a political culture whose self-image was that of high-minded and moral politics. The presentation of history as a morally exemplary tale had strong contemporary relevance in the eighteenth century because of the obvious political importance of a small number of individuals, and because of the notion of kingship and governance as moral activities. As the relationship appeared timeless, it seemed pertinent to apply admonitory tales in a modern context, as with the comparisons of Sir Robert Walpole, Britain's leading minister from 1720 to 1742, indiscriminately with Charles I's unpopular, and eventually assassinated, favourite, the Duke of Buckingham, Henry VIII's Cardinal Wolsey and, a far earlier figure, the Roman Emperor Tiberius's adviser Sejanus. Belief that history possessed a cyclical quality contributed to this, as time was not held to compromise the moral power of Classical exemplars.

Furthermore, the stress in the popular perception of history then (and also now) on personal drives, rather than on impersonal social, economic, institutional or geopolitical forces, ensured that the emphasis was on personality and narrative. A stress on individual free will, or on a providential intervention linked to behaviour, led to a world that was best understood in moral terms, a situation also seen with modern popular history. In William Paterson's play *Arminius*, which was refused a licence for production in 1740, the hero of the title pressed for a valiant rejection of tyranny, while Segestes, the old leader modelled on Walpole, was ready to surrender interests in order to pursue peace with ancient Rome, i.e. contemporary France. In addition, the rivalry between Classical Rome and Carthage could be used to prefigure that of Britain and France in the eighteenth century. In the House of Lords in 1740, at a time when Britain was at war with Spain, John, Lord Carteret, a past and future secretary of state, called Carthaginian strategy a relevant example for current military planning and thereby acquired added authority for his opposition to the Walpole ministry.[13]

Speakers and writers assumed a fair degree of familiarity with history. In the House of Commons' debate on the Address to the Crown in 1755, William Pitt the Elder, the leading critic of the British govern-

THE PUBLIC USE OF THE PAST

ment and, in this case, an advocate of an emphasis on a maritime strategy in war with France, declared 'we have been told indeed that Carthage, and that Spain in 88 [the Armada of 1588] were undone, notwithstanding their navies – true; but not till they betook themselves to land operations and Carthage had besides a Hannibal who would pass the Alps',[14] the last a critical response to William, Duke of Cumberland, George II's militaristic son who was Captain General of the army. In the Commons' debate on the Address in 1770, Sir William Meredith, an Opposition MP, warned of the need to end tyranny at home if the country was to fight successfully for liberty abroad, adding 'our ancestors abandoned King John, in consequence of which he lost all his foreign dominions' to France in 1204, and followed up with a reference to Edward III (r. 1327–77).[15]

The value of historical, particularly Classical, comparisons, however, was contested by a few commentators, indicating that a sense of history as defined by utilitarian factors is not new. The anonymous writer of *Reflections on Ancient and Modern History* (1746) claimed that:

> The best source of civil instruction must be searched for in examples not altogether so remote from our own times. The grand business of the Roman policy was only to contain their own dominions in order and obedience: on the contrary, the interests of modern communities depend entirely on the management of many neighbouring states, equal perhaps in power to themselves.[16]

Less than a month after the speech cited above, Pitt told the House of Commons that 'he would not recur, like Lord Barrington, to the Romans for comparisons; our own days had produced as great examples'.[17] Similarly, in 1771, Philip, 4th Earl of Chesterfield, a former diplomat, wrote to Robert Murray Keith, then preparing himself for a diplomatic career, 'Let modern history be both your study and amusement; by modern history [I mean] from 1500 to your own time, from which era Europe took that colour which to a great degree it retains at this day, and let Alexander and Julius Caesar shift for themselves.'[18] The last remark may not seem controversial today, but was much more so for a society steeped in the Classics.

Although a shift from classical to modern history as a comparative framework began, references to the classics indeed were frequent in works that engaged with new intellectual topics. In his *An Inquiry into the Nature and Causes of the Wealth of Nations* (1776), a key work in the development of the study of economics, Adam Smith, a Scottish professor, used many examples from the Classical world and also treated this world as an appropriate frame of reference. Thus, his chapter 'Of

Colonies' began by discussing the reasons why Greece and Rome established colonies.

Eighteenth-century histories

For societies that were reverential of, and referential to, the past, it was particularly important to have their present purposes set in a favourable historical context. Indeed, the value of the culture of print encouraged government attempts to control the world of publications. That remains an important aspect of the contemporary relationship between the state and history. As is also the case today, however, the ability of states to regulate the world of print varied greatly. It was an aspect of their historical development and, more specifically, of political battles over the prerogatives of government. Indeed, competing readings of history played a major role in these battles, not least over the power and authority of the monarchs in Stuart Britain.

In the United Provinces (the Netherlands), and in Britain from the 1690s, the degree of government regulation over the world of print was limited. Combined with the wealth of these societies and, from the mid-eighteenth century, with growing literacy, this provided opportunities for entrepreneurs to exploit. Partly as a consequence, Europe saw a great flowering in the publication of works of history.[19] In 1731, Voltaire brought dramatic near-contemporary history to a large readership, his *Histoire de Charles XII* being printed ten times in its first two years. His *Siècle de Louis XIV* and his *Histoire de la Guerre de 1741* were similarly successful. Later in the century, the works of Edward Gibbon and William Robertson enjoyed an international reputation. Robertson (1721–93), a Scottish cleric, was elected to academies in Madrid, Padua and St Petersburg.

The widespread and often sympathetic public interest in history clashed with the attitude of many of the *philosophes*, an influential group of fashionable French thinkers, who disparaged much of the past: the Middle Ages for being barbaric, the age of the Reformation for being fanatical and the reign of Louis XIV for its supposed obsession with *gloire*. The *philosophes* also found that history could not provide the logical principles and ethical suppositions that were required to support the immutable laws they propounded, and if they still thought that the past should be investigated and understood, it was largely for utilitarian reasons. Eighteenth-century ministers, trying to abrogate traditional privileges on behalf of modernizing Enlightened Despots, shared in the disparaging of much of the past. The suppression of the Jesuits and that attack on monasticism, which were in part aspects of that assault on traditional privileges in Catholic Europe, led to a loss of institutional continuity, as well as the dispersal of numerous libraries.

Yet, on the part of many writers, there was also a strong interest in the past, reflecting a sense that it had shaped the present and also offered appropriate lessons. The diplomat Joseph Yorke hoped 'that ambitious princes or ministers may forever be obliged to study the history of the war just terminated before they enter upon a new one'.[20] There was also a concern with organic development that is not always associated with Enlightenment thinkers. Interest in the idea of an impartial enquiry into the past was matched by a strong demand for history as *belles-lettres* (literature). A sense of national consciousness was also important, as intellectuals became more willing to attack cultural borrowing, and this encouraged an assertion of past distinctiveness. Joseph II, who founded a German national theatre in Vienna in 1776, had been the dedicatee in 1769 of the *Hermannsschlacht*, a glorification of the struggle of the ancient Germans under Arminius (or Hermann) against Roman invasion, written by the poet Friedrich Klopstock. Klopstock also sought in *Oden* (1771) and in his patriotic plays to replace Classical myths by Germanic ones.[21] In Sweden, Olof von Dalin wrote a scholarly *History of Sweden* (1747–62) commissioned by the Estates, while in Finland Henrik Porthan (1739–1804) founded modern studies in Finnish history and folklore, and in Russia there was a serious controversy over the origins of the people and the language.

In Wales, scholars and antiquaries carved out a distinctive Welsh identity, as descendants of the Ancient Britons, in terms of the ancient language and history of Wales. Some of their claims were totally spurious, notably those made by the remarkable reviver of the bardic craft, Edward Williams (1747–1826), but this was scarcely uncommon in comparable developments elsewhere in Europe. The Welsh tradition that Edward I of England, the thirteenth-century conqueror of Wales, had ordered the execution of all Welsh bards was subsequently discredited. The foundation of the Society of Antiquaries of Scotland in 1780 was important in the development of an interest in Scottish history, as was a focus on the Marians: supporters of Mary, Queen of Scots. Many Scots at the time, however, were suspicious of the Society as promoting an unhealthy interest in a past when Scotland was independent that was best forgotten in a British present.

History was also used to acclaim the cause of English liberty. In the dedication of 1760 for the fourteenth edition of his *A New History of England*, the prolific writer John Lockman 'endeavoured to set the whole in such a light as may inspire the readers with an ardent love for our pure religion, and its darling attendant, liberty; and, on the other hand, with a just abhorrence of popery, and its companion, slavery'.[22]

That year he also published *A History of the Cruel Sufferings of the Protestants and others by Popish Persecutions in various countries.*

The French Revolution which began in 1789 led both to an emphasis on the rejection of the past on the part of radicals (both French and sympathetic foreigners), and to an emphasis on continuity on the part of their opponents. In England, a vocal member of the latter tendency, Edward Nares, vicar of Biddenden, argued that history was a valuable support for religious and conservative views. In a sermon preached in December 1797, on a day of public thanksgiving for recent British naval victories over France's allies, Nares declared:

> From the first invention of letters, by means of which the history of past ages has been transmitted to us, and the actions of our forefathers preserved, it has ever been the wisdom of man, under all circumstances of public and general concern, to refer to these valuable records, as the faithful depositories of past experience, and to deduce from thence, by comparison of situations, whatever might conduce to his instruction, consolation, or hope. Thither the statesman of the present day frequently recurs for the better conduct and support of the commonwealth. Thither the philosopher directs his view to estimate the powers and energy of the human soul, and to form his judgement of its future capacity, by the testimony he obtains of past exertions. Thither the ambitious has recourse to learn how to compass the honours of this world; to enrol himself in the lists of fame, and rival the achievements of former generations. Thither also, in his turn, the religious man applies himself for more sober and rational information; and, bent upon tracing the finger of God in all concerns of importance to the good and welfare of man, is pleased to discover, in the course of human events, a direction marvellously conducive to the final purposes of Heaven, the constant and eternal will of God; and continually illustrative of his irresistible supremacy, his overruling providence, his might, majesty, and power!

Nares contrasted the historical perspective with what he saw as the destructive radical and secular philosophy of present-mindedness:

> the enemy begin their operations on the pretended principle of giving perfect freedom to the mind of man . . . the first step to be taken in vindication of such a principle is to discard all ancient opinions as prejudices; every form of government, however matured by ages, is to be submitted afresh to the judgement and choice of the passing generation.[23]

Nationalists and Whigs

Rapidly rising population and aggregate wealth in the Western world in the nineteenth century increased the general market for historical works, and it extended across generations and classes. The standard historical theme was heroic and the usual frame of reference was nationalistic. In his popular adventure stories for boys, the British war correspondent George Alfred Henty (1832–1902) looked at past as well as present. His historical accounts, which continued to enjoy substantial sales until after the Second World War, included the novels *Under Drake's Flag* (1883), *With Clive in India: or the Beginnings of an Empire* (1884), *St George for England: A Tale of Cressy* [Crécy] *and Poitiers* (1885), *With Wolfe in Canada: The Winning of a Continent* (1887), which stressed Britain's trans-oceanic destiny, and *Held Fast for England: A Tale of the Siege of Gibraltar* (1892): accounts respectively of British victories in the sixteenth, eighteenth, fourteenth and eighteenth centuries.

Alongside the private market catered for by publishers, there was also a major expansion in public history. The establishment of mass schooling, organized and regulated on a national basis, was crucial, not least in leading to a major rise in literacy, but also in increasing the demand for national history and in ensuring that the nation was the prime frame of reference for public history. The growth of academic history at university level enhanced the prestige and position of scholars[24] and the self-consciousness and organizational structures of the profession,[25] and also greatly increased the public weight of the subject, not least because those trained there frequently went on to play prominent roles in politics, government and education.[26] Historians were also called to act as experts, especially on international relations, Sir Charles Webster and Howard Temperly providing advice in this field for the British government in the twentieth century.[27]

The role of history in public consciousness owed much to nationalism, not only in Europe but also in the newly independent states in the New World such as Mexico. The growth of nation states and of national empires were both cause and consequence of *mentalités* that were more focused on the nation, although the political character of this focus was contested by liberals and conservatives.[28] Conversely, the role of ruling dynasties in defining identity and explaining historical development diminished, while, within states, those of regions and localities were not given comparable attention to nations. This emphasis on nations extended to history, for past greatness and pretensions were crucial components of national myths, and the continuity of present and past was stressed.

Such a stress was very pronounced where there were nationalist quests for statehood. The struggle for Italian unification, the Risorgimento, for example drew on a literature of Italian greatness designed to overcome the considerable fissiparous tendencies presented by the multiple sovereignty of the states in the Italian peninsula, as well as what could be presented as the external challenge of Habsburg (Austrian) rule, and the anachronistic universalism of the papacy. In turn, once Italy was united, the Risorgimento played a key role as the foundation myth of the Italian state and nation. This was seen with a greater stress on the Risorgimento in education from the 1880s.

The same was true of German unification, although there, as in other states, it is important to note major differences over the character and, therefore, history of national identity. Thus, in Germany, the presentation of an account of national development centring on a transformation of Prussia into Germany with, in particular, an exclusion of Austria and a marginalization of Catholic Germany, especially Bavaria, was unwelcome to many who offered a different history.[29] Similarly, in Italy, many Southerners resented the Piedmontese takeover which they saw as crucial to the Risorgimento. More generally in this period, current goals and issues were also presented in clashing historical contexts. This was particularly, although not only, significant when territorial disputes were at issue, as between France and Germany. The relevant history ranged across time, with distant episodes disinterred and more recent grievances aired, as with the Territorial Liberation Fund in France in the 1870s, established in response to the loss of Alsace-Lorraine as a result of defeat by Germany in the war of 1870–1.

In Britain the emphasis, especially from the 1830s, was on a Whig interpretation of history, a public myth that offered a comforting and glorious account that seemed appropriate for a state which ruled much of the globe and which was exporting its constitutional arrangements to other parts of the world. The British viewed convulsions on the European Continent, such as the French uprisings in 1830 and 1848 and the Paris Commune of 1870–1, as evidence of the apparent political failure and backwardness of its states and of the superiority of Britain. A progressive move towards liberty was discerned in Britain past and present, a seamless web that stretched back to the supposedly free and democratic village communities of Angles and Saxons applauded by John Richard Green in his *Short History of the English People* (1874).[30] Then, after the setback of the Norman Conquest of 1066, the successful quest for liberty could be traced to Magna Carta in 1215, and to other episodes which could be presented as the constitutional struggles of the baronage (nobility, aristocracy) in medieval England, as well as forward to the extensions of the franchise in 1832, 1867 and 1884. These were seen as arising naturally from the country's development. The 'Glorious Revolution' of 1688–9, in which the Catholic James II of England and VII of Scotland was overthrown by William III, was presented as a crucial episode in this evolutionary move towards national liberty.[31]

British parliamentarians were reminded that liberty had had to be defended: Daniel Maclise received £7,000 for painting *Wellington and Blücher at Waterloo* (1861) and *The Death of Nelson* (1864) for Parliament. His *œuvre*, for example *Alfred the Great in the Tent of Guthruyn* (1852), reflected the demand for an exemplary national history on canvas, especially a history of monarchs and war. Twenty-one years later, the carving of a white horse in a hillside near Westbury that was held to commemorate Alfred's victory over the Danes at Ethandune in 878 was restored. Alfred shared with King Arthur the happy role of providing distinguished ancestry for notions of valiant liberty although, with the idea of the 'Norman yoke', it was believed that these had been superseded due to the Norman Conquest of 1066 and had had to be recovered.[32] Aside from on canvas, there was also a strong sense of the past in nineteenth-century novels, for example those of Sir Walter Scott, such as *The Monastery* (1820), *Kenilworth* (1821) and *Tales of the Crusaders* (1825), or works such as *I Carbonari della Montagna* (1861–2), a Romantic-patriotic novel by Giovanni Verga, a Sicilian supporter of Italian unification. Scott's success reflected a popular market for historical writing that preceded mass education. Hendrik Conscience (1812–83), a Belgian Romantic who had taken part in the 1830 Revolution, wrote historical novels such as *The Lion of Flanders* and *The Mayor of Liège* that produced medieval precursors for the contemporary quest for Belgian liberty. In England, Charles Kingsley (1819–75), a clergyman who was Regius Professor of Modern History at Cambridge from 1860 to 1869, wrote a number of historical novels glorifying heroes from the English past. These included *Westward Ho!* (1855), an account of the Elizabethan struggle with Philip II of Spain, in which the Inquisition and the Jesuits appear as a cruel inspiration of Spanish action, and *Hereward the Wake* (1866) about resistance to the Norman Conquest.

In Britain, as elsewhere, academic historians reflected and sustained national historical myths, a situation that is no longer the case in the West. Captain Montagu Burrows RN, Chichele Professor of Modern History at Oxford, wrote in *The History of the Foreign Policy of Great Britain* (1895),

Happily for the world . . . the Revolution of 1688 once more opened up the way to the resumption of the Tudor foreign policy . . . Not one word

> too much has been said in praise of the benefit conferred upon England
> and the world by the Revolution. From the 5th of November 1688 [when
> William III landed in England] dates the return of England to her old
> place . . . The nation had long been aware of the evils of a departure
> from the principles entwined with its whole earlier history, and exem-
> plified in chief by the great Elizabeth.[33]

Writing in 1922, the influential Cambridge historian Sir Adolphus
Ward was less florid in his language but, to him, the later Stuart monarchs, Charles II (r. 1660–85) and James II (r. 1685–8), had depressed
'the English monarchy to the position of a vassal state' to France, while
William III (r. 1689–1702) was 'one of the most far-sighted of great
statesmen'.[34] The theme of challenge and recovery lent dramatic interest to the tale of national greatness. In France, however, the Revolution
of 1789 was a more troubling presence than the Glorious Revolution of
1688 was in Britain, and it was harder to link it to a pattern of progressive if not apparently peaceful progress. Nevertheless, the Third
Republic established in 1870–1 made much of its role as a modern representation of the Revolution and took steps to foster the history of the
latter.

Alongside the dominance of unilinear and teleological notions of
change, historians shared in a general sense of Western superiority. In
his continuation to Tytler's *Elements of a General History*, Edward Nares,
from 1813 Regius Professor of Modern History at Oxford, offered no
doubt of Europe's civilizing mission: 'Civilized Europe is the only part
of the world that can claim the credit of almost all that has been done
towards the advancement of knowledge since the commencement of
the eighteenth century.'[35] The imperial power and pretensions of the
major Western states were also given a historical component: Europe's
empires were presented as both apogee and conclusion of the historical process, specifically with a linkage to past empires, particularly that
of ancient Rome. The mantle of the latter was appropriated, for
example, by Britain, Italy and Portugal, as each provided accounts that
explained the role of their current colonial expansion.[36] This parallel
was given physical form in the architecture and townscape of imperial
cities.[37]

The sense of Western superiority was also reaffirmed through the
combination of the notion of a ladder of civilization with the findings
of Social Darwinism.[38] This sense led to a presentation of the teaching
of world history in terms of the priorities and progress of Western civilization, an approach that remains influential today, especially in the
USA. Looking back to the Mesopotamians, Egyptians and, more particularly, Greeks, the approach propounded a continuous development

in Western civilization,[39] and Americans, celebrating their European origins and civilizing mission with books such as Washington Irving's *History of the Life and Voyages of Christopher Columbus* (1828), gave themselves a prominent role in this development. This was linked to their downgrading of the Native American contribution. American archaeologists and anthropologists studying Native American cultures appreciated that the surviving landscape and artefacts indicated the achievements of these cultures, but much of American society was very resistant to this perspective and the academic view had only limited impact.

In the nineteenth century, the tension between nationalism and supranational loyalties was to be a major background to public history, and it is one that continues down to the present. The role of the state in defining this history in the nineteenth century ensured a movement from an earlier cosmopolitanism. The earlier intellectual agenda in the West had been dominated by the Classics and the Bible and, with literacy limited and books expensive, much had been published in international languages. This meant, on the European Continent, French, German or Latin. Conversely, in the nineteenth century, nationalism was linked to an emphasis on the history of individual peoples and states,[40] as well as the development of national school systems purchasing educational works in the vernacular,[41] the more widespread growth of the publishing industry and the rise of publication in most of the European languages.

In place of, and in reaction to, the idea of a totally new start, seen with the French Revolution (that had even extended, in a deliberate rejection of the Christian framework, to a new calendar), came an emphasis on regeneration and recovery. In this, the recognition of historical development was linked to a contemporary concern for continuity and roots. This led to a scholarly interest in the roots of national identity[42] and a related public interest in a history that encompassed folklore, costumes and archaeology,[43] and also to the pointed use of cultural and commercial forms, ranging from the museum to the postage stamp, from the map to the flag, and from the souvenir shop to the pantheon of past national heroes, such as the Valhalla built on the towering banks on the Danube in 1842 by Ludwig I of Bavaria, or the French monuments to Vercingetorix, Julius Caesar's leading opponent during the Roman conquest of Gaul.[44]

Arminius was celebrated anew as a liberator against foreign oppression and a unifier of Germans with the Arminius Monument completed in 1875 on an elevation in the Teutoburger Wald. The statue of the armed Arminius has him holding aloft a massive sword of vengeance. The Belgian equivalent was the celebration of Ambiorix, a leader of the Eburones in their revolt in 55–54 BCE against Julius Caesar's occupation. He was presented as a bold leader of the putative 'ancient Belgians' in their fight for freedom and a statue to him was erected in Tongeren. Ambiorix was also discussed in school books as an example of the Belgian love for liberty. The Dutch equivalent was Civilis. Across Europe, exemplary anniversaries were celebrated frequently, and with considerable energy. This was particularly true of heroic battles that supposedly had paved the way to present greatness, for example, in Germany, victories over the French at Leipzig (1813) and Sedan (1870).

Nostalgia as well as power were thus invoked, and the potency of these celebrations rested on the degree to which they could satisfy varied social and cultural drives and demands, in particular marking not only modernization but also the reaction against aspects of it, for example social change. The desire to preserve landscapes, buildings and folklore that supposedly represented national identity and values[45] was an important consequence of the reaction against social change. In Europe, for example, it led to an upsurge in medievalism in the late nineteenth century. This had a number of consequences, including the attempt to provide a historical pedigree for the German Empire acclaimed in 1871 by linking it to the medieval Holy Roman Empire, a quest that led in 1879 to the rebuilding at Goslar of the eleventh-century imperial palace. The large-scale historical paintings in the Reichssaal in the Kaiserpfalz depicted the glorious past when the Salian emperors had lived in the town.

While medieval themes were employed in neo-Gothic buildings across Europe, there was also a quest to preserve medieval buildings. In Britain, the Somerset Archaeological Society purchased Taunton Castle in 1874, and then restored it, John, 3rd Marquess of Bute acquired Falkland Palace in 1887 and began its restoration, and William, Lord Armstrong followed with Bambrugh Castle in 1894. George, Marquess of Curzon bought and helped restore Bodiam and Tattershall castles, before giving them to the National Trust, which had been founded in 1893–5. In Scotland, William Wallace and Robert the Bruce, medieval heroes of the independence struggle against England, were seen as heroes, but heroes who laid the basis for union with England in 1707 by resisting earlier conquest.

In imperial states nationalism, however, pulled in different directions. Alongside the attempt, often in response to contrary pressures from within and without, to strengthen the identity and image of empires, such as Austria-Hungary, Britain and Russia, not least by emphasizing a common cultural consciousness within empires, came efforts on behalf of self-identifying peoples within these and other empires. This was particularly so with the Hungarians, Irish and Poles, but also for example with the Czechs, Croats, Finns, Norwegians, Icelanders and Ukrainians.[46] In each case, the development of historical consciousness served to affirm an identity that in part was more clearly historical because of the lack or limitation of political options, but also where the possibility of a political change encouraged the demand for a distinctive and exemplary history. The development of national languages, such as Finnish, also led to the publication of historical works. These deliberately asserted a spatial coherence and chronological distinctiveness for proto-nations that became central to public cultures that were particularly pronounced in urban and middle-class circles. This process of reifying the intangible community denoted by terms like 'Deutsches Volk' (German people) was taken further with the emergence of discrete 'scientific' disciplines of history and geography.

The arts vied to support national accounts, with institutions such as national theatres and national opera houses being used to the same aim. Musical compositions, such as Brahms's *German Requiem* (1868), celebrated national identity and, sometimes, myths. In Russia, Mikhail Glinka employed folk themes in his operas *A Life for the Tsar* (1836) and *Russlan and Ludmilla* (1842). Giuseppe Verdi (1813–1901), an ardent Italian nationalist, based many of his operas, for example *Don Carlos* (1867), on historical episodes in order to provide stirring calls for liberty. *Má Vlast* (My Country, 1874–9), a cycle of six symphonic poems, was written by Bedřich Smetana (1824–84), a composer who supported Czech nationalism. The last two of the poems, *Tábor* and *Blaník*, commemorated the Hussites who had resisted foreign rule in the fifteenth century.[47] The arts could indeed act as a spur to action. The Belgian revolution of 1830 broke out after the Brussels opera house mounted a performance of Daniel François Esprit Auber's recent opera *La Muette de Portici* (also known as *Masaniello*), based on the Neapolitan revolt against Spanish rule in 1647, with a rousing chorus of 'Amour sacré de la patrie' in the grand finale being the key prompt to action.

Music was not alone. The Polish poet Adam Mickiewicz (1798–1855), who played an active role in the nationalist cause, also wrote a series of patriotic, historical works including *Ancestors* (1823–33), *Books of the Polish Nation* (1832) and *Pan Tadeusz* (1834). Monuments asserted particular identities, as with the celebration of the Magyars in the millennial memorial of the Hungarian Land-taking erected in Budapest in 1896.

These tendencies were not restricted to the Western world. In Japan, the avowed modernization and state-building of the late nineteenth century, which included, for example, the foundation of a compulsory primary school system, were matched by the development of a Western-style history. Indeed, in 1887 Ludwig Reiss, one of the students of the most influential German historian of the period, Leopold von Ranke, was appointed to teach history at the new Tokyo Imperial University. His approach, which incorporated a causal analysis within a chronological framework, seemed to Japanese scholars to be more valuable than the established annalistic Chinese method of historical scholarship.[48] In Japan, as with other countries that responded to Western hegemony, there was both a borrowing of Western forms and an attempt to offer a nationalist history; this involved support for the Meiji restoration of 1868–9. A large proportion of the early scholarship lamented the preceding Edo period (from 1609) as a dark age of the degeneration of imperial rule, while also celebrating its military traditions, although many of these were in fact manufactured by historians and military officers. Nationalist history gave Japan a 'usable past' that matched the requirements of its government in a way that liberal Western perspectives could not. Within European colonies, such as India, nationalist accounts of the past developed to complement political movements for self-government, if not independence.

Towards the close of the nineteenth century, alongside the emphasis on 'scientific' scholarship by university academics,[49] those who propounded the increasingly common organic notions of the nation became readier to draw on, if not create, an often mystical sense of identity between people and place or, as it generally was, race and country. This was a historicist interpretation because it was usually posed in terms of a long-term identity. Although such work became more common, to a certain extent it took up conservative themes seen throughout the century, which included both an overt political and religious engagement and a criticism of what was presented as modern and progressive. In the preface to his major historical work, a biography of Elizabeth I's leading minister William Cecil, 1st Lord Burghley, Nares had declared that:

> he has not sought to qualify himself for an historian in the negative manner prescribed in a motto prefixed to the Memoirs of Horace Walpole: 'Pour être bon historien, il ne faudroit être d'aucune religion, d'aucune pais, d'aucune profession, d'aucune parti'. Believing such negations to be no securities against dangerous prejudices, but perhaps quite the contrary, he acknowledges that he prides himself upon being an Englishman, an English Protestant, a Church of England man, a Divine.

Nares used his account of Tudor England to defend the establishment of the Church of England: 'Catholic Christianity restored'.[50] The presence of religious minorities, however, ensured that confessionalism could prove a divisive form of identity and one that challenged progressive, in Britain Whig, nostrums. For example, the re-establishment of a Catholic hierarchy in England in 1850 lent, in response, renewed vigour to anti-Catholicism, including the celebration of Guy Fawkes' night.[51] Instead, the emphasis was placed on national identity.

Archaeologists, anthropologists and historians were expected to play a role in creating order out of the data they and others accumulated. They did so in large part in terms of cultures, and this emphasis on ethnicities fed into early fascism. Organic notions of the nation drew on, and sustained, a range of political and cultural notions and ideas including the legacies of Romanticism and Social Darwinism. Fictional works, such as Maurice Barrès's novel *Le Jardin de Bérénice* (1890), and the use of folk themes in classical music, for example by Sibelius in Finland, often expressed the historical sense of identity between people and place more clearly than books on history.[52] The German concept of the *Vaterland* (Fatherland) was matched elsewhere. It was consciously echoed and worked on in Meiji-era Japan, the elite of which was significantly shaped by the encounter with German Romanticism.

Such a sense of identity was, however, challenged by variant readings of the national past, and this helped to ensure that they were particularly controversial. This was especially the case with the memory of the French Revolution. Condemned by conservatives, its republicanism was affirmed by their rivals. The centenary of events associated with the Revolution further ensured that it remained a live issue toward the close of the nineteenth century. In January 1891, in response to the criticism of the Revolution, and specifically the Terror of 1793–4, as self-interested brutality in Victorien Sardou's play *Thermidor*, Georges Clemenceau, a prominent republican, told the French National Assembly that the Revolution was a 'bloc from which nothing may be removed'. The government itself banned the play on the grounds of public order: there had been audience disturbances in response to criticisms in the radical press.[53] The Revolution was to continue to be highly contentious in French public memory and François Furet was to argue that the Revolution did not end, in the sense of becoming a non-contentious political issue, until the late-twentieth century.[54] Republics faced particular problems in arguing for historical continuity, as they could not rely on real or spurious dynastic longevity. Nevertheless, the reputations of certain monarchs were adopted for the historical myths of republics, for example Charlemagne in France.[55]

Professional history and the modern nation state grew up in partnership. History found favour in Europe, Japan and the USA because creating a national history would help form national citizens, thus affirming the nation as the primary form of solidarity.[56] Intellectual and cultural developments interacted. Academic historians created a new discipline that freed history from philosophy, as Ranke and other new 'scientific' historians told the story, with the claim that people's thoughts and actions did not follow universal and timeless patterns but were shaped by time and place, an argument that lent itself to the idea of distinctive cultures. Ranke, and particularly his disciples, connected their study of change over time to the state and its public records.[57]

The development of Romantic nationalism and self-enclosing national professionalization catalyzed the new discipline's collapse of its promise to explore influences of time and place into the assumption that the most defining differences were those between nation states. By the turn of the twentieth century, historians had added pedagogy as a civic justification (as formulated, for example, by the American Historical Association's Committee of Seven in the late 1890s): loyalty to, and focus on, the nation state should define the events to be studied in classes on modern history and the perspective from which they should be studied. The organizing narrative was designed to identify and link events from the past by one theme – the nation in which those events occurred. History departments parcelled out the past into mainly national units. The function of history, particularly in the schools, was to provide the vision of a single people with a national destiny. Trying to define and contain experience within national borders, such history was particularly vulnerable to, and suspicious of, boundary-crossing ideas, institutions and people: immigrants, 'half-breeds' and people whose experiences and identities could not be easily corralled. The equivalent in terms of ancient history was a great concern to provide an acceptable account for modern nations of ethnic origins and of patterns of cultural diffusion.

The early-twentieth century

The nationalist character of public history was to be taken further in the early-twentieth century. This was especially so as ideologically-focused regimes sought added legitimacy for their position and goals. To a considerable extent, Fascist Italy and Nazi Germany maintained aspects of the existing tenor of both popular and academic history in their respective countries, and it is important not to allow an emphasis on Fascism and Communism, self-consciously transforming ideologies, to lead to a neglect of the continued role of nationalist public history throughout the West and also, as in the case of Japan, further afield. Indeed, the years before the First World War saw an upsurge in a nationalism that was strongly grounded in a presentation of history. This was particularly the case on the right, which lacked the socialist internationalism that found favour in some circles on the left. Nevertheless, it would be mistaken to imply that the use of history was largely the monopoly of one particular political strand, and on the left there was a liberal nationalism with a historical consciousness as well as a socialism with a strong awareness of radical antecedents.

The First World War saw all the combatants draw on a patriotic historiography as, during what became an unexpectedly long conflict, they sought to sustain the enthusiasm of mass armies and of the crucial civilian workforce. This effort was seen across a range of reference. Past military heroes and victories, such as Horatio Nelson and the battle of Trafalgar of 1805, were held up for emulation, in this case to underline British confidence in naval calibre and success in a more troubling maritime environment that included challenges, such as submarines, that Nelson had not faced. In addition, past ideas and images of heroism and self-sacrifice, for example those of chivalry, were extensively employed,[58] and this contributed to an acceptance, at least on the part of many non-combatants, of the death of many in the war. Academic historians produced efforts to justify war goals.

After the war, there was an immediate need for historical resource in the commemoration of the struggle, most obviously in the design of cemeteries and the staging of anniversaries. These provided an opportunity to underline national identity by providing a history of sacrifice that was, at the same time, a call for the sacrifice not to be in vain. Thus, past, present and future were linked. At a very different level, but often again reflecting themes of commitment, new media, especially cinema, also focused on national history, with films such as, in France, Abel Gance's *Napoléon* (1927) and Carl Teodor Dreyer's *La passion de Jeanne d'Arc* (1928), and, in Britain, *The Private Life of Henry VIII* (1933), *The Iron Duke* (1935), *Victoria the Great* (1937) and *Sixty Glorious Years* (1938).

The political character of the fashioning of history varied greatly, as did the intensity of debate. The facetious note struck in Britain with Walter Sellar and Julian Yeatman's *1066 and All That*, first published in the comic weekly *Punch* in 1929 and then as a book in 1930, was not widely matched. In Germany, the collapse of the Second Reich as a result of its failure in the First World War and the accompanying fall of the other ruling families, such as the Wittelsbachs of Bavaria, ensured that the focus of historical attention shifted from these dynasties. It led, instead, to a largely grim emphasis on the history of the *Volk* (people) and the hardship and dispossession it suffered as a consequence of defeat in the recent war. The Whiggish tone of George Macaulay

Trevelyan's best-selling *History of England* (1926) was far more optimistic.

Fascist history

In Benito Mussolini's Italy, Fascism was presented as a revival of Italian greatness. Considerable attention was devoted to the Roman heritage, not least in archaeology with an important support for excavations. In Rome, Mussolini's works included the laying out of the Via dei Fori Imperiali in 1932. The iconography of Italian Fascism made frequent reference to classical, especially imperial, Rome, not least in its name and its salute. Mussolini's Italy was thus located with reference to the past: it was displayed as the rebirth of ancient glory. Past episodes of success were appropriated to the cause of an exemplary history. Mussolini's Italy was also viewed as the culmination of the drive for independence and unification seen with the Risorgimento. Fascism was presented as realizing the ideal of the 'nation state'. In contrast, Italy's liberal governments of the late nineteenth and early twentieth centuries were condemned, and Mussolini's 'March on Rome' in 1922, a key stage in his seizure of power, was interpreted as regenerating Italy.

Much emphasis was also placed on the contrast between the national humiliation at the hands of Ethiopian forces at the battle of Adua (Adowa) in 1896 and the success of Mussolini's forces in conquering Ethiopia in 1935–6. This was seen in the film *Scipio Africanus* (1937), an account of a Roman general (236– *c.*183 BCE) of the Second Punic War (218–201 BCE), that counterpointed the Roman defeat by the Carthaginian general Hannibal at Cannae (216 BCE) with Scipio's victory at Zama (202 BCE) which had led to the surrender of Carthage, offering a parallel with the contrast between Adua (Adowa) and Mussolini's victory. Zama was in Africa, and the subtext was that Italy should be in the continent. A division of Fascist Blackshirts was used as extras in the film and they were then sent to Africa.

Within the scholarly community, the 'ideal' Fascist historiographical line, however, was supported by relatively few historians, even Fascists. The principal academic innovation indeed was a greater stress on diplomatic history. Mussolini was far more concerned about the public dimension. He wanted to secure not only Italy's place in history but also that of Fascism. In *The Doctrine of Fascism* (1932), which he co-authored, Fascism was presented as 'an historical conception . . . Outside history man is nothing.'

Nazi history

A similar reconfiguration of public history was seen in Nazi Germany, although with the important addition of a marked racist component. The latter ensured that German history was understood primarily as that of the Aryan Germans, part of the process by which the state created in 1871 overlaid earlier identities and loyalties, in this case those of Germans with different ethnic origins. Alongside the traditional nationalist emphasis on conflict with foreign states, which, in the German case, included the role of foreign powers in causing and benefiting from the crisis of the Thirty Years' War (1618–48), the most serious crisis that could be readily recovered in the German historical memory, there was an understanding of German nationalism very much in terms of the *Volk*, and a concentration on ethnic rivalry with non-Aryans, especially Slavs and Jews. As with many other public histories, the vision of the national past was to an extent depoliticized by focusing on these external threats (the Jews treated as a threat to the organic, ethnic concept of Germanness). Thus, in creating a history of, and in terms of, Aryans, serious regional, political, religious, social and economic divisions and differences within Germany were downplayed, if not ignored. Archaeologists were expected to demonstrate the range of the Aryan people and their cultural and economic superiority over others.[59] The focus on racial origins led to a downplaying of the earlier tradition of studying Classical influences in German history, while the stress on the *Volk* challenged Whig progressive narratives of the celebration and protection of the self. Mussolini similarly declared that Fascism was against individualism.

Continuing the pre-Nazi mode of German (and non-German) history, recent history was shaped within a long-standing presentation of national struggle. The Versailles Peace Settlement after the end of the First World War was seen in terms of cruel and inappropriate dispossession and, while academics challenged the war guilt clause of the Versailles Treaty,[60] much public history was devoted to presenting the case for the lost German lands, a theme also taken by other states that had lost territory in the peace settlement: especially Hungary, but also Bulgaria, Turkey and Austria. Budapest had a memorial garden laid out as a map of the old kingdom of Hungary. It both recorded the losses suffered by the Treaty of Trianon of 1920, such as Transylvania to Romania, and made them seem unnatural.

Many professional historians backed the Nazi regime. This was true not only of its foreign policy and the quest for expansion to the east, but also of the attack on the liberal post-war Weimar constitution which few historians had supported.[61] In both academic and popular spheres the depiction of the Nazi regime as the Third Reich looked back to earlier periods of national power and glory. History to Hitler was also a lived process that he encapsulated, so that his personal drama became an aspect of the historic, and thus, at once, historical and timeless, mission of the German people. The cult of personality, and the associated sense of historical mission, were very pronounced in totalitarian regimes.

Spain

Ethnicity was again the issue in Spain where the right-wing Nationalists under General Francisco Franco seized control in the Civil War of 1936–9. In the subsequent presentation of Spanish history, the Jews and Muslims were ignored, the medieval *Reconquista* of Spain from Islam received much attention, and nineteenth- and twentieth-century modernization and domestic politics were denied in favour of an apparently more heroic and united Catholic past. Heroes included Rodrigo Diaz, *El Cid* (*c.*1043–99), who was inaccurately presented as a Spanish patriot when in fact he was a soldier of fortune who fought for Muslim rulers as well as Christians,[62] and also Ferdinand III of Castile (r. 1217–52) under whom much of southern Spain had been conquered from the Moors, and Ferdinand and Isabella, the unifiers of Spain. The Franco regime encouraged an approach to Spanish history that praised unification and emphasized the eternal and unbreakable unity of the country, and the central place of Catholicism and church–state harmony within it.[63] Catholicism indeed played a major role in the regime's self-image and offered a key theme of continuity.

In part, this approach represented an attempt to justify the Nationalist position during the Spanish Civil War, an attempt that continued after Franco's death in 1975. Thus, the Museo del Ejército in Madrid displayed his Civil War car with the description 'The Car the General used during the Crusade'. The Francoist approach emphasized what it saw as moral factors, rather than material ones, when seeking to ascribe value and explain success in both past and present, and this provided a way to join past and present together in opposition not only to Communism but also to what was seen as American materialism. During the Civil War, the Republicans were portrayed as the servants of the Antichrist.

This conflict provided the foundation myth of Francoism, offering rationale and occasion for Franco's power. At the same time, like other public histories, for example that of the Soviet Union, there were shifts in emphasis that reflected changing circumstances and requirements. Thus, in response to growing, albeit very measured, liberalization from the late 1950s, the Franco regime came to devote less attention to this aspect of its history and, instead, to emphasize the value of popular acceptance of governmental continuity. The stress was now on forgetting the war, as an aspect of a national reconciliation that would permit continued conservative ascendancy after Franco's death.[64]

Far from being an aberration, the Francoist stance represented an aspect of a much more widely displayed emphasis in Spanish history on a unified national past and on a distinctly Spanish Catholicism, and against revolution and internationalism. In particular the stance emphasized Spanish unity rather than regional autonomy, especially that of Catalonia with its pronounced separatist character: the Catalans had been prominent in the opposition to Franco. Because they established unity in the peninsula after the post-Roman divisions, the Visigoths, who ruled most of Iberia from the late fifth century until its conquest by the Moors in the 710s, were much admired by the regime and Franco praised the Visigoths when establishing a museum devoted to them in 1969. Since Franco's death, however, the Visigoths have fallen decidedly out of fashion.[65]

Under Franco, a national ethnicity of Spain was on offer and regional ethnicities were ignored. Ethnic concepts of national identity were especially popular with European right-wing movements. For example, French right-wingers, both under Vichy and before, adopted an ethnic notion of nationhood that affected their historical views.

Asian authoritarianism

Similar developments could be seen in Asia. The new regime that took power in Siam (Thailand) in 1932, and that was to cooperate with the Japanese during the Second World War (a position downplayed in subsequent Thai history), offered a nationalist view of the Thai past designed to provide more than the royalist stress on dynastic continuity. The new constitution of 1932 lessened royal authority. The emphasis now was also on 'the Thai people', in part a creation matching the concern with ethnic homogeneity seen in Europe. The Chinese minority assimilated by adopting Thai names and culture. The state was renamed Thailand in 1939. The onward march of this people was presented as validating political developments.

In Japan, there was controversy over the national myth that traced Japan and its emperor back to a legendary past. This myth limited archaeological discussion, while historians who challenged the received view were criticized. Tsuda Sōkichi, a critic of the imperial myth which he claimed had been invented by eighth-century writers, was sentenced in 1942 to two years' imprisonment for *lèse-majesté*. More generally, the nationalist character of most historical scholarship in Japan became more pronounced in the 1930s and early 1940s as censorship effectively made it impossible for more liberal scholars to publish anything for fear of persecution. Nationalist accounts of the relationship between Japan and East Asia were used to justify Japanese expansionism. Naito Konan, an influential Japanese journalist and historian of China, argued that Japan received the baton of Chinese culture from the Chinese after the Song dynasty (960–1127), a mistaken view that neglected the important influence from China over subsequent centuries but one that was employed to support rule of Korea and attacks on China since the Japanese were, in effect, returning Chinese culture to them.

Communist history

Communist public history mirrored that of Fascist states in that the natural didacticism of the state-supported version of the past was extended in a dictatorial context to include no tolerance of different accounts. Appointments were carefully controlled by the state and historians judged insufficiently zealous became targets, as in the Soviet Union from 1929 and in China's Anti-Rightist campaign of 1957–8 and, from 1966, its Cultural Revolution. Soviet historians were pressed particularly hard to support the nostrums of government policy in the 1930s within an anti-intellectual context in which many were purged, which meant being sacked and, generally, imprisoned and killed.[66]

Nevertheless, there were also important differences between Communist and Fascist history that, in part, were an aspect of the contrast between totalitarianism and authoritarianism. In the case of Communist states, there was a more rigid historical model, that of Marxism, and it was important to use history in order to demonstrate the truth of the Marxist approach and to show that the formation of Communist parties, and their seizure and use of power, were the necessary end of the historical process. This sense of purpose was linked to a conviction of the importance of rapid, forced modernization, with the past seen in terms of backwardness. The apparent inevitability of this process permitted the suspension of humanitarian constraints on policy: those killed by the state were necessary victims.

As history was seen as intensely political, there was no room for historians to be anything other than committed to the appropriate doctrine. There was also the problem that the public history on offer was supposed to be at once national and global, as Marxism was a universal model. In place of thinking of history in terms of states, and of the states' system in terms of homogeneous blocks of territory, the standard pattern in nationalist accounts, the emphasis was on a universal struggle that spanned national boundaries: on class struggle in its varied manifestations. This even extended to pre-history: in 1955 the Chinese Communist Party launched a campaign against what it saw as the capitalist mentality in archaeology and the handling of cultural relics. Mao Zedong, the Chinese Communist dictator from the proclamation of the People's Republic of China in 1949 until his death in 1976, expected archaeology to demonstrate the truths of Marxism, and the value(s) of the proletariat, not least the cultural interest offered by the remains of ordinary people and the superiority of the latter.[67]

In discussing history, the Communists were particularly interested in those sections of the past that could be readily interpreted in Marxist terms, and in the history and pre-history of Communist agitation. Considerable attention was devoted to social and economic history, not only that of the industrial proletariat that was awarded a key role in Marxist history but also the earlier history of the peasantry whose history was seen in terms of class struggle. This approach rested on a conviction that class consciousness was well defined, widely held and international (each of which is questionable), and events were portrayed in these terms. A heroic account of the revolutionary struggle was offered. In the Soviet Union, the film industry was nationalized in 1919 and deliberately used to propagate an exemplary account of recent history. This focused on the cruelty of the old order, as in Sergei Eisenstein's film *Strike* (1925), which depicted Tsarist troops shooting workers, and *Battleship Potemkin* (1925), a film produced to commemorate the twentieth anniversary of the unsuccessful 1905 revolution. The tenth anniversary of the 1917 revolution was marked by a series of films that included Vsevolod Pudovkin's *The End of St Petersburg* (1927), Esther Shub's *The Fall of the Romanov Dynasty* (1927), and Eisenstein's *October* (1928).

Communists stressed the continuous nature of struggle and thus looked for episodes in the past that could be seen as similar, an ahistorical process that failed to place enough weight on the specific contexts of particular episodes. The continuing strong sense of history held by Marxists was indicated by the British Rail, Maritime and Transport Union, whose annual general meeting in June 2004 backed a motion for the distribution of free or subsidized copies of classic socialist texts, including *Revolt on the Clyde* (1936) by the Communist MP Willie Gallacher, an account of the 1919 industrial turmoil in Glasgow. This was very much in accord with the traditional partisan trade unionism of a union whose general secretary, Bob Crow, has a bust of Vladimir Lenin, Soviet leader from 1917 to 1924, in his office. Traditional trade union banners often depicted Karl Marx, the key figure in the historical iconography of socialism.

At the same time, Communist history was not a monolith. There were, for example, many shifts and changes over time in Soviet history. These included the shift from a universal to a national perspective, with a greater stress on the state, the methodological shift from economic to ideological determinism and, finally, in the 1980s, in response to the Gorbachev *glasnost* – the movement for openness and modernization designed to strengthen Soviet Communism – calls for a new history that would serve the goals of reform.[68]

The control of the state over Soviet education was very tight, reflecting a strong belief in the importance of its ideological value. Indeed, political education was seen as a goal of the system. The role of central control was such that standardization in the teaching of history was taken further than had been the case under the Nazis. The institutions permitted to teach history were all very much under the control of the state and the Communist Party. Research and publication were focused on research institutes whose agenda were carefully controlled, for example in Latvia, the Institute of Party History, the Institute of History of the Academy of Sciences of the Latvian Soviet Socialist Republic and the University of Latvia. Some themes and individuals were treated as unacceptable for study. Archives shared in this politicization. I can recall a Communist slogan about history being of, and for, the people at the entrance to an East German archive in 1979. Historians were expected to toe the party line as an aspect of the attempt to control what was defined as cultural production. Opening the first Congress of Soviet Writers in 1934, Andrey Zhdanov declared:

> Our Soviet literature is not afraid of the charge of being 'tendentious' . . . in an epoch of class struggle there is not and cannot be a literature which is not class literature, not tendentious, allegedly non-political.[69]

In their history, the Communists offered clear-cut contrasts, as well as a teleology. They propounded a conflict between the world of socialism, i.e. Communism, and that of divided and decaying capitalism; a struggle in which the former was helped by the extent to which allegedly capitalist states could only hold down their workers by force. The strength of Soviet historiography was its concern to highlight social and economic as well as political history, but the weaknesses were readily apparent: the limitations and distortions imposed by the narrow and rigid official ideology, combined with Russocentrism. This led to ahistorical perceptions, and often to exaggerations of what were taken to be developments in the 'forces of production' and manifestations of 'class struggle'. Far too much attention was devoted to Lenin and the Bolsheviks, with the assumption that all history was building up to their inevitable victory in Russia in the Great October Socialist Revolution of 1917. The impact of Communist historical texts was increased by the very rigid nature of the Soviet national curriculum: every school was supposed to teach the same thing to the same class at the same time, and teachers were very much under Party control. The role of religion in history was either neglected or attacked, although Joseph Stalin, Soviet leader from 1924 until 1953, found it expedient to use the unifying religious identity of Orthodox Russia during the Second World War.

The Soviet view of history combined anti-Western Slavophile themes, seen strongly in Russia in the nineteenth century, with more specifically Communist perspectives. In the first case, instead of accepting that Scandinavian raiders/traders/conquerors in effect created the state of Rus by subduing scattered Slav tribes, the Soviets fostered an inaccurate anti-Norse line as it fitted their nationalist and ideological prejudices. Rejecting the idea that Scandinavians had played a major role in western Russia, the Soviets emphasized a largely mythical, organic rise in Slav self-awareness, and thus statehood, in the pre-Kievan era. Archaeologists were expected to support this view, rejecting the work of Scandinavian counterparts. The debate focused on early Russian towns: the Soviets were resistant to the idea that they, and the social developments represented by urban life, had been boosted by the Scandinavians.

A reading of the history of Russia's international position also played a role in Communist policy towards foreign countries. Lenin had been wary of what he termed 'Greater Russian chauvinism', but Stalin, who used such chauvinism to his own ends, was convinced from his reading of early-modern Russian history, especially the Time of Troubles (1604–13), when the Poles occupied Moscow from 1610 to 1612 and Wladyslaw, the eldest son of King Sigismund III of Poland, was proclaimed tsar, that the Poles were a threat to Russia and had to be weakened and brought under control.

Equally, episodes from Russian foreign policy in the past were explained in terms of the current interests of the Soviet state. In 1951, the prestigious Stalin Prize was awarded to L.A. Nikiforov for his *Russko-angliiskie otnosheniia pri Petre I* (1950). This study of the difficult Anglo-Russian relations during the reign of Peter I (1689–1725) was intended as a parallel to current Cold War relations, for the historical episode was presented in terms of a harsh treatment of Russia by Britain, particularly with the naval expeditions to the Baltic during the reign of

George I (1714–21), even though during the Great Northern War (1700–21) an aggressive Russia had played the key role in ending the Swedish hegemony in the Baltic. As was commonplace with Soviet history written during Stalin's ascendancy, Nikiforov used only Russian sources.

The history of Russia served to exemplify Communist themes. The Pugachev rising of 1773–5 was emphasized for the eighteenth century and presented as a peasants' rising (rather than with the emphasis being, as it should have been, on non-Russian participation, especially by Yaik Cossacks[70]), while the peasantry were also shown as taking a major role against the Napoleonic invasion of Russia in 1812 and as heroically contributing to its failure. This contrasted with the pre-Revolutionary emphasis on the role of the elite in Russian history, and with earlier Marxist views that focused on the radical potential of the industrial proletariat, and presented peasants, instead, as anti-revolutionary reactionary forces. Risings outside Russia were also extensively covered in public history during the Communist era and were eagerly appropriated as part of the Communist heritage, whether those of the slaves under Spartacus against the Roman republic, or the Hussites in the fifteenth century in what became the modern Czech Republic, or the German Peasants' War of 1524–5, or the French peasantry in the seventeenth century.[71] Risings against Communist rule, such as that by Soviet sailors at Kronstadt in 1921, and also peasant resistance, however, were ignored. Concern about the presentation of the past extended to the policing of fictional accounts. Boris Pasternak was persecuted for his novel *Doctor Zhivago* (1957), which was set in the Russian Civil War, the formative period of the Communist state. Banned in the Soviet Union, it was first published in Italy.

Similar emphases were seen in other Communist states, while the extensive treatment of Russian history was a characteristic of their coverage of the rest of the world. A benign impression of Russo/Soviet history was offered, both in republics that had been absorbed (after conquest) into the Soviet Union, such as Lithuania, Latvia and Estonia, and in client states, such as Hungary. The emphasis was on the Soviet role in the liberations from Nazi occupation or from Fascist rule and Nazi alliance in 1944–5, and also, where pertinent, Russia's part in earlier liberations from the Ottomans. The latter was very significant in Bulgarian history.[72] Chronology and periodization were also set by the Soviet example. Thus, the October 1917 Revolution was treated as a major turning point.

In East Germany, the Communist state created in the Soviet-occupied zone of Germany, the tone was very different from what had been the case in the age of German nationalism. The focus was on past instances of radicalism, such as the German Peasants' War of 1524–5 (seen in terms of economic, not religious, radicalism), the Jacobin Mainz Republic of 1793 (in fact a fairly atypical episode of popular attitudes), and the German revolution of 1848–9; and Communist opposition to Hitler was emphasized. The 1930s and early 1940s were defined as a 'Nazi era' with responsibility placed on Hitler and the Nazi Party, rather than on the Germans themselves. East Germany was seen as a product of a true German political culture: that of popular radicalism. Inconvenient episodes in Soviet history, such as the Molotov–Ribbentrop pact of 1939 (the alliance between Hitler and Stalin that served as the prelude to their joint attack on Poland), were omitted;[73] just as the Poles were encouraged to ignore extensive opposition to Russian domination in the eighteenth and nineteenth centuries, and not to emphasize the Warsaw Rising of 1944.

Similarly, the Czechoslovaks focused on the fifteenth-century Hussites (presented as a popular force), and the 1680 and 1775 Bohemian peasant risings. These were used to argue that there was a popular nationalism directed against foreign rule, an approach that removed the centuries of Habsburg rule from a comfortable nostalgia and, instead, presented them in a hostile guise. This was amplified by using the palaces of the great aristocratic families as museums, thus apparently demonstrating that the people had been exploited for the profit of these families, the foreign, particularly German, antecedents and interests of whom were emphasized. There was particular criticism of Habsburg policy in the Thirty Years' War which was presented in terms of the suppression of Bohemian liberties after the Battle of the White Mountain.[74]

For Hungary, there was an attempt to run together the unsuccessful 1848–9 war of independence against the Habsburgs, the 'patriotic' war of the short-lived Hungarian Soviet Republic in 1919, and the liberation of Hungary in 1944–5; and in Bulgaria opposition to the monarchy in 1923 was linked to the resistance during the Second World War. When, in 1958, the Bulgarians published an atlas of Bulgarian resistance in 1941–4, they were asserting that Bulgarian identity could be seen in anti-Fascist terms: that the presence of Bulgaria in the eastern bloc was not simply the consequence of Soviet conquest, but that that conquest in 1944 accorded with Bulgarian history. Similarly, in the Soviet republics in Central Asia the emphasis was on a pro-Soviet and Marxist account.

Alongside Communism and Russophilia came the suppression of nationalist views judged inappropriate, such as those from Ukraine in the 1930s. In 1968, Ibrahim Muminov, president of the Uzbek Academy of Sciences, was dismissed for publishing a book querying the critical orthodoxy about Temur (Tamerlane) as a savage barbarian, and all copies were removed on the instructions of the Central Communist Committee of Uzbekistan.[75]

Conversely, what could be presented as acceptable nationalism was lauded, as in the emphasis on the strength of indigenous opposition to Fascism, for example in Bulgaria, Hungary and Czechoslovakia. In the latter, considerable attention was devoted to the Slovak uprising of 1944 which diverted notice from five years of widespread Slovak cooperation with Germany. The Czechoslovak Communist Party inaccurately claimed that it had played the key role in the uprising, and attributed its suppression to 'bourgeois' Slovaks and to the lack of Anglo-American support. As a result of the uprising, there was the usual commemoration, with war memorials, annual celebrations, films and naming, for example the Slovak National Uprising Bridge in Bratislava.[76]

This process was seen even more clearly in Yugoslavia, where Josip Tito's break with the Soviet Union in 1949 encouraged an emphasis on the role of the Communist partisans in what was seen as a 'war of national liberation'. The role of non-Communist partisans (Droza Mihailovíc's Chetniks), as well as of Western assistance and (after the break) of the entry of Soviet forces into Serbia in September 1944, were all minimized, and necessarily so as the war was used to validate the ruling order. This continued to be the case when Yugoslavia faced dissolution. In February 1989, the People's Defence Commission of Slobodan Miloševíc's League of Communists of Serbia attacked the public separatist meeting of Slovene politicians at Ljubljana as an 'insolent attack on the achievements of the National Liberation War, Tito's Yugoslavia. . .'.[77]

More generally, the early history of the Eastern European peoples was appropriated to serve the cause of governments, as well as of state identities and interests. Archaeologists were expected to support the cause of the state. Albanian archaeologists were required to substantiate the links with ancient Illyria proclaimed by the state, based on the idea that the ancient Illyrians were ancestors of the modern Albanians, and to find a wide scope for the Illyrians; this then served to extend the claims of modern Albania. In Romania, the traditional claim for ethnic continuity since the Roman period was maintained, although the Hungarians challenged the Romanian assertion of the historical evidence for the Romanness of Dacia, the Roman Empire north of the Danube.

Nationalist public history thus offered a panacea to help cover the unpopularity of Communism. This was an aspect of the rapid changes in the nationalist/universalist mix in state presentations of history and memory in the Soviet bloc after 1945, as the emphasis shifted between the universalist cause of the proletariat and the particular resonance of the histories of individual states. Thus, in East Germany in the 1980s there was a new emphasis on German heroes, particularly Luther and Frederick the Great, as part of an emphasis on a total history of East Germany that was not restricted to the radical tradition.

A powerful aspect of nationalism was provided by the assimilation of newly acquired territories as boundaries were redrawn after the Second World War and peoples were forcibly moved in order to create more ethnically homogenous states that conformed to processes of identification focused on such homogeneity. This was a multilayered process, including the renaming of cities (German Königsberg becoming Russian Kaliningrad), and the appropriation of regions, such as formerly German but now Polish Silesia, in part through accounts of their history. This process could serve to consolidate states, but also to challenge them as ethnic minorities, such as Magyars in the Transylvanian region in Romania, resisted such appropriation and turned to a different history[78] in order to assert a defiant communal identity. So indeed even more clearly did exiles, such as the Germans expelled from Eastern Europe. Within Yugoslavia, this defiant course was also taken by Croatian and Serbian nationalists, leading Tito, the Yugoslav dictator, to condemn nationalist historiography in the early 1960s, and to imprison prominent individuals such as Franjo Tudjman, who was dismissed from his post in the Institute of the History of the Workers' Movement in 1967 and imprisoned in 1971 and again in 1981 (see pp. 141–2).

As more widely in Communist states, tolerance of different historical views varied in accordance with more general political shifts. Historians were purged as part of the intellectual policing of Communist societies, a process that was particularly acute in the late 1940s and early 1950s. Gheorghe Brătianu, Professor of History at Bucharest University from 1940 until 1947 and a prominent liberal as well as a major historian, was imprisoned, dying in prison in 1953, and publication of his works was forbidden in Romania. In East Germany, non-Marxist historians faced increasing pressure, which led many to flee to the West, and publications that did not reach appropriate conclusions were criticized. Alexander Abusch's *Der Irrweg der Nation* (1947), which searched for Nazi origins not in capitalism but across German history back to Luther, was condemned in 1951.[79] The purging of historians was matched by the destruction of sites that offered an undesirable public memory. The country houses of Prussian junkers (landed gentry) were demolished, while the castle in Berlin, the Stadtschloss, was destroyed to make way for the Palast der Republik, the base for East Germany's parliament.

Recent history was subject to radical revisions as Communist politicians purged each other, leading to the saying 'the past is always changing – only the future is certain'. Across much of Eastern Europe political reform after the Stalin era, however, led to intellectual liberalism and a measure of historical independence, as in Czechoslovakia in 1956–68, Poland from 1956 and Croatia in 1967–72. Among Polish academics, alongside the works of the ideologically committed, such as Boguslaw Leśnodorski's *Les Jacobins polonais* (1965), came those of sceptics such as Jósef Gierowski, Jerzy Michalski and Emanuel Rostworowski. Subsequent reaction, however, especially in Czechoslovakia, led to renewed rigidity, orthodoxy and repression.[80] The latter extended to émigrés, whose historical works were rarely noted in Communist histories and thus tended to circulate secretly.

Elsewhere in the Communist world, there was also an emphasis on the Marxist approach and an attempt to present national history in this mould. After the Communist takeover of China in 1949, there was pressure for a new history to match the new society being forcibly and brutally created. As Communism was the public ideology, it was scarcely surprising that Soviet historiography seemed the appropriate model in terms of content, approach and institutionalization, particularly as the Sino-Soviet break was not to occur for another decade. As a consequence, the number of Chinese scholars employing Western techniques or writing histories of the West went into decline, part of a more general sundering of intellectual links, especially with the USA, that had been important in the first half of the century.

Communist historians favoured an interpretation of Chinese history that forced everything into a safe and unimaginative Marxist framework in which peasant uprisings were seen as the locomotive of history. Much Marxist historiography in China revolved around periodization of Chinese history: somehow shoehorning China's long history into the Marxist paradigm of stages of historical development. What emerged as the orthodoxy was the period of the Shang dynasty (1800–1027 BCE) to Warring States (403–221 BCE) as a 'slave society', with the Warring States and the Qin dynasty ushering in a feudal stage that lasted about 2,000 years. This produced some odd results, from the Western perspective, with the highly centralized Qin administration (221–206 BCE) branded as the quintessence of feudalism. Labelling both Qin and Qing (Manchu, 1644–1911 CE) as feudal did not aid understanding of the differences between them or help with the identification of long-term trends across the two millennia of imperial China. The presentation of Chinese history was very much in line with Marxist orthodoxy as interpreted by Mao Zedong who, in 1939, had discerned Marxist-derived continuity in some very diverse struggles:

> The history of China's transformation into a semi-colony and colony by imperialism in collusion with Chinese feudalism is at the same time a history of struggle by the Chinese people against imperialism and its lackeys. The Opium War [1840–2], the Movement of the Taiping Heavenly Kingdom [1850–63], the Sino-French War [1883–5], the Sino-Japanese War [of 1894–5], the Reform Movement of 1898, the Yi Ho Tuan Movement, the Revolution of 1911, the May 4th Movement [1919], the May 30th Movement, the Northern Expedition [1926–8], the Agrarian Revolutionary War and the present War of Resistance Against Japan – all testify to the Chinese people's indomitable spirit in fighting imperialism and its lackeys.[81]

The volumes later published by the Foreign Languages Press, translated from the *History of Modern China* compiled by members of the history departments of Futan University and Shanghai Teachers' University, and published by the Shanghai People's Publishing House, did not deviate from this line. Significantly, no authors were named. Chapter headings for *The Opium War* (1976) included 'The Covetous British Invaders', 'British Aggression Brings War to China', 'Popular Anti-British Struggles in Fukien, Chekiang and the Lower Yangtze Valley', 'The U.S. and French Invaders Follow Suit', and 'Birth of a Semi-Colonial and Semi-Feudal Society', while Karl Marx was cited more than once. The tone was clear-cut:

> With foreign capitalism undermining China's social economy, the contradiction between the forces of aggression and the Chinese people deepened. The five trading ports became the bases for capitalist aggression against China . . . Foreign gangsters and adventurers gathered in these places where robbery, murder and other crimes were common occurrences.[82]

In the book on the Taiping Revolution of 1850–63, also published in 1976, it was presented as a sequel of the contradictions between foreign aggression and the interests of the Chinese people, and the Taipings were praised for struggling against foreign capitalism as well as feudalism. This permitted a castigation of the Qing (Manchu) dynasty as imperialist 'lackeys'. Yet the revolution itself had been weak:

> The peasant masses want liberation and dare to engage in armed struggle to gain it, but in the midst of success, they are easily carried away and do not see the revolution through to the end. During the triumphant days when the capital was established at Nanking, bad old habits like conservatism, pleasure-seeking and factionalism besieged

the revolutionary ranks. The Taiping heroes lost the strength to hit
back under the onslaught of decadent feudal habits.

Defeat was inevitable because of the stage then of Chinese development, as the episode illustrated Mao's dictum that 'without the leadership of the working class revolution fails'. Yet the Taiping Revolution
was presented as a source of inspiration for later struggles, and as pro-
pelling 'history forward'[83] (see, also, p. 167). There was much concern
in the 1960s and 1970s with peasant leaders in the past, and they were
assessed in terms of their loyalty to what was seen as the revolution of
the time. Aside from the teleological and heroic depiction of recent
history, there was also criticism of what was seen as conservative.
Confucius was condemned as 'feudal', and Confucianism was not to
revive until the period of reform in the last two decades of the twentieth century.

A more abrupt shortening of history was attempted in Cambodia,
where the seizure of power by the Communist Khmer Rouge in 1975
was stated to be the last stage in a popular struggle against hostile
forces, past and present being run together in an ideological vista. 1975
became Year Zero, as the past was swept away by a regime determined
to build the future, even at the cost of killing large numbers of its population including all intellectuals. It was also necessary to come to terms
historically with the international alignments of Communism. Just as
Eastern Europeans were told that they had been friends or bene-
ficiaries of the Russians in the past, so the Vietnamese invasion of
Cambodia in 1978–9, and the subsequent replacement of Khmer
Rouge rule, led to an emphasis on close links between Cambodia and
Vietnam in the past.

Across the Communist world, the domestic resistance to Communist
views of history was expressed not only in terms of an important private
focus on family memory and, frequently, religious continuity, for
example in Lithuania, Poland, Russia and Ukraine. In addition, despite
the efforts of the state to suppress anti-Communist accounts and, alter-
nately, to suppress or to marginalize non-Communist ones, there was a
circulation of hostile literature that challenged Communist viewpoints,
especially on recent history. Thus Alexander Solzhenitsyn, a Soviet
officer in the Second World War, who had been imprisoned for criticizing Stalin's conduct of the war, was subsequently in trouble for his writings, not least for his attacks on Soviet censorship. His novels *Cancer
Ward* (1968) and *The First Circle* (1968), set in the dehumanizing institutions of the Soviet police state, were banned, he was expelled from
the Soviet Writers' Union in 1969, and he was arrested and exiled in
1974 for his description of Stalinist terror in *The Gulag Archipelago*

(1973–8). The collapse of the Soviet control-state, conversely, led in 1990 to the restoration of his citizenship and to his being awarded the Russian State Literature Prize, while Solzhenitsyn increasingly offered a Slavophile/Russian nationalistic viewpoint, to which Orthodox Christianity contributed greatly, that propounded a critique of both Communism and the West, especially consumerism.

Solzhenitsyn's Soviet-era novels captured the atmosphere and psychological world of the Soviet police state in a way that academic studies could rarely depict, although in some respects they were well-researched, scholarly studies. They offered a public history very different from the Public History of the period, which was why they were prohibited. In *The First Circle*, Solzhenitsyn presented the uncertainty of transferred prisoners, and the cruelty and harshness of their treatment:

> will they stop his correspondence for years on end, so that his family thinks he is dead? . . . Will he die of dysentery in his cattle truck? Or die of hunger because the train does not stop for six days and no rations are issued?

In Yugoslavia, as in the Soviet Union, the account of the Second World War was crucially important in asserting the legitimacy of Communist rule. In Yugoslavia, criticism of the wartime role of the Communist partisans was unacceptable as this role was used to justify the Party's post-war monopoly of power, not least the position of Josip Tito, prime minister from 1945 until his death in 1980. Milovan Djilas, a prominent wartime partisan, broke with Tito, as a result of which he was imprisoned. In *Wartime* (1977), Djilas controversially revealed that Tito had secretly negotiated with the Germans in 1942–3, a marked contrast with the Communist public history which emphasized negotiations between the Germans and the rival Chetniks, in order to delegitimate the latter, and presented the Communists as very different to the Chetniks. There was a parallel with the pro-Resistance myths in France that supported the political position of Charles de Gaulle from 1945 (see p. 108).

Other critics in Eastern Europe engaged directly with Marxist notions of history. Thus Jan Patočka, a Czech philosopher of history, provided accounts that broke from the materialist nature and teleology of the latter. In his *Platon a Europa* (*Plato and Europe*, 1973), which began as private lectures, he emphasized the value of the unconstrained pursuit of knowledge, while, in *Heretical Essays in the Philosophy of History*, which was illegally published in 1975, Patočka also came to the unacceptable view that history lacked meaning, a radical break from the Communist approach. As a consequence, to Patočka, history scarcely recorded the progress of the working class, which was the goal of Communist history. Patočka's political allegiance was underlined by his role as the author of the Charter 77 of human rights, while the response of the authorities was demonstrated by the fact that his works were not published until after the Czech Communist Party fell from power in 1989.

Conclusions

The situation in recent decades is the subject of Chapters 5, 6, 7 and 8, but enough has been said to indicate the close links between public history and national politics. The relationship was less insistent in the liberal democracies of the West, which did not shoot historians nor, on the whole, transform museum exhibits after changes of government, but even there the links were very important, not least as state and private historical activities were often closely related, for example through corporatism. In Western states, and even more elsewhere, the relationship between public history and national politics was also persistent in the shape of all, or some, of school syllabi and textbooks, as well as public influence over the presentation of history in the media, and the symbolic treatment of the past in celebrations. Each merits detailed consideration, and each contributes to a situation in which independent academic history has scant impact on public views. Instead, state control of, or at least influence over, higher education in most countries is important, although the role of the state in secondary education was, and is, more important in moulding public attitudes to history than that of the academic profession. The state's role in secondary education was also an aspect of the expansion of historical consciousness in an increasingly democratic age.

Notes

1   G.J. Whitrow, *Time in History: Views of Time from Prehistory to the Present Day* (Oxford, 1989).
2   P. Nabokov, *A Forest of Time: American Indian Ways of History* (Cambridge, 2002).
3   J. Demos, *Circles and Lines: The Shape of Life in Early America* (Cambridge, Mass., 2004).
4   W. Haller, *Foxe's Book of Martyrs and the Elect Nation* (London, 1963).
5   P. Meyvaert, '"Rainaldus est malus scriptor Francigenus" – Voicing National Antipathy in the Middle Ages', *Speculum*, 66 (1991), 743–63; C. Beaune, *The Birth of an Ideology: Myths and Symbols of Nation in Late-Medieval France* (Berkeley, CA, 1991); T. Turville-Petre, *England the Nation: Language, Literature, and National Identity, 1290–1340* (Oxford, 1996); A.P. Smyth (ed.), *Medieval Europeans: Studies in Ethnic Identity and National Perspectives in Medieval Europe* (Basingstoke, 1998).

6   G.W.S. Barrow, *Robert Bruce and the Community of the Realm* (2nd edn, Edinburgh, 1988).

7   L. Scales, '*Germen Militiae*: War and German Identity in the Later Middle Ages', *Past and Present*, 180 (August 2003), 80–1.

8   F.J. Levy, *Tudor Historical Thought* (London, 1967); R Helgerson, *Forms of Nationhood: The Elizabethan Writing of England* (Chicago, 1992); G. Brennan, *Patriotism, Power and Print: Language, Literature and Nationalism in Sixteenth-Century England* (Cambridge, 2003); D. Woolf, *The Social Circulation of the Past: English Historical Culture, 1500–1730* (Oxford, 2003).

9   W.B. Smith, 'Germanic Pagan Antiquity in Lutheran Historical Thought', *Journal of the Historical Society*, 4 (2004), 357.

10   Earl of Ilchester (ed.), *Letters to Henry Fox* (London, 1915), pp. 13–14, 9.

11   R. Browning, *Political and Constitutional Ideas of the Court Whigs* (Baton Rouge, La., 1982); T.P. Wiseman, *The Myths of Rome* (Exeter, 2004).

12   P. Conisbee, *Painting in Eighteenth-Century France* (London, 1981), p. 8.

13   W. Cobbett (ed.), *Parliamentary History of England* (35 vols, London, 1806–20) vol. XI, col. 719.

14   Horace Walpole, *Memoirs of King George II*, edited by J. Brooke (3 vols, New Haven, Conn., 1985) II, 70.

15   Cobbett, XVI, 1038–9.

16   *Reflections on Ancient and Modern History* (Oxford, 1746), p. 23.

17   Walpole, *Memoirs*, II, 87.

18   Chesterfield to Keith, 4 Aug. 1771, BL. Add. 35003 fol. 197.

19   K. O'Brien, *Narratives of Enlightenment: Cosmopolitan History from Voltaire to Gibbon* (Cambridge, 1997) and K. O'Brien, 'The History Market in Eighteenth-Century England', in I. Rivers (ed.), *Books and Their Readers in Eighteenth-Century England: New Essays* (London, 2001), pp. 105–33.

20   Yorke to Edward Weston, 22 Feb. 1763, BL. Add. 58213 fol. 208.

21   V. Lange, *The Classical Age of German Literature* (London, 1982), p. 50.

22   J. Lockman, *A New History of England* (London, 1794 edn), pp. ix–x.

23   E. Nares, *A Sermon, Preached at the Parish Church of Shobdon* (London, 1798), pp. 1–2, 4–5.

24   B.G. Smith, 'Gender and the Practices of Scientific History: The Seminar and Archival Research in the Nineteenth Century', *American Historical Review*, 100 (1995), 1150–76.

25   D. Goldstein, 'The Organisational Development of the British Historical Profession, 1884–1921', *Bulletin of the Institute of Historical Research*, 55 (1982), 180–93; D.D. Van Tassel, 'From Learned Society to Professional Organization: The American Historical Association, 1884–1900', *American Historical Review*, 89 (1984), 929–56; M.D. Rothberg, '"To Set a Standard of Workmanship and Compel Men to Conform to It": J. Franklin Jameson as Editor of the American Historical Review', Ibid., 89 (1984), 957–95; P. den Boer, *History as a Profession: The Study of History in France, 1818–1914* (Princeton, NJ, 1998).

26 D. Goldstein, 'The Professionalization of History in Britain in the Late Nineteenth and Early Twentieth Centuries', *Storia della Storiografia*, 3 (1983), 3–26; R. Jann, *The Art and Science of Victorian History* (Columbus, OH, 1985); P. Slee, *Learning and a Liberal Education: The Study of Modern History in the Universities of Oxford, Cambridge and Manchester, 1800–1914* (Manchester, 1986); R. Soffer, *Discipline and Power: The University, History, and the Making of an English Elite, 1870–1930* (Palo Alto, CA, 1994); W. Keylor, *Academy and Community: The Foundation of the French Historical Profession* (Cambridge, 1975).

27 C.A. Cline, 'British Historians and the Treaty of Versailles', *Albion*, 20 (1988), 43–50.

28 C. Crossley, *French Historians and Romanticism* (London, 1993).

29 J. Breuilly, 'Historians and the Nation', in P. Burke (ed.), *History and Historians in the Twentieth Century* (Oxford, 2002), p. 69; S. Berger, *Inventing the Nation: Germany* (London, 2004).

30 A. Brundage, *The People's Historian: John Richard Green and the Writing of History* (Westport, Conn., 1994).

31 O. Anderson, 'The Political Uses of History in Mid-Nineteenth Century England', *Past and Present*, 36 (1967), 87–105; J. Burrow, *A Liberal Descent: Victorian Historians and the English Past* (Cambridge, 1981).

32 R. Strong, *And When Did You Last See Your Father? The Victorian Painter and British History* (London, 1978); N.J. Higham, *King Arthur: Myth-Making and History* (London, 2002).

33 M. Burrows, *The History of the Foreign Policy of Great Britain* (London, 1895), pp. 32, 34–5.

34 A. Ward and G.P. Gooch (eds), *The Cambridge History of British Foreign Policy 1783–1918*, I (Cambridge, 1922), pp. 38–9.

35 E. Nares, *Continuation* (London, 1822), p. 417.

36 M.E. Chamberlain, 'Lord Cromer's "Ancient and Modern Imperialism": A Proconsular View of Empire', *Journal of British Studies*, 12 (1972), 61–85.

37 F. Driver and D. Gilbert (eds), *Imperial Cities: Landscape, Display and Identity* (Manchester, 2003).

38 P.J. Bowler, 'From Savage to Primitive: Victorian Evolutionism and the Interpretation of Marginalised Peoples', *Antiquity*, 66 (1992), 721–91; D. Goldstein, 'Confronting Time: The Oxford School of History and the Non-Darwinian Revolution', *Storia della Storiografia*, 45 (2004), 3–27.

39 D.A. Segal, 'Western Civilisation and the Staging of History in American Higher Education', *American Historical Review*, 105 (2000), 779–803; P.N. Stearns, *Western Civilization in World History* (London, 2003).

40 S. Bann, *The Clothing of Clio: A Study of the Representation of History in Nineteenth-century Britain and France* (Cambridge, 1984); P.J. Geary, *The Myth of Nations: The Medieval Origins of Europe* (Princeton, NJ, 2002).

41 V.E. Chancellor, *History for Their Masters: Opinion in the English History Textbook 1800–1914* (Bath, 1970).

42   S. Berger and P. Lambert, 'Intellectual Transfers and Mental Blockades: Anglo-German Dialogues in Historiography', in Berger, Lambert and P. Schumann (eds), *Historikerdialoge: Geschichte, Mythos and Gedächtnis im deutsch-britischen kulturellen Austausch 1750–2000* (Göttingen, 2002), pp. 18–26.

43   P. Levine, *The Amateur and the Professional: Antiquarians, Historians and Archaeologists in Victorian England, 1838–1886* (Cambridge, 1986).

44   D.A. Bell, *The Cult of the Nation in France: Inventing Nationalism, 1680–1800* (Cambridge, Mass., 2001), pp. 201–2. See, more generally, E. Hobsbawn and T. Ranger (eds), *The Invention of Tradition* (Cambridge, 1983).

45   T.M. Lekan, *Imagining the Nation in Nature: Landscape Preservation and German Identity, 1885–1945* (Cambridge, 2004).

46   R.J. Finlay, 'Controlling the Past: Scottish Historiography and Scottish Identity in the Nineteenth and Twentieth Centuries', *Scottish Affairs*, 6 (1994), 127–48; M. Pittock, *Celtic Identity and the British Image* (Manchester, 1999); T. Snyder, *The Reconstruction of Nations: Poland, Ukraine, Lithuania, Belarus, 1569–1999* (New Haven, Conn., 2003), p. 128.

47   A. Fauser and M. Schwartz (eds), *Von Wagner zum Wagnerisme* (Leipzig, 1999); H. White and M. Murphy (eds), *Musical Constructions of Nationalism: Essays on the History and Ideology of European Musical Culture, 1800–1945* (Cork, 2001).

48   J.A. Thomas, 'High Anxiety: World History as Japanese Self-Discovery', in B. Stuchtey and E. Fuchs (eds), *Writing World History 1800–2000* (Oxford, 2003), p. 316.

49   P.B.M. Blass, *Continuity and Anachronism: Parliamentary and Constitutional Development in Whig Historiography and in the Anti-Whig Reaction between 1890 and 1930* (The Hague, 1978); E. Fuchs, 'English Positivism and German Historicism: The Reception of "Scientific History" in Germany', in B. Stuchtey and P. Wende (eds), *British and German Historiography, 1750–1950* (Oxford, 2000).

50   E. Nares, *Burghley* (London, 1828) I, xx–xxii, 3.

51   D. Cressy, 'The Fifth of November Remembered', in R. Porter (ed.), *Myths of the English* (Cambridge, 1992), p. 81.

52   K. Passmore, *Fascism* (Oxford, 2002), p. 2.

53   L. Winnie, 'Un'bloc'ing the French Revolution', *European Review of History*, 11 (2004), 97–8.

54   F. Furet, *Penser la Révolution française* (Paris, 1978).

55   G.R. Morrissey, *Charlemagne and France: A Thousand Years of Mythology* (Notre Dame, Ind., 2003).

56   D. Thelen, 'The Nation and Beyond: Transnational Perspectives on United States History', *Journal of American History*, 86 (1999), 965–75.

57   G. Iggers and L. Powell (eds), *Leopold von Ranke and the Shaping of the Historical Discipline* (Syracuse, NY, 1990).

58   A.J. Frantzen, *Bloody Good: Chivalry, Sacrifice and the Great War* (Chicago, 2003).

59   B. Arnold, 'The Past as Propaganda: Totalitarian Archaeology in Nazi Germany', *Antiquity*, 64 (1990), 464–78.

60   H.H. Herwig, 'Clio Deceived: Patriotic Self-Censorship in Germany after the Great

War', in K. Wilson (ed.), *Forging the Collective Memory: Government and International Historians through Two World Wars* (Oxford, 1996), pp. 87–127.

61   M. Burleigh, *Germany Turns Eastwards: A Study of 'Ostforschung' in the Third Reich* (Cambridge, 1988); K. Schönwälder, 'The Fascination of Power: Historical Scholarship in Nazi Germany', *History Workshop Journal*, 43 (1997), 133–54; H. Schleier, 'German Historiography under National Socialism: Dreams of a Powerful Nation-State and German *Volkstum* Come True', in S. Berger, M. Donovan and K. Passmore (eds), *Writing National Histories: Western Europe since 1800* (London, 1999), pp. 176–88.

62   R. Fletcher, *The Quest for El Cid* (New York, 1990).

63   J. Hillgarth, 'Spanish Historiography and Iberian Reality', *History and Theory*, 24 (1985), 23–43.

64   P. Aguilar, *Memory and Amnesia: The Role of the Spanish Civil War in the Transition to Democracy* (Oxford, 2002).

65   R. Collins, *Visigothic Spain 409–711* (Oxford, 2004), pp. 1–3.

66   C.E. Black (ed.), *Rewriting Russian History: Soviet Interpretations of Russia's Past* (New York, 1956); G.M Enteen, *The Soviet Scholar-Bureaucrat: M.N. Pokrovskii and the Society of Marxist Historians* (University Park, Pa., 1978).

67   M.L. Galaty and C. Watkinson (eds), *Archaeology under Dictatorship* (New York, 2004).

68   D. Brandenberger, *National Bolshevism: Stalinist Mass Culture and the Formation of Modern Russian National Identity, 1931–1956* (Cambridge, Mass., 2002); R.W. Davies, *Soviet History in the Gorbachev Revolution* (Basingstoke, 1989).

69   *Soviet Writers' Congress 1934* (London, 1977), p. 21.

70   J. Alexander, *Autocratic Politics in a National Crisis: The Imperial Russian Government and Pugachev's Revolt* (London, 1969).

71   A.D. Lublinskaya, *French Absolutism: The Crucial Phase, 1620–1629* (Cambridge, 1968), but see Y.-M. Bercé, *History of Peasant Revolts: The Social Roots of Rebellion in Early Modern France* (Ithaca, New York, 1990).

72   M. Todorova, 'Historiography of the Countries of Eastern Europe: Bulgaria', *American Historical Review*, 97 (1992), 1105–17.

73   A. Dorpalen, *German History in Marxist Perspective: The East German Approach* (London, 1985); A.L. Nothnagle, *Building the East German Myth: Historical Mythology and Youth Propaganda in the German Democratic Republic, 1945–1989* (Ann Arbor, Mich. 1999).

74   J.V. Polisensky, *The Thirty Years' War* (London, 1971).

75   J. Marozzi, *Tamerlane* (London, 2004), p. 172.

76   M.D. Brown, 'The S.O.E. and the Failure of the Slovak National Uprising', *History Today*, 54, no. 12 (December 2004), 44–5.

77   Ex inf. Colin Fleming.

78   N. Davies and R. Moorhouse, *Microcosm: Portrait of a Central European City* (London, 2003); Snyder, *Reconstruction of Nations*.

79   J. Connelly, *Captive University: The Sovietization of East German, Czech and Polish*

Higher Education, 1945–1956 (Chapel Hill, NC, 2000); M. Fulbrook, 'Dividing the Past, Defining the Present: Historians and National Identity in the Two Germanies', in S. Berger, M. Donovan and K. Passmore (eds), *Writing National Histories: Western Europe since 1800* (London, 1999), p. 219.

80   M.B. Petrovich, 'Continuing Nationalism in Yugoslav Historiography', *Nationalities Papers*, 6 (1978), 161–77; I. Banac, 'Historiography of the Countries of Eastern Europe: Yugoslavia', *American Historical Review*, 97 (1992), 1084–104.

81   Mao Zedong, 'The Communist Revolution and the Chinese Communist Party', in his *Select Works* (Beijing, 1967), II, p. 314.

82   *The Opium War* (Beijing, 1976), p. 115.

83   *The Taiping Revolution* (Beijing, 1976), pp. 172–3, 178.

5

Confronting the past

Apologies

In 1997 the recently elected 'New Labour' British prime minister, Tony Blair, marked the commemoration of the 150th anniversary of the Great Famine in Ireland by issuing a statement declaring that those 'who governed in London at the time failed their people by standing by while a crop failure turned into a massive human tragedy'. This admission of guilt was criticized by Northern Irish Unionists, committed to defending the historical legacy and memory of the Union between Britain and Ireland, as well as by conservative commentators in Britain, the *Daily Telegraph* claiming that Blair had given support to 'the self-pitying nature of Irish nationalism'. The Famine certainly plays a major role in the nationalist account of Irish history, both in Ireland and in the Irish diaspora, particularly in the USA. The Famine allegedly demonstrated that Ireland had been harshly treated when linked to Britain, and therefore showed that Irish commentators who defended the link were, at best, mistaken.

Blair was not alone in apologizing, which indeed became the norm across much of the West in the 1990s and 2000s, although there had been earlier examples, as when Willy Brandt, the German chancellor, apologized for Germany's role in the Second World War. In 1993, President Clinton signed a joint resolution of both houses of Congress which formally apologized to the native Hawaiians for American governmental complicity in the overthrow of Hawaiian independence: the native monarchy had been overthrown a century earlier. Five years later, he apologized for America's role in the slave trade. Anniversaries proved particularly appropriate for apologies. In 2004, Heidemarie Wieczorek-Zeul, German Minister for Economic Cooperation and Development, apologized formally for the brutal German suppression of the 1904 Herero uprising, admitting that its policy and practice amounted to genocide. The site of the apology was also significant: where the uprising broke out in Namibia. The same year, Gerhard Schröder, the German chancellor, attended the annual commemoration of the Warsaw uprising of 1944 against German occupation and apologized for its brutal suppression.

In turn, there were demands for more apologies and, in some cases, for reparations. The Second World War is the key issue in China's negotiations with Japan about reparations and apologies. This has become a particularly hot issue in the last few years with, for example, concern about an 'orgy' held by Japanese businessmen in Zhuhai on 18 September 2003, the anniversary of the Manchurian crisis. In 2004, the Polish government pressed Britain and other Second World War Allied powers to apologize for failing to do enough to help the Polish resistance to the Germans. The same year, however, the German envoy in Namibia, Wolfgang Massing, declared that the German government was unwilling to respond to pressure for reparations for German conduct in its former colony. Demands for compensation were addressed both to the government and to German companies that allegedly had profited from the colonization of Namibia, including Deutsche Bank and the Deutsche Afrika Linie which had shipped out troops.

The pressure for apology can well lead to a disproportionate account of the past. For example, there has been an extensive literature devoted to the Japanese-Americans interned, with suffering but minimal violence, by the USA during the Second World War, but far less attention to other American ethnic communities during the Second World War, such as Greek, Serb or Polish Americans, each of which was well aware of the acute suffering of their European relatives as a consequence of German aggression. Thus, the theme of suffering visited on fellow Americans during the war offers an unbalanced account of the Home Front.[1] At a different level, German pressure for British apologies for bombing German cities in the Second World War not only fails to recover the historical context of the policy and its benefits, not least gravely weakening the German air force and thus greatly helping the process of defeating German forces on the ground, but also suggests an inappropriate equivalence with an earlier German use of terror bombing.

Calls for apology can play a major role in international (and also domestic) politics, and, indeed, are playing an increasing one. This is true not only of areas ruled by European colonial powers, but also of Eastern Europe. Anger there is directed against both Germany and Russia. On 10 September 2004, 320 MPs in the Polish parliament passed a motion instructing the government to demand compensation from Germany for its actions in 1939–45, in order to right the wrong of 'the enormous material and spiritual destruction caused by German aggression, occupation and genocide'. Two months earlier, the mayor of Warsaw announced that he had appointed a group of statisticians and economists to calculate building by building the heavy damage done to Warsaw by the Germans so that, if necessary, they could be presented with a bill.

This was in part in response to calls from the heads of German expelled-citizens' organizations for compensation from Poland for the 3 million Germans driven from their homes by the Poles at and after the close of the war. The resolution in the Polish parliament pressed the German government to 'stop encouraging its citizens to bring lawsuits against Poland' (the Schröder government had not in fact done so), and called on the Polish government to press its German counterpart to resist such claims. The Czechs had also expelled about 3 million Sudeten Germans at and after the close of the war. The wife of Edmund Stoiber, Gerhard Schröder's conservative opponent in the last German election, was from a Sudeten refugee family and he made much of the refugee issue. German pressure for compensation entrenched differences and led the Czech parliament in 2003 to pass a resolution applauding President Beneš who was in large part responsible for the post-war policy. These moves in turn further harmed relations. The Czech step was seen as provocative in Germany, while in September 2004 President Kwasniewski pressed Poland's MPs not to vote in favour of the resolution as he claimed it could harm relations with Germany for years.

Across Eastern Europe the ethnic violence of the 1940s, including forcible resettlement after the Second World War, fuelled demands for apology and reparations, demands that strengthened after the end of Communist rule. For example, Ukrainians complained about forced resettlement by the Polish government in 1947, while Poles complained of Ukrainian brutality in 1943. Anger and grief about the Second World War played a major role in popular historical consciousness,[2] just as, earlier, the struggle to come to terms with the mass bereavement of the First World War had played a major role in interwar collective memory.[3]

Coming to terms with the past

Coming to terms with the past has been a particularly difficult aspect of public history as, in many respects, it represented a reversal of previous claims or, at least, the recovery from the twilight of episodes that hitherto had been thought best left forgotten. Thus, on behalf of the

Catholic Church, Pope John Paul II apologized in 2004 for the sack of Constantinople (now Istanbul), then the centre of Orthodox Christendom, by the Fourth Crusade in 1204. This apology was seen as a way to serve the current purpose of improving relations with the Greek Orthodox Church, an indication of the continued role of historical disputes in a rift (between Catholicism and Orthodoxy) based on theological differences that originated centuries back. John Paul II has also apologized for Christian anti-Semitism, the Crusades, the actions of the Inquisition and the treatment of Galileo, and, in 2004, was pressed to apologize for the brutal suppression of the Knights Templars in the early fourteenth century.

The process for redress was not therefore restricted to the events of recent centuries. In 2004, the Socialist-dominated government of Aragon, a region of Spain that was based on an independent medieval kingdom, indicated that it was ready to abandon the heraldic shield of Aragon – which portrayed four severed Moorish heads – as it was seen as insensitive to the Muslim minority: Aragon had been founded and then expanded at the expense of Muslim Moorish principalities, themselves based on earlier conquests. In turn, the opposition conservative People's Party criticized the proposed step. On the whole, left-wing parties were far keener to apologize than conservative counterparts, which tended to have a greater sense of affinity with past governments and which saw demands for apology as signs of weakness and self-hatred.

In many respects, the process of apology was a matter of a re-evaluation of aspects of imperialism and colonialism. Thus, for the British there were calls to confront the Irish legacy (which also in fact divided the Irish), leading to the long-running 'Bloody Sunday' inquiry into events in Londonderry in 1972 that concluded in 2004 after six years. Reconciliation led even the terrorists of the Irish Republican Army to apologize for some of their killings: in July 2002 this extended to all 'non-combatants' killed in Northern Ireland and to contrition for 'past mistakes'. The British were also expected to apologize for other imperial episodes, such as the Amritsar Massacre of 1919 in India, which, indeed, had been controversial at the time and had led to a government inquiry and to a legal case.[4] A state visit by Queen Elizabeth II to India proved controversial when her husband, the Duke of Edinburgh, failed to show the expected contrition over Amritsar.

For the French, there was similar pressure to look at past difficulties in relations with Algeria, pressure that owed much to the large Algerian immigrant community in France and that, in part, was a response to the underrating (if not deliberate covering up) of the Algerian war of 1954–62 in French public memory. The controversial nature of this conflict was kept alive by artistic representations, not least showings of the film *The Battle for Algiers* (1965), but also by the expression of the views of participants. In 2000, former generals disputed the employment of torture in Algeria: General Massu admitting and regretting it, while General Aussaresses claimed that it had been necessary and was subsequently denounced for excusing war crimes in his account of the war.[5]

It was not only imperial policing that was at issue. There was also a wider claim that the nature of imperialism had been expropriatory, that many Western institutions rested on this violence and that redress was required. This ranged from pressure for the return of artefacts from museums and scientific collections, for example body parts gathered for anthropological research, to the emotive issue of slavery and the slave trade. The former led to difficulties between Australia and British museums in 2004, as the Australian government responded to Aboriginal pressure that it should not return loaned exhibits to Britain. Slavery and the slave trade brings the USA fully into the picture for its role as including, in the Southern states, a major slave society until 1865, leaving it open to the rhetoric of redress, and indeed to demands for compensation. Furthermore, prior to the late nineteenth century American imperialism was largely directed against contiguous peoples and powers, principally Native Americans but also Mexico and, to a minor extent, the British in Canada. As a result of this imperialism, Native- and, to a lesser degree, Mexican-Americans currently express grievances.

These aspects of confronting the past were of varied importance in First World countries, as public cultures and legal systems proved very differently open to such pressures. There is more concern in Britain about the treatment of former colonies than there is in Spain, although, of course, most of the latter's became independent far earlier. Furthermore, the nature of these pressures is in part moulded by the character of domestic politics, in particular the responsiveness to ethnic minorities. Pressure for a reconsideration of empire indeed is felt both in the metropole and in former colonies. In 2003, Jack Straw, the British foreign secretary, blamed British colonialism for many of the world's international disputes.[6]

This pressure for reconsideration has an important symbolic side, seen, for example, with the removal of statues from the imperial period. Thus, the statues of imperial rulers, proconsuls and generals were moved from prominent places on avenues, boulevards and squares, and destroyed or consigned to curious dumps where they act as a register of the twists of fate. This is a modern counterpart to the remains of the rule of the fictional Ozymandias, 'king of kings', described by Percy Bysshe Shelley in his poem of that name, written in 1817:

> Two vast and trunkless legs of stone
> Stand in the desert
> . . .
> And on the pedestal these words appear:
> 'My name is Ozymandias, king of kings:
> look on my works, ye Mighty, and despair!'
> Nothing beside remains . . .

India is a prominent example of a former colony where the statues of foreign rulers have been (re)moved, but the same is also true of the treatment of Soviet-era statuary in former Communist states, as many of these statues were seen not only as the legacy of a discarded ideology but also as the products of Soviet or Russian imperialism. One of the most interesting uses of these statues is in Budapest, where the Statue Park sets up around 40 of these Socialist Realism statues in a park with a set visitors' trail and explanations provided from a pretty strongly anti-Communist angle.

The movements of statues can be complicated. In commemoration of the major contribution of West Africa colonial troops in the First World War, the French government in 1923 erected a monument depicting two soldiers, one African, the other French, in the centre of Dakar, the capital of their colony of Senegal. In 1985, the now independent government of Senegal moved the monument to a far more marginal setting: in a Catholic cemetery (most Senegalese are Muslims) on the city outskirts. This was at a time of popular protests against the government's French links, to which another response was the renaming of a central square Place Soweto. In 2004, however, the statue was moved back to the centre of Dakar. The military museum established in the city in 1997 also commemorated cooperation.

In the former imperial metropoles (including Russia but not France) there is frequently the sense of a discarded past. In Britain it led, in the early 2000s, to a series of minor controversies, each indicative of the definition of a new post-imperial public history. There were calls, for example, by Ken Livingstone, the left-wing mayor of London, to remove the statues of imperial generals, such as Havelock and Napier, from their plinths in London's Trafalgar Square and elsewhere. There were also complaints about a lack of state support for the new Museum of the Empire in Bristol. In 2004, a House of Commons' committee recommended the removal of imperial designations from the honours system, for example ending the title Member of the Order of the

British Empire. Such titles were now seen by some as anachronistic. The vast majority of those offered them still accepted, but the official view of appropriate nomenclature had changed.

Historical writing registered these changes in official Western culture. Scholarly history in the West became far less prone from the 1960s than it had been to offer a teleological account of past, present and future, in which, at least due to the process of improvement, a benign element was discerned. For example, the 'consensus historians', such as Richard Hofstadter and Daniel Boorstin, who were so influential in the USA from the Second World War until the mid-1960s were challenged by revisionist radicals keener to draw attention to tensions within American society.[7]

More generally, the teaching and writing of the history of Western civilization were increasingly relativized by being put into a global context; and this new world history was no longer presented in terms of the traditional idea of a ladder of civilization dominated by the West and defined by its criteria. Such a concept, instead, appeared increasingly redundant in a Western culture that, to a certain extent, was unsure of its purpose and that anyway preached relative values: a product of cultural changes summarized as 'political correctness', as well as of scholarly shifts, including anthropological insights. This helped to ensure that the historical process, let alone goal, was understood far less than hitherto as the triumph of the West. Greater interest in other cultures and societies contributed to this shift in scholarly studies, and both, to an extent, affected public history, at least in so far as education in the Western world was concerned.

This was particularly seen in former colonies where the majority of the population were the descendants of European emigrants. In the USA, there was increasing interest in the history of African-[8] and Native Americans and of women, as well as in the world outside the earlier definition in terms of North America and Europe. Engagement with these issues led to an explicit call for the public acceptance of different viewpoints,[9] and this interest affected not just educationists but also fund-raisers. The leaflet distributed in 2004 by the Monticello Fund, the preservation and educational organization linked to the house of Thomas Jefferson, did not focus on his role as one of the Founding Fathers of the American constitution. Instead, there was an emphasis, in illustrations and text, on the Native Americans: 'the Entrance Hall filled with daylight and art objects representing American natural history and Native American cultures . . . the Indian Hall, containing re-creations of Native American objects sent by Lewis and Clark to Jefferson, greets every visitor to Monticello. The Entrance Hall Museum was Jefferson's way of reminding each guest that a wider world lay beyond Monticello.' Displays of archaeological work on the estate in the 2000s also devoted more attention than hitherto to the slaves on whom it had depended. In 2004, the National Endowment for the Humanities awarded the Thomas Jefferson Foundation one of the first eight of its America's Historic Places grants (under the 'We the People' initiative) to aid in restoration and interpretation of the workrooms, storage areas and slave quarters. Tours offered in 2005 included Plantation Community and Enslaved Domestic Workers Tours, while in February 2005, as part of African-American History Month, an exhibition of paintings of African-American life at Monticello was held.

By the early 2000s the prime issue in relations between Native Americans and public authorities was the gambling licences sought by the former (gambling ironically helped fund a series of museums), but there were other sources of tension. In 2004, an attempt by a group of re-enactors to follow the overland route to the Pacific Ocean of the Lewis and Clark expedition of 1804 led to a confrontation with Native Americans who objected to the celebration of a journey that to them marked the start of the end for traditional Native American culture. The re-enactors alleged that they received threats of violence, while the Native leader, Alex White Plume of the Pine Ridge Reservation, declared, 'Lewis and Clark brought the death and destruction of our way of life'.[10] In contrast, 'Discovering the Legacy of Lewis and Clark', a leaflet produced by the Lewis and Clark Interagency Partnership, declared 'The Corps of Discovery encountered the diversity and generosity of many Indian Nations as they traveled across the land and waters. The expedition survived and succeeded because of the shelter, supplies, good will, and cooperation of Native American people they met. Now, as then, the people, cultures, and land have much to share.' Celebrating the bicentennial of the expedition was also presented as a way to affirm American identity:

> Lewis and Clark's spirit of discovery embodies the American character – their documentation of what they thought and whom they met, their desire to cooperate with the American Indians they encountered in peace and friendship, their persistence and resolute determination to reach their final destination and return, their resourcefulness and courage. The multi-year Bicentennial Commemoration of the Lewis and Clark Expedition provides an unprecedented opportunity to remind us of our humanity and proud history, and to restore and preserve America's abundant natural resources and cultural diversity.

This was not the sole area of competing memory. Established by an Act of Congress in 1989, the National Museum of the American Indian, which cost $219 million and opened on a prominent site on the National Mall in Washington in September 2004, was criticized by some Native activists, for example members of the American Indian Movement, for downplaying the role of violence in the conquest of the Americas, although in fact a tour of the museum indicates that the disruptive nature of European contact is clearly discussed. The public theme in the museum was one of reconciliation, the museum director, W. Richard West Jr., a member of the Cheyenne and Arapaho tribes, declaring at the opening 'At long last the culturally different histories, cultures and peoples of the Americas can come together in new mutual understanding and respect.' Earlier in 2004, at the annual Independence Day Celebration and Naturalization Ceremony at Monticello (where the oath of citizenship was taken on the steps of Monticello), West offered a version of the official account of multiculturalism past, present and future: 'The demographics of the United States will change dramatically and materially within a generation, requiring that all American citizens respect and honor anew cultural difference and the vast benefits that diversity can bring to America's future – just as it has in enriching this country's past cultural heritage.'[11]

Hawai'i posed particular problems for the American public engagement with the past, as there was a strong sense of ethnic consciousness among much of the indigenous population which led, from the 1970s, to political pressure: the assertion of cultural identity, especially from the 1960s, was followed in the 1970s by debate over land rights and self-determination. As in Australia, land rights were a major issue. Native advocates argued that ceded land was in fact stolen.[12] Pressure led to the State Constitutional Convention of 1978 creating an Office of Hawaiian Affairs. Furthermore, under the Carter (Democratic) administration, the US Congress created a Native Hawaiians Study Commission. The Reagan (Republican) government that took office in 1981 changed the direction of policy, and the membership of the Commission. In place of the six Hawaiians and the three Mainlanders (Americans from the continental USA) under Carter, there were now three and six respectively. The commission's draft report of 1982 denied that there was an issue, as it found American policy in the overthrow of the monarchy in 1893 acceptable. The major final report, published in 1983, supported this view, but the three Hawaiians produced a conflicting version.

Tension, however, continued and 1993, the centenary of the overthrow, saw much public debate and dissension. The Hawaiian state's flag, that of the old monarchy, was widely flown without that of the USA, and the state legislature issued a resolution condemning the events of 1893 and thus the legitimacy of current arrangements. It declared that 'the United States military committed the first overt act to overthrow the independent nation of Hawai'i . . . an overt act of military aggression against a peaceful and independent nation'.[13] Claims of dispossession continue to serve as the basis for sectional demands on behalf of those of Hawaiian descent, for example for special educational provisions, that exclude the large numbers (a majority of the population) with non-Hawaiian antecedents. This issue at the same time highlighted problems of definition, which in 2003 included the case of Brayden Mohica-Cummings, an 'Anglo' adopted by a Hawaiian. He was excluded on the grounds of race from Kamehameha Schools, Hawai'i's well-funded guardian of indigenous culture and customs, but this was overturned by the US District Court of Hawai'i. The court's earlier views on the issue of race and discrimination – a 1997 ruling – had been overturned by the Supreme Court in 2000, and in 2003 the District Court followed the Supreme Court. The dispute revealed the extent to which a perception of historical wrongs clashed with constitutional prescriptions of uniformity. One of the Kamehameha Schools trustees, Douglas Ing, declared that the trust sought 'to rectify past imbalances to the Hawaiian people' and another that the 2003 court decision ignored 'centuries of injustice to the Hawaian people', while the Supreme Court minority in 2000 argued that the majority had failed to recognize 'a history of subjugation at the hands of colonial forces'.[14] Although there are differences, the position in Hawai'i has parallels with the situation concerning the Maori in New Zealand, while in Fiji there is opposition to the Indians who settled under British imperial rule.

In Australia, Canada and New Zealand in recent decades the sense of history became less focused on Britain, the 'mother country' of their constitutions and the source of the majority of their immigrants over the previous quarter-millennium. The new interpretation of the past, seen for example in Charles Manning Clark's nationalistic *A History of Australia* (1962–87), placed less of an emphasis than hitherto on state formation, a process in which the colonial power, Britain, was dominant, and instead emphasized subsequent history, particularly social history, a slant that directed attention to domestic pressures. Clark, nevertheless, was of his time in having relatively little to say about women or Aborigines, and was criticized on that head by radical historians of the following generation. The opening words of the first volume were 'Civilization did not begin in Australia until the last quarter of the eighteenth century', and Manning continued 'The early inhabitants of the continent created cultures but not civilizations . . . Of the way of these three peoples before the coming of European civilization, little need, or indeed can, be said . . . the failure of the Aborigines to emerge from a state of barbarism.'[15] In the Epilogue to his last volume, however, Clark responded to such criticism and, indeed, accepted the absence of a canonical (established, even definitive) account in the modern, liberal Australia that he praised:

> Women wrote their own history. Aborigines wrote their history, main-
> taining that their ancestors were not immigrants, but were always there,
> and that white man's history was a catalogue of 'white lies'. The New
> Left wrote their history. Accounts of the past became part of the strug-
> gle for power in Australia. In an age of doubt about everything, even the
> past lost its authority.[16]

At the same time Manning was still determined to argue his case, using his authority as a major historian to condemn what he disliked: the weight of the past, the impact of the petit-bourgeois and the consequences of the British link.[17]

More generally, there was a greater willingness, especially in New Zealand, to give due weight to the historical experience of Native peoples. This was as part of a questioning of the previous emphasis on a consensual approach to national history, but can also represent an attempt to develop that. For example, in 1932 the Waitangi National Trust estate was purchased by Lord Bledisloe, the Governor-General, and given in trust to the people of New Zealand to enjoy. The estate included where the treaty of Waitangi of 1840 was signed between the Maori chiefs and the British, establishing the basis of British sovereignty over New Zealand. The theme of the commemorations held there, for example the treaty Centenary Celebrations in 1940, and of the permanent displays, was one of inclusion. For instance, the brochure handed out there in 2004 declared:

> Though debate continues over the interpretation of its parts, the Treaty
> is best understood as a whole. It is an agreement between two peoples to
> live and work together in one nation. This agreement is as relevant
> today as in 1840, for it guarantees the rights of both Maori and non-
> Maori citizens in Aotearoa, New Zealand.

Similarly, the preface to the *New Zealand Historical Atlas* (1997), its research a beneficiary of state support and published in part by the Department of Internal Affairs, noted that 'a large part of the *Atlas* is concerned with the Maori experience of New Zealand . . . it will be plain to even the casual reader that this is an atlas of Maori as well as Pakeha [White or European] history'. This relationship, however, was far from static, and was itself put under pressure from Maori demands. In response to these, the Waitangi Tribunal, established by the government in 1975 to investigate alleged breaches of the Treaty of Waitangi of 1840, provided the context for a re-examination of the treatment of the Maori, and thus for both the foundation myth of modern New Zealand and much of its history.[18] The extent to which calls for a greater awareness of Maori perspectives, including a shift of emphasis from the Treaty to the subsequent Maori Wars with British settlers and forces, entail a rejection of assimilation and also challenge good relations is controversial.

In Australia, greater emphasis on the Aborigines from the 1970s was in part associated with an emphasis on social and other divisions that subverted the dominant myth of nation-building,[19] but the treatment of Aborigines was particularly controversial, linking as it did past and present, history and politics. Left-wing politicians tend to side with what is termed by its critics the 'black arm-band' historical view: claims that the British colonizers acted in a brutal and genocidal fashion, and that this was the unacceptable foundation of modern Australia. In contrast, conservative politicians, such as John Howard the prime minister, find critics of this view, who treat it as an exaggeration, more conducive. Thus, in the early 2000s there were claims by the most prominent critic, Keith Windshuttle, in his *The Fabrication of Aboriginal History. Volume I: Van Diemen's Land 1803–1847* (2002), that Henry Reynolds, Lyndall Ryan and other scholars had exaggerated the numbers of Aborigines killed by the early colonists. Australian academics in turn were very critical of his work. *Whitewash. On Keith Windshuttle's Fabrication of Aboriginal History* (2003), a volume edited by Robert Manne,[20] argued that his account did not stand up to scholarly discussion, and there were also claims that Windshuttle had been taken up by influential circles in the media, especially *The Australian* newspaper, as part of an assault on the academic profession. Windshuttle's critique of the subject had already been clearly expressed in his *The Killing of History: How Literary Critics and Social Theorists Are Murdering Our Past* (1996). At the July 2004 meeting of the Australian Historical Association, Stuart Macintyre claimed that the history wars in Australia were in accord with the 'political dimensions' of the Howard government's 'abandonment of reconciliation, denial of the stolen generations, its retreat from multiculturalism and creation of a refugee crisis'.

Aboriginal politicians also play a role in the debate, which is directly linked to their calls for land rights and self-determination. The issue of the degree of conflict in the past between Aboriginal groups is another aspect of dissension, as it moves attention away from the colonists–Aborigines confrontation.[21] The debate still simmers along and is not without its effect: historians of all hues are now much more wary of using the term 'genocide' in connection with colonial Australia. Reynolds in fact was always cautious of doing so, and his much disputed guesstimate of 20,000 Aborigines killed – though challenged by Windshuttle as unsubstantiated – did provide some corrective to the wholesale massacre view.

The impact of changing views can be seen by comparing the centenary with the bicentenary of the beginning of British settlement in Tasmania. On 22 February 1904, in front of several thousand spectators, the governor unveiled a monument to the founder and praised the settlers. No Aboriginal people were known to have been present, and no mention was made of the subsequent massacre of Aborigines on 3 May 1804. In 2004, in contrast, no formal ceremony was held to mark the landing on 22 February 1804 and, instead, on 3 May the massacre was commemorated from the Aboriginal perspective. The monument erected in 1904 was covered with a white sheet splattered with blood as a mark of respect to the victims of the massacre, and the secretary of the Tasmanian Aboriginal Centre declared 'They killed us off in this place 200 years ago, stole our land, took away our people and imposed their religion on us. But our presence here today shows they have not destroyed us.' From the academic perspective, settler narratives no longer dominate the account. After Aboriginal pressure, including the disruption of a re-enactment of the 1804 landing held in 1988 to celebrate the Australian bicentenary, Risdon Cove, the site of both landing and massacre, was declared an Aboriginal Historic Site and transferred to the Tasmanian Aboriginal Land Council. This, however, was challenged in the early 2000s by Reg Watson, a leading member of the Anglo-Keltic Society, who claimed that the government was bowing unnecessarily to Aboriginal pressure. Similar charges had been made by Pauline Hanson, the leading right-wing populist Australian politician.[22]

A related controversy led in 2004 to the replacement of the director of the National Museum of Australia because the Howard government saw the contents of the museum as overly devoted to the Aborigines, not least in the First Australians Gallery, the largest of the museum's permanent exhibitions. This was a public controversy, not one conducted simply in the corridors of power.

In Canada, the stress on the Native peoples followed on from the earlier emphasis on Québécois nationalism from the 1960s, although they were very different in character, and the Québécois had scant sympathy for the Native peoples in Quebec. Québécois nationalists stressed their French roots and identity in order to make a separatist case.

The equivalent in Latin America was a greater interest in the pre-colonial past, and also in the Native population during the period of rule by Spain and the colonial elites from the sixteenth to the early nineteenth centuries. The two were separate tendencies but were also linked, for, by emphasizing the vitality and survival of pre-conquest societies, a perspective was offered on the colonial period. This had a political slant with the scholarship devoted to the widespread insurrection against Spanish colonial rule in Peru in 1780–1 headed by Túpac Amaru, a descendant of the last Inca rulers. Recovering this history of resistance served to legitimate independent statehood, as it was presented as a prelude to the successful fight in the early nineteenth century for independence from Spain.[23] At the same time, there was a social dimension in that independent Latin America was dominated by the descendants of Spanish settlers, while the Native people were still excluded from economic and political power.

Academic work has contributed to the reconsideration of the role of the Native population of Latin America. In place of earlier neglect, there has been an emphasis on the contribution of Native allies, and, to a lesser extent, blacks, in the Spanish conquest of what became Latin America, and also on the process of cultural interaction between Spanish and Native societies in Mexico and elsewhere, and on the extent to which, as a result of Native cultural persistence, the conquest was incomplete. As a result, the conquest of the core areas of Meso-America and the Andes was, it is now argued, more protracted than the Spaniards initially claimed, and later believed. Furthermore, it is suggested that when warfare did end in these areas it was displaced, taking on multiple forms of domination and repression, but encountering a diverse set of methods of Native resistance. Spanish superiority is therefore presented as a myth.[24]

Although extensive, the process of apology has marked limits. It is difficult to see the American government apologizing for what the Mexicans refer to as the war of aggression: the American conquests of 1846–8. Nevertheless, in part in response to the cultural renaissances of indigenous peoples,[25] the pressure for, and practice of, apology is an important aspect of confronting the past in the modern world. It is also one of the principal public uses of history. This was demonstrated in December 2004 when Michel Barnier, the French foreign minister, insisted Turkey take responsibility for the mass slaughter of about 1.5 million Armenian Christians in 1915, a genocide the Turks have consistently minimized and attributed to spontaneous popular action. Barnier declared: 'Turkey should face up to the requirement of remembrance. The European project itself is founded on reconciliation.'

Notes

1   I would like to thank Roger Lotchin for sending me a copy of his paper 'Turning the Good War Homefront Bad: The Historians Counterattack on the Greatest Generation'.

2   N. Tumarkin, *The Living and the Dead: The Rise and Fall of the Cult of World War II in Russia* (New York, 1994); C. Merridale, *Night of Stone: Death and Memory in Russia* (London, 2000).

3   J.F. Vance, *Death So Noble: Memory, Meaning, and the First World War* (Vancouver, 1997).

4   D.G. Boyce, 'From Assaye to the *Assaye*: Reflections on British Government, Force, and Moral Authority in India', *Journal of Military History*, 63 (1999), 655–68.

5   *Le Monde*, 23 Nov. 2000.

6   Interview with John Kampfner, *New Statesman*, 18 Nov. 2003.

7   J. Higham, 'The Cult of Consensus: Homogenizing American History', *Commentary*, 27 (1959), 93–100; G. Wise, *American Historical Explanations: A Strategy for Grounded Inquiry* (Homewood, Ill., 1973); D.J. Singal, 'Beyond Consensus: Richard Hofstadter and American Historiography', *American Historical Review*, 89 (1984), 976–1004; J. Wiener, 'Radical Historians and the Crisis in American History, 1959–1980', *Journal of American History*, 76 (1989), 399–434.

8   A. Meier and E. Rudwick, *Black History and the Historical Profession, 1915–1980* (Urbana, Il., 1986).

9   P. Limerick, *The Legacy of Conquest: The Unbroken Past of the American West* (New York, 1987), p. 27 and 'The Battlefield of History', *New York Times*, 28 Aug. 1997, Section A, 19.

10   Associated Press report in *The Virginian Pilot*, 26 Sept. 2004.

11   K. Curtis, 'On Independence Day', *Monticello*, 15, no. 2 (Winter 2004), 7.

12   M. Chait, 'Healing Hawai'i: The Recovery of an Island Identity. A socio-historical study of Hawaiian cultural resistance from the 1840s to the 1990s' (unpublished D.Phil. thesis, Oxford, 1999).

13   S.R. Fischer, *A History of the Pacific Islands* (Basingstoke, 2002), pp. 253–5.

14   R.M. Rees, 'Hawaiian History Can't Be Reduced to Race', *Honolulu Advertiser*, 31 Aug. 2003, Section B, 1, 4.

15   C.M.H. Clark, *A History of Australia. I* (Melbourne, 1962), pp. 3–5.

16   C.M.H. Clark, *A History of Australia. VI* (Melbourne, 1987), p. 499.

17   Ibid., pp. 496–7.

18   C. Orange, *The Treaty of Waitangi* (Wellington, 1987).

19   R. Pascoe, *The Manufacture of Australian History* (Melbourne, 1979).

20   See also L. Ryan, 'Waterloo Creek, northern New South Wales, 1838', in B. Atwood and S. Foster (eds), *Frontier Conflict. The Australian Experience* (Canberra, 2003), pp. 33–43.

21   Atwood and Foster (eds), *Frontier Conflict*.

22   L. Ryan, 'Risdon Cove and the Massacre of 3 May 1804: Their Place in Tasmanian

History', *Tasmanian Historical Studies*, 9 (2004), 107–23; A. Curthoys, 'Mythologies', in R. Nile (ed.), *The Australian Legend and its Discontents* (St Lucia, Queensland, 2000), pp. 11–41.

23   C.D. Valcárcel, *Túpac Amaru: Precursor de la Independencia* (Lima, 1977).
24   M. Restall, *Seven Myths of the Spanish Conquest* (Oxford, 2003).
25   J. Sissons, *First Peoples. Indigenous Cultures and their Futures* (London, 2005).

6

Western Europe and the USA

Confronting the past was not simply a matter of the imperial and colonial legacy. There were also aspects of domestic history that created issues. The most divisive were those of politics and war during the twentieth century. These divisive issues varied greatly by state but spanned confronting the experience of civil war, which was especially strongly felt in Spain (although largely ignored in Ireland); of defeat and collaboration, which was particularly pointed in France, but not only there; of defeat, and of responsibility for a brutal totalitarianism, and for the Holocaust, which was the case for Germany and also, although its public history was far more evasive, of Austria; of Fascist rule and defeat in Italy; and of defeat in the Vietnam War for the USA. These issues were important not only in the immediate aftermaths of the episodes in question, but also in the longer term, helping to affect politics and to ensure that the public account of the past was highly contentious.

France and Vichy

The defeat of France by Germany in 1940 led to the fall of the Third Republic, the occupation of much of the country by German forces (and a small sliver by Italy), and the creation of a collaborationist regime in the rest of France. Based in Vichy, this was a conservative government that presented an account of the past that was at once nationalist and highly conducive to its purposes in the then current political atmosphere. In particular, still fighting the 1790s, this account was in part the anti-French Revolution: the focus was on a Catholic and conservative presentation of French domestic history that was anti-liberal, leading to particular hostility to Jews and Freemasons, as well as unsympathetic to cities, particularly Paris. As a result, Vichy took up themes from France's divided history and contested collective memories, most recently not only the French Fascist movement, the Action Française, but also the conservative reaction to the Popular Front of the 1930s.[1] Vichy also presented the Third Republic (1870–1940) and its politics as decadent and weak, and in large part responsible for defeat in 1940, indeed, as a failure.

At the same time, the Vichy account of history served the cause of alliance with Germany by emphasizing anti-British themes, sharpened by the British attack on the French fleet at Mers-el-Kébir in 1940, an attack that was commemorated in Vichy propaganda.[2] Opposition to Britain, which was also the base of the Free French movement led by Charles de Gaulle, helped ensure a stress on Joan of Arc, an icon from the early fifteenth century, and on other episodes when conflict with Britain could serve to underline ideas of French identity and bravery, both otherwise compromised by defeat in the recent war with Germany.[3] Joan's memory was strong because she had been made a saint in 1920, the same year in which France designated a national holiday to her memory. The use of French icons by Vichy and the Nazis was also seen with the establishment of the Charlemagne Division to fight for the Germans.

After the Second World War there was a punishment by the French of French collaborationists, with possibly up to 10,000 killed and 40,000 detained. There was also a major rejection of the psychological grip of Vichy. This involved not only a rewriting of the public history offered by Vichy but also, far more significantly for post-war French politics, a particular shaping of the years from defeat in 1940 to liberation in 1944. The post-war French myth offered an account of 1940–4 in which Vichy was largely excised from the collective memory, and in which most of the French were said to have supported the Resistance to German occupation.[4] Amnesty laws for wartime collaboration were passed in 1951 and 1953. This was a necessary aspect of the emphasis on national honour.

The process of myth-making, however, was divisive as Communist prominence in the Resistance was written out of the Gaullist myth, instead providing a separate Communist myth emphasizing the role of the working class and the Soviet Union in the Resistance. This led to rival, indeed contested, commemorations of Resistance episodes and heroes. Much was made of the latter. In a key act of commemoration, the ashes of Jean Moulin, a major Gaullist Resistance figure captured by the Gestapo in 1943 who died after torture, were transferred to the Panthéon in 1964. Responsibility for his capture was bitterly contested. Alternative readings that cast doubt on the strength of support for the Resistance and for de Gaulle were marginalized. In Alain Resnais's documentary about the Holocaust, *Nuit et brouillard* (1955), a film commissioned by the

'Comité d'histoire de la 2e Guerre mondiale' with the support of the Ministry of Veterans, the French licensing authorities censored a shot briefly showing the kepi of a French policeman among those guarding deportees.[5]

This process was given added force by the search for assurance and prestige that finally culminated in the formation of the Fifth Republic in 1958 and the presidency of de Gaulle (1958–69). His refusal to collaborate during the war was presented as the quintessential cause of the new France, and the fact that he was now president apparently vindicated the French of 1940–4 and, more generally, French history, as did the exaggeration of the popularity and effectiveness of the Resistance. This included an exaggeration of the role of the Free French in the Normandy landings and in the subsequent capture of Paris. Some 30 films about the Occupation were produced in the period 1958–62. Similarly, the role of the Resistance was exaggerated in Italy, especially by the Communists, in order to provide an acceptable recent national pedigree.

This situation was to change, in part because of developments specific to France itself, but in part due both to the greater weight that the Holocaust came to play in the collective Western consciousness and to the less reverential approach to the past that was an aspect of the cultural changes of the 1960s. Scholarship played a role, not least the book of an American scholar, Robert Paxton, *Vichy France: Old Guard and New Order, 1940–1944* (1972). In place of the presentation of Vichy and collaboration as something forced on France by the Germans, Paxton, by extensively employing German archival material (the French archives were closed to him), argued that the Vichy regime had been popular and also keen to collaborate in order to win German support for a reconfiguration of French society that was to mark the triumph of an anti-liberal ideology. This approach was unacceptable to many of those in academic authority in France, and there were difficulties in publishing a French translation. Similarly, a documentary about the Occupation in Clermont-Ferrand, an industrial centre near Vichy, *Le Chagrin et la Pitié* (*The Sorrow and the Pity*), released in 1971, was not shown on French television for 12 years. Louis Malle's film *Lacombe, Lucien* (1973) created considerable controversy because it made Fascism seem attractive and presented its protagonist as working voluntarily for the Gestapo.[6]

Although post-war views about laudatory wartime conduct continued to be expressed, as in François-Georges Dreyfus's *Histoire de Vichy* (1990), nevertheless growing interest in Vichy's complicity in the Holocaust, and the less deferential character of French society, especially after the unrest of May 1968, combined to provide a more conducive atmosphere for the pursuit of the truth by journalists, scholars and others. Politics also played a major role, as scores were settled with those who could be tainted for their role under Vichy, most prominently François Mitterrand, president from 1981 until 1995, and the friend of René Bousquet, chief of police under Vichy, who was assassinated in Paris in 1993 just before he could be tried for his role in rounding up Jewish children for deportation to slaughter in Germany. Attention was also directed at the ambivalent role of the powerful French Communist Party during the Nazi-Soviet Pact of 1939–41. Judicial proceedings further helped encourage interest and controversy, especially the trials in 1994 of Paul Touvier, head of the collaborationist *milice* in Lyons,[7] and in 1997–8 of Maurice Papon, a former secretary-general at the Préfecture of the Gironde, who had played a major role in the deportation of Bordeaux's Jews and later became a government minister.[8] The former was sentenced to life imprisonment, the latter to ten years but immediately appealed. Papon's role in arresting Jews had first been revealed in the press in 1981.

The Vichy period was put under the spotlight, not least when a number of films were set there. The situation led to pressure for a new public memory, and this was grasped in 1995 when Mitterrand's political opponent and successor, Jacques Chirac, accepted national responsibility for the wartime treatment of the Jews, a major condemnation of the Vichy regime, and a step Mitterand had refused to take in 1992. Thus, the Holocaust helped focus a more complex refashioning of the recent French past, creating a demand for the recognition of events and memories that had been ignored in the public account.[9]

The weight of the past continues to play a role in current French politics. With the right divided between the Gaullists and the far-right National Front, both struggled for appropriate historical references.[10] The Gaullists argued that the National Front looked back to Vichy, and indeed it did make such references, not least in the 2002 presidential election when the Vichy slogan 'Work, Family, Country' was deployed. The relationship between past and present was at stake in France in 2004 when President Chirac sought an appropriate context for a call to act against a rising wave of anti-Semitism and racism. He travelled to Le Chambon-sur-Lignon, a village in the Massif Central that had sheltered Jews from the Holocaust, in order to declare: 'Faced with the rise of intolerance, racism and anti-Semitism . . . I ask the French to remember a still recent past. I tell them to remain faithful to the lessons of history, a so recent history.' Praising Chambon as a model for modern France because its people had rejected 'the infamy of the Vichy regime', Chirac linked a call for modern vigilance to a demand that the horrors of the past be understood. Later that year, the French education ministry distributed

DVDs with excerpts of *Shoah* (1985), a film about the Holocaust, to schools as part of its attempt to combat anti-Semitism.

Confronting the recent past, in the shape of the Second World War, was also related to public rereadings of earlier episodes in national histories. This was made dramatically clear in Paris in 1989 when state-sponsored celebrations of the bicentenary of the French Revolution were challenged by posters drawing a parallel between the Revolutionaries' brutal suppression of popular opposition in the Vendée in 1793 and genocide, with its obvious echoes in more recent history. The previous year, the popular film *Chouans!* had drawn attention to another uprising against the Revolution. The extent to which the Revolution led necessarily to tyranny was controversial, not only in academic circles[11] but also in popular ones no longer willing to accept the doctrine of French statist liberalism. Furthermore, this reinterpretation had an impact on the global understanding of the Revolution as icon and inspiration of modernity.[12]

In an earlier instance of the reverse process, the term Bonapartism was applied to de Gaulle by his critics. Napoleon's legacy has proved less divisive than that of the Revolution. It was particularly favoured by the Gaullists. Dominique de Villepin, a neo-Gaullist who became Interior Minister in 2004, is a biographer of Napoleon who does not feel it inappropriate to keep in his office a bust of a man who was in practice a dictator.

Germany and the Holocaust

The Holocaust helped force a recognition of the past in West Germany to an even greater extent, but there also, there was a chronology similar to that in France. Post-war occupation had led to the punishment of many members of the wartime regime and to the dismantling of the state and its apparatus. This process, however, was less than complete in Germany not only because of the serious inherent difficulties of the task but also because of the desire to integrate West Germany into the West as the front line against Communism. This led to the reformulation of German nationalism with the creation of a 'new' free Germany and, in particular, a new German army. Such a goal required an acceptable presentation of recent history. This was characterized by a widespread desire to present Naziism not as something inherent within Germanness but rather as an aberration that had gained support and power due to the particular circumstances of the 1930s, especially the Depression.

Others, therefore, could be presented as bearing the burden of responsibility for the Nazis and, indeed, in part this involved a reiteration of criticism of the Allies in the 1920s and 1930s for the supposedly harsh peace terms after the First World War. The whitewashing of the recent German past led to an emphasis on limited, and/or misguided, support for Hitler prior to his seizure of power in 1933, and to coerced support thereafter. There was also a stress on resistance to Nazi policies, particularly on the July 1944 bomb plot, which seemed particularly appropriate as it had been mounted by conservative elements, not Communists. The role of the latter in the resistance was neglected.[13]

This approach was also seen in the business community, which sought to shake off claims that it had played a major role in the Nazi rise to power. Individual companies such as Siemens produced favourable, and misleading, accounts of their activities.[14] In addition, in the 1950s relatively little attention was paid to the Holocaust, while the denazification of the German historical profession (as of much else in West, and even Communist East, Germany) was very incomplete.[15] This was important for the training of the next generation of historians.

As in France, the situation subsequently changed. In part, this was due to the pressures on the collective myth of general social and cultural changes, specifically the rise of a generation that did not feel responsibility for Naziism, and also the decline of deference towards the former generations. In part, the shift was due to a growing awareness of the atrocities committed by the Nazi regime. This was matched by a growing focus on the Holocaust from outside Germany,[16] and by the widespread determination to treat it as the defining moment in public responsibility. The attempt to contain the effects on Germany's image by blaming the atrocities specifically on the Nazis was challenged, especially in a debate about the complicity of the military, which was indeed pronounced.[17] Thus, in place of the notion of the Germans as in some way victims of the Nazis[18] (an idea pushed especially hard in Austria) came the view that they had collaborated.

In turn, this was challenged by attempts to put the post-war expulsion of Germans from Eastern Europe on the agenda. For example, the West German Ministry for Refugees published *Documents on the Expulsion*. In part, this was an attempt to shift the focus of attention on atrocities, and to suggest that the Germans were not uniquely guilty of anti-societal behaviour. In response, for example, to the stress on the brutal conduct of the German army came attempts to argue that the Soviet army was as bad, attempts that ignored the extent to which the Soviet presence in Germany in 1945 was a consequence of the German invasion of the Soviet Union in 1941. There were also claims that those who focused on atrocities were motivated by left-wing politics.

Blame-shifting also affected the response to the claim that, in attacking the Soviet Union, Hitler had in fact pre-empted a planned Soviet assault on Germany, a problematic thesis pushed hard by Viktor Suvorov in *Ice-breaker: Who Started the Second World War* (1990). There was also interest in the Germans as victims of Allied bombing, although the presentation of the latter in terms of mass murder ignored the role of the Germans in bombing, the strategic goals of the latter and its success in destroying the German air force. Hermann Knell's *To Destroy a City: Strategic Bombing and Its Human Consequences in World War II* (2003), which had a considerable impact in Germany with its account of the British air force's destruction of Würzburg in March 1945, inaccurately presented German policies in the 1930s and the attack on the Soviet Union as defensive and preventive. This literature was very popular. Appearing in 2002, Jörg Friedrich's *Der Brand: Deutschland im Bombenkrieg 1940–1945* went into its thirteenth edition in 2003.[19] In October 2004, the issue of whether the British would apologize for their bombing campaign was stoked up in the mass-circulation German press prior to a visit by the Queen. 'Sagt die Queen jetzt Sorry?' (Will the Queen say sorry?) asked *Bild* on 28 October, beside a picture of a British bomber and under a reminder of those killed at Dresden. Recent British work had emphasized the degree to which Dresden was a major centre in the German military-industrial complex.[20]

More generally, the emergence of the Holocaust as a central issue in the collective memory of France, Germany and the USA from the 1970s, and more particularly in the 1990s (as well as a legitimate academic subject and not simply an aspect of the Second World War), rested on complex social, cultural and political reasons.[21] These included a reaction against Holocaust denial on the resurgent extreme right.[22] Such denial was criminalized in France. Growing interest in, and reference to, the Holocaust marked not only an important change in how people saw the 1940s, but also the development of a wider frame of reference. The capacity of historical works to ignite public interest in this field was shown by the response to Daniel Goldhagen's depiction of the Germans as *Hitler's Willing Executioners* (1996), and with the 2000 libel trial arising from David Irving's work. The former juxtaposed an often critical scholarly response with a more engaged populist reception accepting Goldhagen's somewhat simplistic case, especially in the USA,[23] while the latter indicated that historical evidence could be deployed effectively within the constraints of legal cases. The libel trial served as an opportunity to assert that there were historical truths, in this case the horrors of the Holocaust.[24] The American concern about the Holocaust led in the 1990s to the Nazi War Crime Disclosure Act of 1998, and to the opening of the large United States Holocaust Memorial Museum in Washington.[25]

In German historiography there was a controversy about the relationship between the Nazis and longer-term trends in German history, and this had a direct relevance to attempts to legitimate the West German political system, and a link with challenges to the dominant conservative (and gerontocratic) character of post-war West German historical scholarship. Fritz Fischer's *Griff nach der Weltmacht: Die Kriegszielpolitik des kaiserlichen Deutschlands, 1914–1918* (1961), a book translated into English as *Germany's Aims in the First World War* (1967), focused on the primacy of domestic policy, particularly the response by the conservative elite to rising socialism. Condemning conservatism and capitalism, Fischer undermined the attempt to present Wilhelmine Germany as a model for post-1945 West Germany and the Nazis as an aberration. Fischer instead argued that there was an essential continuity from Wilhelmine Germany through to the Hitlerian regime.[26] This acted as a parallel to the Japanese scholarship that criticized post-1945 Japan by discerning elements of continuity with wartime Japan.[27]

Separately in Germany, the *Historikerstreit* (controversy among historians) of 1986–7, which linked discussion of the Holocaust to the question of how best to present national history, was played out in a very public fashion with many articles appearing in prominent newspapers. In part, it was a product of the attempt by historians close to Chancellor Helmut Kohl, the leader of the Conservative Christian Democratic Party which gained power in 1982, to 'normalize' German history, which was taken to mean make it more acceptable in order to ground national identity. Kohl saw this as a necessary basis for patriotism, national pride and spiritual renewal, a theme taken up more generally on the German right.[28] In the controversy, the degree to which the Holocaust arose from specific German characteristics was debated, as was the extent to which the German state had a historical mission, specifically to resist advances from the east, i.e. the Soviet Union, an approach pushed by conservatives such as Andreas Hillgruber. This led to the claim that its iniquities had to be considered against this background.[29] The argument that the Germans had to fight on to resist the Soviet advance was also that of German generals in the final stage of the war. This self-serving argument did not stop them also mounting a fierce resistance to Anglo-American forces, while fighting on of course provided more time for the Holocaust.[30]

The conservative argument influenced more than the presentation of the twentieth century, and was not only advanced within Germany. In 2000, a translation of Theodor Schieder's biography of Frederick the Great was published in England. Schieder (1908–84) had pursued his career during the Hitler years, which was glossed in the introduction by writing that his account was 'firmly within an established German – and German nationalist – tradition' and that he had been involved 'with the *Ostforschung* School of German historians who emphasized their nation's decisive contribution to the development of "Slavic areas in Eastern Europe"'. Schieder's work indeed presented a sense of mission and of history as clear-cut process. In contrast to scholarship emphasizing the value of the Holy Roman Empire, Schieder saw it as anachronistic, while the Habsburg monarchy was presented as 'an hermaphrodite', in short an aberration compared to Prussia.[31] Parallel to the debate about Germany, conservative Japanese historians, especially from the 1960s, tried to defend aspects of the authoritarian and bellicose Japan of the 1930s and early 1940s.

Separately from, but related to, debates among historians, the controversial nature of the recent German past has a direct impact on German domestic and, possibly, foreign policy. This was seen in October–November 2003 when a controversy arose over a speech by Martin Hohmann, a backbencher from the then opposition Christian Democratic Party, declaring that Germans should not, as a result of their support for Hitler, be treated as a 'guilty people'. Hohmann's comparison indeed was designed to deflect criticism onto those whose brutal treatment under Hitler formed the prime charge, the Jews, because he claimed that they were themselves guilty of a prominent role in Communist atrocities, a claim also made on behalf of anti-Semitic nationalists in Eastern Europe. After a fortnight's controversy, Hohmann was expelled from the Christian Democrats. Concerns that his attitude was related to and might encourage anti-Semitism were linked, possibly less accurately, to claims that anti-Semitism was related to growing opposition to Israel's policies towards the Palestinians.

This was not an isolated episode. In Nuremberg, criticism of the granting in 1997 by the city council of honorary citizenship to Karl Diehl, a local industrialist who had used concentration camp workers, led to a bitter controversy, in which the majority of the council supported Diehl.[32] Further south, Munich has been reluctant to acknowledge its role as the early centre of Nazi movement.

The official federal governmental memorialization in Germany was reflected powerfully in the Memorial to the Murdered Jews of Europe, finally finished in 2005 after long controversy. A large work, the size of two football fields, built close to the site of Hitler's bunker in Berlin, its design, however, was a source of dispute, as was the extent to which it represented a break with the past. The need to coat the stones (designed to represent a Jewish cemetery) with anti-graffiti spray reflected anxiety that they could be defaced by neo-Nazis. Furthermore, as another cause of controversy, this spray was manufactured by Degussa, a subsidiary of which produced the Zyklon B gas used in the death camps. The memorial was presented not simply as a response to the past but also as a warning. In July 2004, Wolfgang Thierse, the Speaker of the German parliament, praised it not just as a memorial to mark the Holocaust but also for being 'about the future: a reminder that we should resist anti-Semitism at its roots'.

Memorials and cemeteries are important sites for contestation as well as commemoration. Thus, President Ronald Reagan of the USA caused a stir on a state visit to West Germany in 1985 when, joining the German Chancellor, Helmut Kohl, he visited the military cemetery at Bitburg, because it contained the graves of SS guards. Reagan indeed described the soldiers as as much victims of the Nazis as those who had suffered in concentration camps, a bizarre equivalence.[33] The pressure from the Federation of the Expelled for a centre to commemorate the Germans driven from Eastern Europe at the close of the war has led to controversy.

A more insistent memorialization of the Nazi regime and its iniquities was offered by print and, even more, the visual media, and this made their coverage particularly sensitive. In 2004, there was controversy inside and outside Germany over the coverage of Hitler's last days in the film *Der Untergang* (*The Downfall*), financed by the German state television network ARD. Released in September 2004, the film, which showed him as popular with his staff in order to demonstrate his humanity, minimized the evil of his policies. In an interview in September 2004 the film's producer, Bernd Eichinger, further accentuated concern by referring to the German *Volk* or people, a term beloved by the Nazis. Interest in Hitler in 2004 was also bolstered by the German mass-circulation press, especially the newspaper *Bild* and the magazine *Der Spiegel.*

Anti-Semitism, past and present, was also an issue elsewhere in Europe. Claims that all, many or some Poles had taken anti-Semitism to murderous extent during the Second World War and indeed, as in fact happened, that the killing of Jews continued after the end of war,[34] proved both embarrassing to Polish apologists and also a factor affecting foreign views of Poland. These claims affected the anti-German and anti-Soviet 'victim status' account of Polish history by suggesting that the Poles had their own victims. In turn, this led to the argument that anti-Semitic aspects of the Polish response to the rising of the Warsaw Ghetto against the Germans in 1943 and of the Warsaw rising the following year had been overlooked by Polish historians.[35]

Italy

In Italy, the treatment of the Jews was an issue in the contest over the reputation of Mussolini, not least over the popularity of the Fascist Salò republic in northern Italy in 1943–5. This contest was directly linked to the legitimacy of political groupings – from Communists to neo-Fascists – that looked back to the 1940s and earlier for evidence of their probity and of the iniquity of their opponents.[36] As a result, the reputation of Mussolini has a greater resonance in Italian politics than that of Hitler or Tojo in those of Germany or Japan. The widespread positive re-evaluation of Mussolini and Italian Fascism, beginning with the work of Renzo De Felice in the 1960s, the differentiation of both from the Nazis, and the decline in the reputation of the Communists, were aspects of the shift that gathered pace following the end of the Cold War, with Italy sharing in the general development in Eastern Europe (see pp. 138–42). The role of the Resistance was reduced,[37] not least by emphasizing the extent of civil war in 1943–5 and also with the argument that part of it had been compromised by its Communism.

These changes in reputation were also related more directly to political developments in Italian politics, not least the restructuring of the right linked to the decline of the Christian Democrats; not that the two were separate. The Italian Social Movement (MSI), the Fascist Party, has itself broken with its past in order to move from the political margins. As late as 1992, the MSI marked the 70th anniversary of Mussolini's seizure of power by donning black shirts and giving the Fascist salute, but in 1994–5 the leader, Gianfranco Fini, changed the MSI into the more moderate Alleanza Nazionale. This kept some aspects of Fascist social thinking, but sought acceptance, not least by a rejection of anti-Semitism. Distancing himself from the party's legacy, in 1996 Fini declared that the verdict on Mussolini was 'best left to the historians'.

Defining public histories

Throughout Europe there was the problem of defining public histories, and, indeed, both the public and history, in response to changing political realities. These reflected a range of issues, not only political but also social. Political ones were more prominent, however, because alongside differences over international alignments, especially in Eastern Europe (see Chapter 7), there were also profound questions about national identity. These focused on relations with proto-nations, such as Catalans in Spain, and Scots and Welsh in Britain, but this relationship was more widespread as it was also an aspect of the tension between nationalism and regionalism. For example, in Italy in the 1990s the separatism of the Northern League led to a distinctive account of regional and national history. Across Europe, this was a dialogue in which the European Union came to play a major role. As so often, control over education was an important issue. Thus, the level at which teaching was overseen was controversial and changes emerged when it was transferred from the national to the regional level.

In Belgium, this occurred from the early 1960s as Flanders and Wallonia became the key governmental areas, and this led to a shift in the treatment of Belgian history. Governmental changes were made more contentious by the political context. Flemish nationalists presented Flanders as suffering a millennium of foreign oppression and claimed that, once independent in 1830, Belgium had served as a system to benefit the Walloons. The problem of national identity was more complex when groups claimed it transcended state boundaries: in the case of Europe, Basques in both France and Spain posed this issue, and, outside Europe, Kurds in Iran, Iraq and Turkey.

Britain

Within countries there was also a more general contesting of the national past that led to particular controversies over individual works. Thus, in Britain, the publication of Norman Davies's best-selling national history *The Isles: A History* (1999) led to a response that threw considerable light on the controverted character of history and on the potential role of the historian as a public figure, a task for which current academic models leave scant room. *The Times* was in no doubt of what it had bought: on 1 November 1999, the Features section of the newspaper began a serialization of excerpts from the work heralded with 'In the most controversial history book of the decade, Norman Davies traces the story of our islands . . . He finds that much of the history we have been taught is untrue.' The Features section included a piece by Davies stating 'It would be hard to find another country that is so befuddled about its past', as well as 'The real story of the Battle of Hastings'. The newspaper's leader that day proclaimed 'A history which rescues our past from anachronism . . . It effortlessly supersedes the attempt of journalists and generalists to lend coherence to the national narrative . . . History is presented in all its complexity', and so on. No suggestion of limitations or debate, and apparently no alternative to the 'microscopes' of academic specialism and the flaws of the ignorant generalist, bar Davies.

In the *Daily Mail*, however, four days later, Andrew Roberts, a conservative columnist and popular historian, began: 'This is a dangerous book, written at a dangerous time', a reference to New Labour's assault on the role of history in British culture. Later in his piece, Roberts claimed: 'Because this book is so unrelentingly critical of so many aspects of British institutions and "Old Britain" – especially the

Monarchy – it has been hailed in *bien pensant* New Labour circles as intellectual justification for their ideological preconceptions in favour of devolution, regionalism and pooling British sovereignty through closer European integration.' Roberts, who saw Davies's book as an assault on 'the legitimacy of the British nation state', wrote: 'With will-power and self-confidence, the present threats can be overcome . . . United we stand, Daviesed we fall.'

On 23 December 1999, Nigel Jones followed up by launching a strong attack on Davies in *The Times*:

> it is no coincidence that this determined attempt to airbrush England and Englishness out of the historical narrative comes at precisely the moment when the Government should be actively seeking to subsume our age-old national identity in a remote, centrally-directed, unelected, inor-ganic foreign body . . . our own 'cultural cringe': the idea that continen-tal Europe is, by definition, a superior entity, that all roads lead to and from Rome; and that European notions, whether pronounced by Popes, by despot monarchs, by committees of public safety and Nuremberg rallies, or promulgated by philosophers from Rousseau to Marx to Nietzsche, are, ipso facto, the bee's knees. This is the self-hating England exemplified by James I, Charles I and James II, Harley and Charles James Fox, Philby *père et fils*, Lytton Strachey and Sir Oswald Mosley; and in our day, by the likes of Edward Heath, Hugo Young, Ken Clarke and Chris Patten . . . As a leading light in what might be called the 'collaborationist' school of historians, Davies deplores each and every event that gave these islands their unique distinctiveness – from the continental shift that let in the Channel . . . down to the Reformation.

Ironically, the use of the term 'collaborationist' was indicative of a frame of reference that was continental as well as historical.

In practice, Davies's emphasis on nations as imagined political com-munities was to a considerable extent a matter of stating the obvious. It is readily apparent that British political entities were in large part created, and that this creation owed much to the formulation and dis-semination of new images. This, however, does not lessen the value of such entities. Nor is it the case that an understanding of the role of moulding identities in the past necessarily justifies the replacement of existing practices and ideas that give people a sense of continuity, iden-tity and values. The emphasis on the 'invention of tradition' fails to consider adequately the consensual aspect of 'manufactured' tradi-tions, more specifically the extent to which they reflect a popular will, and also to give adequate consideration to the raw materials from which traditions evolve.[38] Furthermore, to prove that there is no one conception of national interest, or single constitution, that has lasted without change or criticism for a long period, is not the same as arguing that all conceptions or constitutions are of equal value, or that it is a good idea to reject existing systems in favour of an untried future. Evidence of artifice and/or contestation does not undermine the need to place an emphasis on consent on the part of much of the population.

Varied views about British national identity can draw on a rich tradition of informed scholarship that is alive to different interpretations, but it is disappointing that so many of the generalists writing for the public market ignore this tradition. This was abundantly clear in Britain at the start of the new millennium. It was decided at a very senior ministerial level to include no section on history in the Millennium Dome at Greenwich (which ensured that the issue of what to include did not cause controversy), and although a handbook for immigrants prepared in 2004 under the auspices of the Home Office included 21 large-print pages on national history, the government decided that history should not form part of the citizenship tests introduced in 2005. The British Broadcasting Corporation, however, spent a large sum of money (allegedly £400,000 per episode) to produce *A History of Britain* (2000–2) presented by Simon Schama, and he found favour with the government, receiving a CBE (Companion of the Order of the British Empire) in the 2001 New Year's Honours List.

Schama, who described himself as 'a born-again Whig', devoted much attention to what he has referred to as the 'soap opera' of the past, but his television series was lambasted for its approach. In *The Times* of 28 September 2000, Magnus Linklater pointed out that Schama's approach to Britishness 'blithely ignore[d] the entire canon of recent historical work'. Two days later, the anonymous reviewer in *The Economist* warned that Schama 'runs the risk of reducing the history of Britain to little more than a soap opera of bloodthirsty warring kings, jealous siblings, and revolting barons . . . [and] risks the charge of banality'. In the *Times Higher Education Supplement* of 8 December 2000, Christopher Haigh found 'too much drama . . . a Hollywood version . . . a messy soap opera in costume' rich in error.[39]

More characteristic of public history, whether British or not, is the failure on the part of authors (including Schama) and others to make due allowance for contrasting popular responses to historical developments, or for different approaches to national history. This is serious, as the latter are not only part of the fascination of history but also central to its civic importance, not least as a reminder of the limitations of authoritarian accounts. This simplification, or, as it is frequently termed, dumbing down, is linked to a persistent and mistaken tendency to underrate the intelligence of the public. They encounter competing analyses in political debate, so why not for history?

The official call for a rewriting of history is often both explicit and pointed, both in Britain and elsewhere. The Commission on the Future of Multi-Ethnic Britain, which reported in 1999, declared that 'Britishness, as much as Englishness, has systematic, largely unspoken, racial connotations', and called for a change in historical treatments, specifically 'reimagining' to challenge racism. The demand for the inclusion of ethnic minorities in national history offers a very different account to that provided by such earlier staples as Winston Churchill's *A History of the English Speaking Peoples* (1956–8), although, in their own way, such works shared in a concern with the cultural consequences of ethnic identity. A quest for inclusion characterized the *Oxford Dictionary of National Biography* (2004), a work that registered changes since the *Dictionary of National Biography* was published from 1885 until 1901, not least with the state contributing much of the £25 million cost. A publicity flyer, '*Oxford DNB* and history', that accompanied the publication, accurately noted:

> Many new entries chronicle the lives of particular Welsh, Scottish, Irish, or, indeed, purely regional significance. Others record the impact of 'foreigners', as visitors, travellers, or permanent settlers. Pre-independence America and parts of the British empire/Commonwealth have been particular areas of growth. Linguists, artists, religious leaders, and nationalist politicians now take their place alongside the administrators and loyalists who dominated the *DNB*'s coverage, reflecting more fully the experiences of countries under British rule. 'National' as well as historical diversity will be a defining characteristic of the *Oxford DNB*.

Godfrey Smith's review in the *Sunday Times* claimed 'The *DNB* is not just a prodigious piece of scholarship; it is also a mirror of Britishness', while the editor claimed 'we are parts of a network that has rewritten the history of Britain, encapsulating this generation's view of national history'.[40] The euphoria of publication was responsible for such claims but, despite governmental support, the marginal character of the work (as of other scholarship) to the views of most of the generation was readily apparent. Writing in the *Daily Telegraph* on 25 September 2004, Christopher Howse declared: 'The *DNB* should be in the national curriculum. Every home should have a set. Sell the car and buy the new *DNB*.' The second-hand car market recorded no changes.

Debate in Britain about history and national character draws not only on the contested terrain of real or alleged racism, but also on

Britain's uneasy relations with the movement for European unity.[41] In 1962, Hugh Gaitskell, the leader of the Labour Party, warned in a television interview that entry into the European Economic Community (the basis of the European Union) 'means the end of Britain as an independent nation; we become no more than Texas or California in the United States of Europe. It means the end of a thousand years of history.' Gaitskell should have been talking about England not Britain, which, as a state, does not have such a long political history, but his comment captured the location of political concerns about identity in a historical context. For Gaitskell, Second World War memories of the Commonwealth supporting Britain meant a lot. The following year, *The Living World of History* (1963), a popular children's history, did not suggest that Britain's future lay with European unity, and indeed made no mention of the European Economic Community. Instead, the book presented the Victorian period as the great age of British achievement and used Lady Butler's heroic painting of *The Charge of the Scots Greys* at the battle of Waterloo in 1815 as its endpapers. The academic counterpart was the careful separation of British from European history in teaching and research.[42] This approach appeared less relevant with Britain's membership in the European Union from 1973, while the rise of Scottish and Welsh nationalism undermined the British perspective.

What was, and is, certainly under threat was the self-contained and Whig approach to British history, an approach already largely overthrown in academic circles as a result of scholarly work as well as intellectual assaults from left and right, but now also challenged in the public realm.[43] The Whig approach had emphasized a Protestant identity for the nation, respect for property, the rule of law and parliamentary sovereignty as a means to secure liberty and order, and a nationalistic self-confidence that combined a patriotic sense of national uniqueness with a xenophobic contempt for foreigners, especially Catholics. The positive contributions of Protestantism and liberty to prosperity and social development were stressed, but a very partial account of the latter was offered, concentrating on the growth of a strong middle class.

Despite challenges, at the popular level of the bulk of the population in Britain, aspects of traditional history and conventional historical images are still common, generally reflect Whiggish notions and often have little to do with academic developments, as can be seen, for example, with Sir Roy Strong's commercially-successful but intellectually-limited *The Story of Britain* (1996); and the same is true of other states with a past liberal historical tradition of progressive change.

Furthermore, the academic works that sell best and are most accessible to the general reading public are generally those written in a traditional fashion. Biographies and narratives are at a premium, and there is also a huge trend of republishing books written years ago. In combination, narrative and the Whig approach offer a readily accessible, and thus popular, means to produce a clear account of a highly complex subject: human history.[44]

Strong himself criticized academics for writing badly and failing to provide an accessible narrative framework. A relevant perspective is offered by David Cannadine's brief account of recent historiographical trends in which he notes that historians are less interested in explaining how, why and when and, instead, have moved 'from explanation to meaning, from causes to understanding'.[45]

There is a parallel in the reading of fiction, where continued popular preferences tend to defy powerful academic literary fashions, most of which are unintelligible to fellow academics, let alone the reading public. The persistent popularity of the detective novel is especially noteworthy. This literature places a stress on the role of chance and individuals, offers a strong narrative structure and, in most cases, a powerful moral element. The genre indeed offers exciting often exemplary stories, which are precisely what are sought by most readers of history. A story (i.e. narrative) is required in order for history to make sense. Another parallel is offered by modern Western symphonic music, which generally has limited popular appeal.

Decolonization in Europe

Within Western Europe it is also possible to see the impact of decolonization on national history. One major consequence was a lack of interest in periods of colonial rule. Thus, Norwegian history is presented with relatively little concern for the long centuries of rule by the crowns of first Denmark and then Sweden prior to 1905; and the Finns, similarly, do not devote proportionate attention to their period under Russian rule from 1809 until 1917.

In Ireland, the positive aspects of English control from the twelfth century to 1921 are underrated. Museum displays on Irish history concentrate on the glories of Celtic civilization in the 'Dark Ages', emphasizing Ireland's contribution to European culture at a time when Europe was assailed by barbarians. There is then relatively little on the period of English rule, until the story resumes with the struggle for independence and subsequent history. As a consequence, the positive aspects of the centuries of English rule are neglected in favour of an image of lost centuries, their gloom punctuated by cruel episodes, such as the fate of Wexford and Waterford at the hands of Oliver Cromwell and his invading English Protestant troops in 1649, and the Irish

Famine of 1846–8. This neglects the major role played by the Irish in the development of the English, and then the British, Empire. It also ensures that the riches of Anglo-Irish culture, famously represented by the writers Jonathan Swift and Oscar Wilde, are undervalued.

The emphasis on Irish nationalism in the twentieth century led to a marked neglect of the large number of Catholic volunteers who had fought for George V in the First World War. This extended to a failure to put much effort into constructing or maintaining war memorials. In contrast, the far smaller number involved in the Easter Rising of 1916 against British rule were actively commemorated. Their defiance was seen as a central episode in winning Irish independence, and thus was a crucial element in the Irish foundation myth. That a survivor of the rising, Eamon de Valera, leader of Sinn Féin in 1917–26, was in power for most of the period from 1932, as president of the Executive Council (1932–7), prime minister (1937–48, 1951–4, 1957–9) and president (1959–73), contributed greatly to this situation, and also to the continuing ambivalence about the commemoration of the Irish Civil War of 1922–3 as he had been a member of the defeated rebels in the latter.[46] An academic revisionism critical of the IRA and the eulogization of armed struggle became pronounced in some scholarly circles from the 1970s to the 1990s,[47] but it is far less clear that it had a comparable impact on the public use of history.[48]

With Scotland, which had not been a colony, the increased expression from the 1960s of a distinctive historical tradition separate to that of Britain was widely linked to pressure for autonomy, if not independence. Much focused on the Anglo-Scottish Union of 1707, which was widely presented in public discussion as a measure detrimental to Scotland and maybe obtained partly through bribery: the theme of disunity, indeed treason, as a cause of national weakness was one that could also be applied to present issues. In practice, although the passage of the measure through the Scottish Parliament of 1706 in part depended on successful political management as well as corruption, there were also important issues of self-interest. The Scottish economy was in a poor state, there was a determination not to be shut out from English and colonial markets, the civil war of 1689–91 had underlined the difficulty of independence from England, and the powerful leadership of the Presbyterian Church, whose privileged position in Scotland was written into the treaty, accepted the Union as a political necessity because there was no good Protestant alternative: the refusal of the exiled Stuarts to convert to Protestantism lessened Scottish options.[49] These points, however, were not well ventilated in public discussion: academic caveats were unwelcome. The new Scottish history sees itself as discarding myths rather than creating new ones,[50] but the public reading of the Scottish past is already slanted. Thus, the new museum of Scottish history in Edinburgh greatly downplays the role of the Scots in the British Empire. Wales has witnessed a similar process as far as its British identity and role are concerned.

Alongside the assertion of national historical identities within Europe against allegedly colonial accounts and imaginations, there are also instances of historical clashes between states. This was seen in 2004 when Spain complained about the celebrations for the tercentenary of British rule over Gibraltar. The fact that this represented the democratic will of the vast majority of Gibraltarians was of no consequence to the Spanish state because the loss of territory in 1704 still rankled.

The USA

In the USA, the presentation of the past was involved in the culture wars[51] that became increasingly vexed as an important strand of political disagreement focused on the content of higher education. The content of social history and cultural studies, increasingly prominent forms of academic history in the USA,[52] was a matter of particular contention. This content was criticized by conservatives concerned not only about the empirical basis of such work but also about what they saw as a malign and disruptive political stance, for example an emphasis on social division in American history and on non-conventional sexual behaviour, and a failure to give due weight to religious roots.[53] In turn, radicals used history to support their case that modern America had departed from its founding ideals.[54]

These tensions and debates affected a profession responding to shifts in historical methodologies and the boundaries of historical inquiry.[55] This is a benign remark that underrates the bitterness of much of the debate, bitterness stemming from a self-conscious embrace of new approaches and from the deliberate politicization of the issue by both sides. The scope of new approaches even included the designation of the subject, some feminist historians adopting the term 'herstory'. 'History' is not a reference to masculinity but rather a derivation from the Latin 'historia', but the use of this etymological inaccuracy was designed to make a postmodern intervention in order to challenge conventional assumptions.

Concern over the designation of the subject was an instance of a more general preference for presentation (in the shape of language or discourse) over, or as, content, that was seen in the work of radicals keen to challenge earlier methods of discussing the subject. Their approach drew on literary theory, and sometimes extended to the argument that the discourse was the prime constituent of reality and, because it necessarily varied and was a matter of controversy, that the latter could not be recovered.[56] Related to this was the attempt by the often self-appointed representatives of groups that considered themselves, or could be presented as, marginal to offer a discourse that focused on their concerns and that frequently entailed a demand for apologies.

The treatment of counterfactual history provided a good instance of the relationship between historical methodology and often politicized controversy over content as well as method. Those who adopt the counterfactual 'what if?' approach are sometimes condemned as conservatives unhappy with the course of developments,[57] and the methodology therefore seemingly located politically, although it is apparent that counterfactuals in part reflect the fact that at any one moment various developments seemed possible to people and the sole guarantee was that what was going to happen was not known. Aside from particular political and military turning points, it is possible to consider different developments in public culture or environmental policy and, indeed, such options play a major role in economic modelling and social planning. Comparative history also encourages a measure of counterfactualism.[58]

In the USA in the 1990s and 2000s, controversy also arose from standards of scholarship, with questionable practices by some historians being used by critics to argue (generally in a very sloppy fashion) that the profession as a whole was unscholarly. This was a particularly pointed aspect of America's culture wars and was a crucial issue in the public realm, with an anti-professionalism and a populism becoming increasingly assertive. The influential gun lobby took grave exception to Michael Bellesiles's book *Arming America: The Origins of a National Gun Culture* (2000), which challenged the association of American identity with personal ownership of guns by arguing that in the colonial and early national period many Americans did not have guns, while those who had did not make much use of them. The archival research on which the thesis was based, and Bellesiles's interpretation, were both subject to considerable and powerful scholarly criticism that also served as an opportunity for more political attacks.[59] In 2002, the National Endowment for the Humanities (NEH), a federal government body whose agenda was particularly partisan under the administration of President George W. Bush (2001–), withdrew its name from an NEH-funded fellowship at the Newberry Library that had been awarded to Bellesiles so that he could continue his research. Lynne Munson, the NEH deputy chair, referred to the need for 'high scholarly and ethical standards', while Bellesiles claimed that the NEH's measure 'should send chills through academics everywhere. The spirit of Joe McCarthy stalks the halls of the NEH . . . I regret that my name has been associated with an agency that values so little the principles of the First Amendment, due process, and academic freedom.'

More generally, the charge on the American right was that the academic profession was overly liberal (a term that has a different location and connotation in the USA to those in some other national political cultures). It was claimed that this liberalism led to bias in teaching, marking and appointments, and that it was an aspect of the misleading of the young and the corruption of an intellectual tradition. In early 2004, one conservative commentator, David Horowitz, not only continued to record cases of alleged bias but also pressed Congress and state legislatures to employ a legislative remedy in the shape of an Academic Bill of Rights designed to encourage a plurality of beliefs in appointments and in tenure decisions. The contrast between the contours of American popular interest in history and the subject, practice and tone of much academic writing was also used to criticize the profession as a whole, although, in practice, the charges of plagiarism used to sow doubt more widely largely related to popular writers.

Within the profession, what was seen as an overly liberal establishment, many of them products of the Vietnam generation, and, more specifically, the politicization of the historical profession, were both challenged in April 1998 with the formation of The Historical Society (THS). This was an organization that, in its own words, sought to reject the jargon-laden debates and political agendas that it saw as all too prevalent. While this rejection represented a conscious challenge to what was seen as the norms of the dominant American Historical Association (AHA), the goals of the new body were presented in an inclusive fashion. Eugene Genovese, the founding-president of the society, and a scholar whose intellectual pedigree was originally on the left, made openness and accessibility its goals, implying that these were not shared by the AHA:

> The Society extends from left to right . . . and promotes frank debate in an atmosphere of civility, mutual respect, and common courtesy. All we require is that participants lay down plausible premises, reason logically, appeal to evidence, and prepare to exchange criticism with those holding different points of view. Our goal is to promote an integrated history accessible to the public.

His criticism of existing academic practices was blunt and public. In an opinion piece in the *Los Angeles Times* of 31 May 1998, Genovese wrote 'The demand that historians privilege race, class, and gender is occurring in an atmosphere that uncomfortably resembles the McCarthyism of the

1950s. It is being imposed by presiding cliques that have made ideological conformity the primary criterion for holding office.' As with the appeasement of the 1930s in foreign policy, McCarthyism was a historical episode that could be widely (even recklessly) applied to discern and describe unwelcome tendencies. Genovese claimed in his THS presidential address of 1999 that the two flagship professional historical associations in the USA (the AHA and the Organization of American Historians) 'have taken one political position after another'. He also linked the historical establishment's political pronouncements to an effort to drive dissidents out of these organizations. Genovese's self-description as a middle-of-the-road figure lashing out against 'political positions' was ironic as he is a long-standing taker of such positions himself, and it is also unclear whether his language of inclusiveness is rhetorical or real.

Another founding member of the THS, Marc Trachtenberg, again courted publicity, writing an opinion piece in the *Wall Street Journal* of 17 July 1998 in which he condemned what he presented as dominant themes in American academic history: relativism, the marginalization of specialisms such as diplomatic history, the emphasis on faddism, and the brutal use of patronage to mould both profession and subject.

The state of the profession in universities was not the sole issue of discussion. There was also a more general debate about the value of multiculturalism in American society and intellectual life, and its impact on the teaching of history. Bilingual education was a related issue, with the Bilingual Education Act of 1968 increasingly opposed from the late 1970s leading, in the No Child Left Behind Act of 2001, to support for English-only teaching. Supporters of multiculturalism in history referred to recovered voices, and critics to a fragmentation that harmed any sense of unity and that made it difficult to produce more than a series of histories of minorities.[60]

This debate acted as a background to the controversy over the release in 1994 of the draft National History Standards intended to act as a voluntary system of guidance to state Boards of Education and other bodies, offering outlines and study guides for the teaching of American and world history.[61] The pressure for these standards reflected widespread public and professional anxiety about the limited knowledge of history of many young Americans, including students at good universities, and the belief that the failure to teach much history at high school level was the key factor. History had been largely replaced by social studies.[62] This pressure led to the establishment of the National Center for History in the Schools at the University of California, Los Angeles, whose work on formulating Standards was funded from October 1991 to the tune of $2.2 million by the NEH and the US Department of Education.

In response to then fashionable norms, the emphasis in the draft Standards was on social not on political history and, more specifically, on groups held to have been hitherto underrated, especially women and African–Americans. The draft Standards conformed to the new multicultural agendas then being advocated by many academics (and others). The draft Standards led to a controversy touched off in October 1994 by Lynne Cheney, a Republican who, when head of the NEH under President George H.W. Bush (another Republican and self-proclaimed 'Education President'), had both supported the project and allocated management of it to the Los Angeles Center. Condemning the draft Standards for 'their unqualified admiration for peoples, places, and events that are politically correct', Cheney saw their consequence as anti-American, in that they focused on negative aspects and individuals, such as the Ku Klux Klan and Senator Joseph McCarthy, and not on praiseworthy ones such as George Washington and the Wright Brothers. Similar double standards were alleged in the treatment of world history, specifically a running down of the value and values of the West, and an account of the Cold War that placed the two sides (the West and the Communist world) on an equal footing. The Cold War was presented in the draft Standards as leading

> to the Korean and Vietnam wars as well as the Berlin airlift, Cuban missile crisis, American interventions in many parts of the world, a huge investment in scientific research, and environmental damage that will take generations to rectify. It demonstrated the power of American public opinion in reversing foreign policy [a reference to the abandonment of American participation in the Vietnam War], it tested the democratic system to its limits, and it left scars on American society that have not yet been erased.

There was no comparable critique of the Soviet Union and China. The Standards also broke with the conventional popular approach in ignoring the established pantheon of heroes, both because the authors contested the interpretations that led to these choices and because they were opposed to the emphasis on great men in history.

The controversy over the draft Standards in part reflected the sensitivity of the issue of the Native Americans. Its presentation of them in positive terms was accompanied by a criticism of their treatment at the hands of the colonists. Neither aspect allowed for the greater complexity of Native cultures that includes much that would now be found undesirable or limited (for example, illiteracy or the absence of the wheel), as well as a relationship with colonists that was not simply adversarial. Aside from trade and military co-operation, what has been termed the 'middle ground' of shared cultural space between colonists and Natives also involved intermarriage. The latter is not a subject that fits with the notion of coherent ethnic blocks, let alone with relationships that were not adversarial, but it was important not only in what became the USA, for example in Hawai'i, but also in other frontier areas of Western activity, such as around Hudson Bay and in West Africa. Furthermore, as more mixed-race children were born, so the prospects of such marriage increased.[63] There was also a clash in the draft Standards between the essentially static values offered by an emphasis on, and praise for, Native Americans and by a stress on relations between different cultures, and the nature of American (and not only American) society as changeable, especially with reference to individual striving for betterment and the collective pressures for change flowing from democracy and purchaser consumerism. The latter, however, were not seen in positive terms. Instead, the emphasis was on a working-class solidarity expressed through popular activism.[64]

The National Standards rapidly became a subject for political controversy. Two Republican senators, one, Robert Dole, the presidential candidate in 1996, introduced amendments to ban the employment of federal money for the implementation of these draft Standards. They also required that such money be spent only on those who 'have a decent respect for United States history's roots in Western civilization'. Lynne Cheney had put the issue squarely in a political light. She argued that the election as president of Bill Clinton in 1992, which had led to her fall from office, had led to the project for the Standards going wrong because, she claimed, it led radical historians to drive forward their ends. Other conservative columnists, such as Charles Krauthammer and Patrick Buchanan, and radio commentators such as Rush Limbaugh, followed suit, unsurprisingly so as the Standards' criticism was not restricted to the early history of America. Conservatives could not expect to warm to being asked to assess President Reagan as 'an agent of selfishness'.

In January 1995, the Senate condemned the draft Standards as irresponsible and malevolent by a vote of 99 to one, the latter, Richard C. Shelby, a Republican senator from Alabama, seeking even stronger action. Later that year, the draft Standards were also attacked by the secretary of education. In turn, the director of the Center, Gary Nash, the president of the Organization of American Historians, claimed that the critique was an assault on a cohort of scholars, and the draft Standards were approved by the American Historical Association and the Organization of American Historians. Once the controversy broke out, the draft Standards were supported by many prominent historians as well as by liberal publications, such as the *New York Times*, although some major historians who were not right-wing, such as Diane Ravitch and Arthur Schlesinger Jr., offered important criticisms of particular interpretations in the Standards. After the Standards were revised under the auspices of the Council for Basic Education, not least to provide a different account of the Cold War, and released in 1996, the controversy became far less heated, although its legacy was divisive, bolstering the convictions of both sets of protagonists.[65]

These and other debates, in part defined as contention over 'the uses to which a largely consensual modernist account of the Founding of a unified nation ought to be put within the postmodern cultural politics of an ethnically mixed society',[66] were not restricted to academic circles. Instead, the culture wars in the USA took on much of their energy because of the large degree of, often vitriolic, public participation. This ranged across American history, from relations between colonists and Native Americans to the treatment of recent events. American military history proved especially contentious. Many foreigners were surprised that the military records of the presidential candidates during the Vietnam War played such a major role in the 2004 campaign, but this reflected a long-term political engagement with such issues. This was multifaceted, relating not only to events during specific conflicts but also to their commemoration.

The controversy over the Second World War Memorial provides a good example. In 1987, Congresswoman Marcy Kaptur proposed such a memorial, but it was not officially opened and dedicated until 2004, significantly on Memorial Day, 29 May. There were serious disputes over location and funding. The memorial was designed for the central axis of the National Mall in Washington around the Rainbow Pool and between the Lincoln and Washington Monuments. The use of so much of the Mall's open space for this purpose was controversial. An opponent, Judy Feldman, President of the National Coalition to Save our Mall, declared 'if we don't have our public space and our commons, where do we go to celebrate, to demonstrate?', and this Coalition mounted a successful lawsuit to prevent construction of the memorial. Under political pressure, however, Congress overturned this. The funds raised for the memorial indicated the extent of popular support. The first $7 million had been raised through the sale of government commemorative coins, but the remainder of the $175 million required was raised through private donations, as was another $20 million for a trust to cover maintenance costs. The design of the memorial also reflected the nature of the Constitution. Columns that are part of the memorial have the name of every state and American territory engraved upon them, while they are linked by a bronze rope signifying the bond between the states.[67]

The treatment of the Second World War is bound up with the concept of the 'Greatest Generation', those Americans who came of age in the 1940s and fought the war. They have been widely honoured, not least as part of an implicit, and often explicit, critique of the '1960s' generation' that is held to have abandoned their values and with damaging cultural and social consequences for the USA. Politics plays a role in this controversy, with the Republicans particularly keen to appropriate the myth of the 'Greatest Generation' (which is ironic as the war was waged by Democratic administrations). Thus, military history, in the sense of the popular portrayal of the Second World War, is directly linked to present-day 'culture wars'.

Controversies in the USA are often bitter, especially when they relate to ethnic issues. The treatment of African-American history is particularly contentious, and the emphasis on race and ethnicity certainly seems to be changing the way it is taught. For example, in 2000, in response to discussion of the Interior Appropriations Bill, the National Park Service submitted to Congress a report assessing the educational information at Civil War sites and recommending that much be updated, not least to illustrate the 'breadth of human experience during the period, and establish the relevance of the war to people today'. Representative Jesse Jackson Jr. and other members of Congress had complained that many sites lacked appropriate contextualization and, specifically, that there was often 'missing vital information about the role that the institution of slavery played in causing the American Civil War'. The treatment of the Civil War is particularly contentious, with the issue of slavery (rather than states' rights) highlighted in order to criticize ante-bellum Southern culture and to present the South as 'un-American' or 'anti-American'. Thus controlling and defining the past become an aspect of current politics.

Charges of exploitation and of historic wrongs explaining present circumstances are contested, especially from the 'white South' with its aggressive and self-righteous[68] sense of historical grievance. This situation is exacerbated when other issues such as gender are involved. Thus, the charge that Thomas Jefferson had had an affair with an African-American servant, Sally Heming, led to contention in the 1990s and early 2000s, with one affronted American participant walking out of a University of Virginia Jefferson Symposium I attended in 1998. The charge was seen by some as an assault on the integrity of the Founding Fathers, while the emphasis on the relationship seems to obscure Jefferson's achievements and is nearly always taken out of context.

The controversy also reflected the degree to which a strong sense of identity held by many (but by no means all) ethnic groups in America could lead to contention over historical issues or, more usually, symbols. In the early 1920s, when the 'New Italian' immigration (from southern Italy, not the earlier northern Italians who could be seen as more 'European', even Alpine) was under attack, the Viking origin of America became more popular and Columbus's role in 'discovering' the New World and beginning European links with the Americas was played down. In the 2000s, in contrast, the now well-established Italian–Americans did not take kindly to often ahistorical criticism of the consequences for Native Americans of the voyages of Christopher Columbus, as Columbus Day celebrations were important to their sense of self-identity. Some commemorations, for example Santa Barbara's 'Old Spanish Days', were not particularly contentious, but they all underline the variety of American public culture. In the American tradition, these particular celebrations are designed to complement the inclusive theme of national memory, seen most particularly with Fourth of July celebrations.[69] In many countries, the relationship is far more tense.

Alongside an emphasis on American academic and public history as responding to political shifts, can come a stress on elements of continuity, not least the notion of American exceptionalism and recognition of the diversity of the national experience.[70] This is an important instance of the dangers of simplifying past generations of scholarship and discussion in order to make the present appear more novel. If the intensity of the 'culture wars' of the recent past is notable, they are not the first in American history. In their context and consequences they pale into a mellow echo compared to the situation in all too many other countries.

Notes

1   R. Gildea, *The Past in French History* (New Haven, Conn., 1994).

2   B. Bowles, 'Newsreels, Ideology and Public Opinion under Vichy: the Case of "La France en Marche"', *French Historical Studies*, 27 (2004), 439, and '"La Tragédie de Mers-el-Kébir" and the Politics of Filmed News in France, 1940–1944', *Journal of Modern History*, 76 (2004), 347–88.

3   E. Jennings, 'Reinventing Jeanne: The Iconology of Joan of Arc in Vichy Schoolbooks, 1940–44', *Journal of Contemporary History*, 29 (1994), 711–34.

4   H.R. Kedward, *In Search of the Maquis: Rural Resistance in Southern France 1942–1944* (Oxford, 1993), p. 228; S. Farmer, *Martyred Village: Commemorating the 1944 Massacre at Oradour-sur-Glane* (Berkeley, CA, 1999).

5   A. Duncan, 'The Problematic Commemoration of War in the Early Films of Alain Resnais', in W. Kidd and B. Murdoch (eds), *Memory and Memorials: The Commemorative Century* (Aldershot, 2004), p. 210.

6   P. Jankowski, 'In Defence of Fiction, Resistance, Collaboration and Lacombe,

Lucien', *Journal of Modern History*, 63 (1991), 457–82; J. Chapman, *Cinemas of the World: Film and Society from 1895 to the Present* (London, 2003), pp. 277–8.

7   R.J. Golsan (ed.), *Memory, The Holocaust and French Justice: The Bousquet and Touvier Affairs* (Hanover, NH, 1996).

8   N. Wood, *Victors of Memory: Trauma in Postwar Europe* (Oxford, 1999), pp. 113–42; R.J. Golsan, *Vichy's Afterlife: History and Counter-history in Postwar France* (Lincoln, Nebr., 2000).

9   H. Rousso, *The Vichy Syndrome: History and Memory in France since 1944* (Cambridge, Mass., 1991) and *The Haunting Past: History, Memory and Justice in Contemporary France* (Philadelphia, 2002); A. Colombat, *The Holocaust in French Film* (Meutchen, NJ, 1993); B.M. Gordon, 'The "Vichy Syndrome" Problem in History', *French Historical Studies*, 19 (1995), 495–518; H. Rousso and E. Conan, *Vichy: An Ever-Present Past* (Hanover, NH, 1998); S. Fishman *et al.* (eds), *France at War: Vichy and the Historians* (Oxford, 2000); B. Bowles, 'Screening *les Années Noires*: Using Film to Teach the Occupation', *French Historical Studies*, 25 (2002), 21–40; A. Nossiter, *France and the Nazis: Memories, Lies and the Second World War* (London, 2003); J. Jackson, *France: The Dark Years, 1940–1944* (Oxford, 2003).

10 N. Atkin and F. Tallett, 'Towards a Sixth Republic? Jean-Marie Le Pen and the 2002 elections', in N. Atkin and F. Tallett (eds), *The Right in France* (London, 2003), pp. 293–304.

11 F. Furet, *Penser la Révolution française* (Paris, 1978), translated as *Interpreting the French Revolution* (Cambridge, 1981); S. Kaplan, *Farewell Revolution: The Historians' Feud, France 1789/1989* (London, 1995).

12 J. Klaits and M. Haltzel (eds), *The Global Ramifications of the French Revolution* (Cambridge, 1994).

13 S. Berger, *Representations of the Past: The Making, Unmaking and Remaking of National Histories in Western Europe after 1945* (Pontypridd, 2002), pp. 5–6.

14 S.J. Wiesen, *West German Industry and the Challenge of the Nazi Past 1945–55* (Chapel Hill, NC, 2001).

15 D. Bloxham, *Genocide on Trial: War Crimes Trials and the Formation of Holocaust History and Memory* (Oxford, 2003).

16 L.S. Dawidowicz, *The Holocaust and the Historians* (Cambridge, Mass., 1981); C. Browning, *Ordinary Men: Reserve Police Battalion 101 and the Final Solution in Poland* (New York, 1992).

17 O. Bartov, *The Eastern Front, 1941–1945: German Troops and the Barbarisation of Warfare* (Basingstoke, 1985); H. Heer, 'The Difficulty of Ending a War: Reactions to the Exhibition *War of Extermination: Crimes of the Wehrmacht, 1941 to 1944*', *History Workshop Journal*, 46 (1998), 187–203.

18 M. Sargeant, 'Memory, Distortion and the War in German Popular Culture: The Case of Konsalik', in W. Kidd and B. Murdoch (eds), *Memory and Memorials.: The Commemorative Century* (Aldershot, 2004), p. 199.

19 See also J. Friedrich, *Brandstätten: Der Anblick des Bombenkriegs* (Berlin, 2003) and

N. Stargardt, 'Victims of Bombing and Retaliation', *Bulletin of the German Historical Institute of London*, 26, no. 2 (Nov. 2004), 57–70.

20   F. Taylor, *Dresden: Tuesday, 13 February 1945* (London, 2004).

21   R. Hilberg, *The Politics of Memory* (Chicago, 1996); P. Novick, *The Holocaust and Collective Memory* (London, 1999); T. Judt, 'The Past is Another Country: Myth and Memory in Postwar Europe', in I. Déak, J.T. Gross and T. Judt (eds), *The Politics of Retribution in Europe: World War II and its Aftermath* (Princeton, NJ, 2000), pp. 293–324; N. Finkelstein, *The Holocaust Industry: Reflections on the Exploitation of Jewish Suffering* (New York, 2000); H. Marcuse, *Legacies of Dachau: The Uses and Abuses of a Concentration Camp* (Cambridge, 2001); J. Massad, 'Deconstructing Holocaust Consciousness', *Journal of Palestine Studies*, 32 (2002), 78–89.

22   D. Lipstadt, *Denying the Holocaust. The Growing Assault on Truth and Memory* (London, 1993).

23   R.A. Shandley (ed.), *Unwilling Germans? The Goldhagen Debate* (Minneapolis, 1998); G. Eley (ed.), *The 'Goldhagen Effect': History, Memory, Nazism – Facing the German Past* (Ann Arbor, MI, 2000).

24   R.J. Evans, *Telling Lies about Hitler: History, the Holocaust and the David Irving Trial* (London , 2001); P. Longerich, *The Unwritten Order: Hitler's Role in the Final Solution* (Stroud, 2001).

25   J.E. Young, *The Texture of Memory: Holocaust Memorials and Meaning* (New Haven, Conn., 1993); A. Landsberg, *Prosthetic Memory: The Transformation of American Remembrance in the Age of Mass Culture* (New York, 2004).

26   J.A. Moses, *The Politics of Illusion: The Fischer Controversy in German Historiography* (London, 1975).

27   J.V. Koschmann, 'Introduction', in Y. Yamanouchi, J.V. Koschmann and R. Narita (eds), *Total War and 'Modernisation'* (Ithaca, NY, 1998), p. xi.

28   S. Taberner and F. Finlay (eds), *Recasting German Identity: Culture, Politics and Literature in the Berlin Republic* (Woodbridge, 2002).

29   C.S. Maier, *The Unmasterable Past: History, Holocaust, and German National Identity* (Cambridge, Mass., 1988); R.J. Evans, *In Hitler's Shadow: West German Historians and the Attempt to Escape from the Nazi Past* (London, 1989); P. Baldwin (ed.), *Reworking the Past: Hitler, the Holocaust, and the Historians' Debate* (Boston, 1990); J. Knowlton and T. Cates, *Forever in the Shadow of Hitler? Original Documents of the Historikerstreit, the Controversy Surrounding the Singularity of the Holocaust* (Atlantic Highlands, NJ, 1993); S. Berger, *The Search for Normality: National Identity and Historical Consciousness in Germany since 1800* (Oxford, 1997).

30   M. Hastings, *Armageddon: The Battle for Germany 1944–45* (London, 2004), pp. 198–200, 438.

31   T. Schieder, *Frederick the Great*, edited by Sabina Berkeley (Harlow, 2000), p. 93.

32   N. Gregor, '"The Illusion of Remembrance": The Karl Diehl Affair and the Memory of National Socialism in Nuremberg, 1945–1999', *Journal of Modern History*, 75 (2003), 594–633.

33 G. Hartman (ed.), *Bitburg: In Moral and Political Perspective* (Bloomington, Ind., 1986).

34 On the 1946 Kielce pogrom in which about 40 Jews were killed, T. Piotrowski and I.C. Pogonowski, *Kielce July 4 1946, Background, Context and Events* (Toronto, 1996).

35 For a generally sympathetic account of the Polish perspective, N. Davies, *Rising '44: The Battle for Warsaw* (London, 2004).

36 C. Levy, 'Historians and the "First Republic"', in S. Berger, M. Donovan and K. Passmore (eds), *Writing National Histories: Western Europe since 1800* (London, 1999), pp. 265–78.

37 R. De Felice, *Fascism: An Informal Introduction to its Theory and Practice* (New Brunswick, NJ, 1977); B. Painter, 'Renzo De Felice and the Historiography of Italian Fascism', *American Historical Review*, 95 (1990), 391–405; N. Zapponi, 'Fascism in Italian Historiography, 1986–93: A Fading National Identity', *Journal of Contemporary History*, 29 (1994), pp. 547–68.

38 A.D. Smith, *The Nation in History: Historiographical Debates about Ethnicity and Nationalism* (Cambridge, 2000).

39 For a more sympathetic account of media history, D. Cannadine (ed.), *History and the Media* (Basingstoke, 2004).

40 *Oxford Dictionary of National Biography Newsletter* 10 (Nov. 2004), 1.

41 J.G.A. Pocock, 'History and Sovereignty: The Historiographical Response to Europeanisation in Two British Cultures', *Journal of British Studies*, 31 (1992), 358–89.

42 K. Robbins, 'Insular Outsider? "British History" and European Integration', in K. Robbins (ed.), *History, Religion and Identity in Modern Britain* (London, 1993), pp. 45–58.

43 F. Füredi, *Mythical Past, Elusive Future: History and Society in an Anxious Age* (London, 1992).

44 For the academic side, J.P. Kenyon, *The History Men: The Historical Profession in England since the Renaissance* (2nd edn, London, 1993).

45 R. Strong, 'Britain, a True Story', *New Statesman*, 13 Sept. 1996, 32–3; D. Cannadine, 'New Key in Same Old Lock', *Times Higher Education Supplement*, 28 June 2002, 23.

46 A. Dolan, *Commemorating the Irish Civil War: History and Memory, 1923–2000* (Cambridge, 2003).

47 C. Brady (ed.), *Interpreting Irish History: The Debate on Historical Revisionism* (Dublin, 1994); D. Ferriter, *The Transformation of Ireland 1900–2000* (London, 2004), pp. 22–3, 531, 747–51.

48 For the strength of public myths, T.W. Moody, 'Irish History and Irish Mythology', *Hermathena*, 124–7 (1978–9), 7–25; and R. Foster, *The Irish Story: Telling Tales and Making It Up in Ireland* (Oxford, 2002). For the failure to note IRA outrages, T.P. Coogan, *Wherever Green Is Worn: The Story of the Irish Diaspora* (London, 2001).

49 C.A. Whatley, *'Bought and Sold for English Gold': Explaining the Union of 1707*

(Edinburgh, 1994); J. Robertson (ed.), *A Union for Empire: Political Thought and the British Union of 1707* (Cambridge, 1995).

50 M. Ash, *The Strange Death of Scottish History* (Edinburgh, 1980); M.G.H. Pittock, *The Invention of Scotland: The Stuart Myth and the Scottish Identity, 1638 to the Present* (London, 1991); R.J. Finlay, 'New Britain, New Scotland, New History? The Impact of Devolution on the Development of Scottish Historiography', *Journal of Contemporary History*, 36 (2001), 383–93.

51 T. Gitlin, *The Twilight of Common Dreams: Why America Is Wracked by Culture Wars* (New York, 1995).

52 L. Hunt (ed.), *The New Cultural History* (Berkeley, CA, 1989).

53 For a stress on social division, G.B. Nash, *The Urban Crucible: Social Change, Political Consciousness, and the Origins of the American Revolution* (Cambridge, Mass., 1979); and R. Raphael, *A People's History of the American Revolution: How Common People Shaped the Fight for Independence* (New York, 2002). For a criticism of this emphasis, F. McDonald, *Recovering the Past: A Historian's Memoir* (Lawrence, Kan., 2004), and, more generally, G. Himmelfarb, *The De-Moralization of Society: From Victorian Virtues to Modern Values* (New York, 1995).

54 D.D. Joyce, *Howard Zinn: A Radical American Vision* (Amherst, Mass., 2003).

55 N. Glazer and R. Ueda, *Ethnic Groups in History Textbooks* (Washington, DC, 1983); G. Himmelfarb, *The New History and the Old: Critical Essays and Reappraisals* (2nd edn., Cambridge, Mass., 1987); T. Bender, P.M. Katz, C. Palmer and the AHA Committee on Graduate Education, *The Education of Historians for the Twenty-first Century* (Urbana, Ill., 2004).

56 B. Palmer, *Descent into Discourse: The Reification of Language and the Writing of Social History* (Philadelphia, 1990); J. Appleby, L. Hunt and M. Jacob, *Telling the Truth about History* (New York, 1994); L. Duggan, 'The Theory Wars, or, Who's Afraid of Judith Butler?', *Journal of Women's History*, 10 (1998), 9–19.

57 R.J. Evans, 'Telling it Like it Wasn't', *Historically Speaking* 5(4), Mar. 2004, 11–14, criticizing N. Ferguson (ed.), *Virtual History: Alternatives and Counterfactuals* (London, 1997).

58 R. Lebow, P. Tetlock and G. Parker (eds), *Unmaking the West: Alternative Histories of Counterfactual Worlds* (Ann Arbor, MI, 2005).

59 P.C. Hoffer, *Past Imperfect: Facts, Fictions, Fraud – American History from Bancroft and Parkman to Ambrose, Bellisles, Ellis and Goodwin* (New York, 2004). For a regional example of bellicosity, W.E. Lee, *Crowds and Soldiers in Revolutionary North Carolina: The Culture of Violence in Riot and War* (Gainesville, Fla., 2001).

60 G. Himmelfarb, 'Some Reflections on the New History', *American Historical Review*, 94 (1989), 663–4; A.M. Schlesinger, *The Disunity of America* (New York, 1992); R. Lerner, A.K. Nagai and S. Rothman, *Molding the Good Citizen: The Politics of High School History Texts* (Westport, Conn., 1995); S.P. Huntington, *Who Are We? The Challenges to America's National Identity* (New York, 2004), pp. 174–7.

61 C. Crabtree and G.B. Nash, National Center for History in the Schools, *National Standards for World History: Exploring Paths in the Present* and *National Standards of*

United States History: Exploring the American Experience (Los Angeles, 1994). The world history issue had already led to J. Konvitz, *What Americans Should Know: Western Civilization or World History: Proceedings of a Conference at Michigan State University* (Lansing, MI, 1985).

62   American Council of Trustees and Alumni, *Losing America's Memory: Historical Illiteracy in the 21st Century* (2000).

63   R. White, *The Middle Ground: Indians, Empires and Republics in the Great Lakes Region, 1651–1815* (Cambridge, 1991); E. Hinderaker, *Elusive Empires: Constructing Colonialism in the Ohio Valley, 1673–1800* (Cambridge, 1997); K.Y. Daaku, *Trade and Politics on the Gold Coast, 1600–1700* (Oxford, 1970), pp. 96–114.

64   For a critical view, see J.P. Diggins, 'The National History Standards', in E. Fox-Genovese and E. Lasch-Quinn (eds), *Reconstructing History. The Emergence of a New Historical Society* (London, 1999), pp. 253–75.

65   G.B. Nash, C. Crabtree and R.E. Dunn, *History on Trial: Culture Wars and the Teaching of the Past* (New York, 1997); see also the perceptive review by S. Wilentz in the *New York Times*, 30 Nov. 1997.

66   J.C.D. Clark, *Our Shadowed Present: Modernism, Postmodernism and History* (London, 2003), p. 196.

67   It is also instructive to read J.C. Scruggs and J.L. Swerdlow, *To Heal a Nation: The Vietnam Veterans Memorial* (New York, 1985).

68   A. Lieven, *America Right or Wrong: An Anatomy of American Nationalism* (London, 2004).

69   C.L. Bushman, *America Discovers Columbus: How an Italian Explorer Became an American Hero* (Hanover, NH, 1992); F. Fernández-Armesto, 'Columbus: Hero or Villain?', *History Today* (May, 1992).

70   E.F. Fitzpatrick, *History's Memory: Writing America's Past, 1880–1980* (Cambridge, Mass., 2002), pp. 11–12.

7

The ex-Communist and ex-authoritarian world

The rapid process of change in the Communist and Third Worlds that arose from the collapse of Communism and from decolonization posed particular problems for public history. Within Europe, and also further afield, there was the need to consider the totalitarian legacy in states that were no longer governed by Communist or authoritarian right-wing, if not Fascist, systems. This shift had already become apparent in the last decade of Communist rule in Europe, with an openness in some countries, especially Hungary, to a wider historical tradition and a less dogmatic approach.

The situation changed radically with the political changeovers of 1989–91. Explicit attacks on the historical role of Communist parties and the Soviet Union were now freely ventilated. In Eastern Europe, Russia no longer appeared, as it had done in Communist Party propaganda, as a liberator. Instead, there was a focus on atrocities by the advancing Red Army in 1944–5, not least the large-scale rape of women not only in Germany and Austria but also across Eastern Europe. There was also greater interest in episodes that had been previously neglected, such as the Hungarian rising of 1956 which had been harshly suppressed by Soviet forces. Interest was accompanied by denial. Eastern Europeans came to see themselves as victims of Communist rule who had played no role in the regime and Communism was presented as a foreign ideology. Some historical museums ignore, or at least downplay, the Communist years, but others are bitterly critical. The controversial House of Terror Museum in Budapest makes the Fascist and Communist periods in Hungary morally equivalent and makes much of the harshness of the latter, ending with a mural of photographs of former Party officials, still alive today, whom it blames for the crimes of Communism. A sense of national victimization drowns out the sufferings of others, especially of Jews. Former Communist leaders such as Tito were disparaged. As another rejection of the past, the pursuit of compensation for property seized under the Communists, which led to legislation such as the Lithuanian law of 1990 for the 'Rehabilitation of Persons Repressed for Resistance to the Occupying Regime', engaged many, although it also proved a divisive issue.

In place of former Communist premiers, right-wing leaders from the early 1940s, such as the Romanian Ion Antonescu, dictator from 1940 until 1944, were now proclaimed favourably as anti-Soviet nationalists. In power, Antonescu had persecuted Jews and collaborated with Hitler. He was executed for war crimes in 1946, but in the 1990s Romanian cities rushed to name streets after him. Although not seen as anti-Semitic acts, this process was an aspect of the expression of traditional themes that included anti-Semitism, and it was not until 2004 that the Romanian President, Ion Iliescu, made the first official acknowledge-ment of the country's role in the Holocaust. The previous year he had established an international panel to report on the subject. Iliescu was an ex-Communist, and it is unclear whether a right-wing leader would have made the same decision. Throughout Eastern Europe there was a reluctance or failure to acknowledge the degree of local complicity in the Holocaust.[1] Furthermore, in Bulgaria, Croatia, Hungary and Slovakia, regimes that had collaborated with Hitler received far more sympathetic attention than had been the case under the Communists, and there was less sympathetic support for the wartime partisan resis-tance to them. In Lithuania, the process of exonerating anti-Communists extended to include celebration of 'heroes' who fought with the SS.

In Slovakia Jozef Tiso, a priest who had headed the pro-Nazi wartime regime and been executed after the war, was, after the end of Communist rule, publicly proclaimed by right-wingers as a patriot. Furthermore, right-wing Slovak nationalists celebrated the gaining of Slovak independence in 1939, a direct consequence of Hitler's invasion of Bohemia and Moravia. This was linked to their campaign for the renewed dissolution of Czechoslovakia: the separation of Slovakia from Bohemia and Moravia, eventually achieved in 1993. In 2000, there was considerable contention in Slovakia over proposals to establish a memorial to Tiso. In Serbia, there was a more understandable attempt to rehabilitate the Chetniks, the largely Serb nationalist-royalists who had fought both the German occupiers and the Communists. Their leader, Draza Mihailović, executed by the post-war Communist govern-ment in 1946, was now honoured. Similarly, in the former Soviet Union, anti-Communist leaders from the Russian Civil War, such as Admiral Kolchak and Ataman Semenov, were praised.

The expression of right-wing views was more marked than elsewhere in Europe, in large part because of the Communism that was being rejected, but although this extremism attracts attention, it is important to understand the diversity of Eastern European historical consciousness. It includes liberal strands. The variety of views were related to controversies about recent history, not least the transition from Communism. In Poland, for example, there was a major division between those who endorsed the 'Round Table' settlement of 1989 as avoiding bloodshed, and those who criticized it because they thought it provided cover for ex-Communists to pillage the state. This was not so much a left–right divide as an elitist–populist one that affected historians as well as politicians.

As part of reconstruction, previously blank periods in national records could now be studied.[2] Communist states, like other totalitarian regimes, worked in part by creating an all-pervasive sense of surveillance and fear, focused on a regime that was felt but could not be seen or located: prison camps existed, but few knew their location or extent. Terror works on ignorance, on the ungraspable nature and undefined scope of the arbitrary power of the oppressor. The authoritarian state needs to locate its opponents, to understand and control dissidence, but does not wish to be understood, other than as a comprehensive force. The end of Communist rule transformed the situation. For example, in Estonia, Latvia and Lithuania it was possible (indeed encouraged) to probe their earlier period of independence between the First World War and Soviet occupation in 1940. It was also possible to work on the harsh aspects of Sovietization, both in 1940–1 and from 1944. In Poland it became possible to assess episodes in recent history that had previously been openly considered only by émigré historians, for example the Nazi-Soviet Pact of 1939 and what followed: the Soviet invasion of 17 September 1939, and the subsequent large-scale Soviet killing of Poles. The Home Army, the non-Communist Polish resistance, which under Communist rule had been condemned as reactionary if not worse, was reinterpreted as a patriotic organization. There was also far more official concern than under Communist rule in these states about the Christian character and history of the Eastern European states and of Russia.

This process extended to the sites of Soviet oppression, such as secret police headquarters and prison camps. Under the Soviets, these had not officially existed, an aspect of the extent to which there was a secret state that entrapped and destroyed real or alleged critics, making them disappear. Bringing this history to light was an important aspect of the post-Communist world.[3] It represented a deliberate attempt to recover what had been hidden, to validate the victims and to match the openness of liberal societies, as well as a way to damn the Communists and thus underline the acceptability of the new start. Secret police head-quarters were thrown open, for example in Vilnius (Vil'nia) in Lithuania, and details of cruelties there were displayed. The statue of Felix Dzerzhinsky, the founder of the Soviet secret police, in front of the KGB headquarters in Moscow was destroyed in 1991. The archives of Communist states and parties were opened for examination. This was a continuation of the *Glasnost,* or openness, of the last years of the Soviet regime, which had permitted a greater openness about events such as the Katyn massacre of Polish officers by the Soviets in 1940, an episode they had earlier blamed on the Nazis. In Belarus, the mass graves at Kuropaty, where the Soviet NKVD had slaughtered at least 100,000 people between 1937 and 1941, were exhumed from 1988,[4] reviving and popularizing Belarussian nationalism in the crucible of anger.

Nationalist themes that had largely been followed during the Communist years only when they conformed to state policy, for example Hungarian claims to Transylvania, and Bulgarian claims to Macedonia and hostility to the Turks, were voiced more frequently after the fall of the Communists. In turn, Macedonia's emergence from the chaos of Yugoslavia as an independent republic in 1991 angered neighbours, especially Greece which sees the name as part of Greek heritage and fears that it will serve to encourage claims to territory now in Greece that can, historically, be seen as part of Macedonia. The definition of the latter had long been a cause of contention.[5]

After the end of Communist rule, the theme of lost Hungary was taken up with renewed vigour, leading in 2004 to the offer of citizenship to those of Hungarian descent living in what had formerly been Hungary. Against the wish of the Socialist government, the measure was pressed by Fidesz, the conservative opposition party, as a way to compensate for territorial losses under the Treaty of Trianon in 1920. In Croatia, Franjo Tudjman, a former general who had set himself up in the 1960s as a revisionist historian, became president in 1990. Tudjman used his history to support his virulent Croatian nationalism, attacking the Yugoslav public myth associated with Tito. Instead, Tudjman argued that the Croat role in the resistance to the Nazis had been minimized by Tito, and himself played down the iniquities of the Croat Ustashe regime that had collaborated with Hitler. In his book, *Bespuća povijesne zbiljnosti* (*The Wastelands of Historic Reality,* 1989), Tudjman greatly minimized the numbers killed in Jasenovac, the concentration camp in which large numbers of Serbs were slaughtered during the Second World War by the Ustashe regime. As president, Tudjman considered bringing back to Croatia for an official state funeral the body of Ante Pavelic, the head of the regime. He was keen to present Croatia as a bulwark of Christian European civilization and to contrast it with a Balkans that in his view lacked all three characteristics. Tudjman also used historical arguments to justify his ambitions for Bosnia, which he claimed had been part of Croatia, or a Catholic kingdom linked to Croatia, until Muslim settlement after the Ottoman conquest.[6]

Nationalist themes were also pushed hard in the former Soviet Union. These included an emphasis on ethnic distinctiveness which echoed much of nineteenth-century nationalism. Distinctiveness could include an apparently exemplary longevity, as with Ukrainian statements about Aryan descent, while the Chuvash looked back to the Sumerians. The interaction of political interests, historical claims and ethnic distinctiveness was seen in Belarus from 1989 as Belarussian activists revived their earlier claims to Vilnius, claims that had been pushed earlier in the century, especially in 1939 and 1945. These activists saw Belarussian independence as the rebirth of the extensive Grand Duchy of Lithuania and, both on that basis and with regard to the Belarussian population in the region, claimed Vilnius for Belarus. The problem of assessing ethnicity was demonstrated anew with the claim that Lithuanian Poles were in fact Belarussians. Ethnic distinctiveness also posed a challenge to the role of ethnic minorities, such as the Bulgarian Turks.[7]

Conversely the views and alleged interests of such minorities could be taken up by foreign states that shared ethnicity and in some eyes nationhood with these minorities. This was pushed further in the case of diasporas. Many used the fall of Communism to press for their interests in the areas whence they had been expelled and also to argue for border changes. The Polish minority in Lithuania called for territorial autonomy, while there were also demands for border revisions. More generally, the emphasis on distinct sovereign states made no sense of previous political arrangements such as the overlapping categories of empires, composite states, and the Polish-Lithuanian federation. By making these arrangements, and the related identities, seem irrational, such views seriously distorted the historical experience of these regions.

The recovery of nationalist voices both repeated and challenged state viewpoints, part of the long-standing tension between nation and state as the source of identity. It proved harder to advocate compromise over the alleged interests of nations than over those of states. The challenge was seen not only in the disintegration of Yugoslavia, which had neglected or sought to suppress nationalist perspectives, but also of Czechoslovakia. In the latter case, the public expression of Slovak separatism proved very important.

Renaming places was an aspect of contention and also part of a more general rejection of Communism and the Russian link. This can be seen in the renaming of towns, mountains, buildings and streets named after Stalin[8] and other Soviet leaders. This process could also be seen in Russia, with Leningrad being called St Petersburg anew. The renaming of holidays was another cause of dispute. After the end of Communist rule, 7 November, the anniversary of the Russian Revolution, hitherto as Revolution Day an annual holiday, was renamed the Day of Accord and Reconciliation. Proposals in 2004 to end the holiday led to a Communist protest, the Party leader, Gennadi Zyugnov, declaring 'People suffered for this holiday, and no one has the right to trample on our history.'

In Mongolia, the Caucasus and Central Asia the end of Communist rule and Soviet dominance led to a rejection of histories that had emphasized cooperation with Russia and, instead, a revitalization of heroes presented now very much from a national perspective, such as Chinggis Khan in Mongolia and Temur (Tamerlane) in Uzbekistan. Temur's statues have replaced those of Communist figures and there is considerable pride in his conquests. In 1993, President Islam Karimov unveiled a statue in the centre of Tashkent, while in 1996 a museum dedicated to him was opened, and a new Order of Amir Temur was created to honour outstanding service to Uzbekistan. The Amir Temur Fund organized conferences on Temur and streets, schools and villages were named after him as the government sought an acceptable basis for legitimacy that distanced it from the Soviet era.[9] The Uzbek government also focuses on Abdulla II (r. 1582–98) because he both unified the state and increased it significantly by conquest.

As an instance of the contested histories created by the end of the Soviet dominance, the three republics that gained independence in the Caucasus – Armenia, Azerbaijan and Georgia – have clashing public histories that are linked to frontier conflicts, for example over the region of Nagorno-Karabakh between Armenia and Azerbaijan. Governments in the region also seek to strengthen themselves by reference to the past, and this provides a means to claim both distinctiveness and legitimacy. When in 2004 Mikhail Saakashvili became president of Georgia, he first went to a revered monastery, founded by Georgia's most famous monarch, in order to receive a blessing.

In those parts of the Caucasus that remained in the Russian Federation, most obviously Chechnya, modern reference to heroic opposition to Russian conquest in the nineteenth century, for example by Shamil, was designed to build on a tradition of ethnic strife. Conversely, those who co-operated with the Russians did not emphasize a history of political opposition and Islamic identity.

Recreating non-Communist public and academic histories, and expressing a stronger interest in national distinctiveness, took place within a context in which national perspectives and solutions inter-acted with a world order dominated by the West and by capitalism. The consequences of this dominance provide an instance of the more general process of understanding past and present circumstances after defeat, one in which learning from the victor involves not just simple adoption or imitation but, rather, a complex process of assimilation and cultural adaptation.[10] This was particularly the case in the former East Germany as it lost not only its Communist past but also its terri-torial integrity, being united with the more populous, prosperous and assertive West Germany. The German government cleared out East German historians from their professional positions and also offered a new memorialization of recent and earlier history. There was an effort to provide an acceptable national history that included the former East Germany,[11] while academics were replaced on the grounds that they had supported the intellectual dictatorship of East German Communism.[12] Most new appointees were West Germans. Museums were also transformed, and members of the former regime tried.[13] The treatment of East German history became a source of academic contro-versy.[14] A degree of public nostalgia for the Communist past in East Germany was accentuated by the extent to which German unification was seen in terms of conquest by West Germany, but, nevertheless, it was limited.

More positively, the end of Communist rule enabled scholars in the former Eastern-bloc countries to gain access to Western literature and archival sources. This represented a welcome opening out to the wider world that was truly a cause of liberalization. More specifically, the works of émigré writers were now published and circulated freely in former Communist states.

The relationship between the decline of Marxism as a viable social theory for academic, especially historical, research and the fall of Communism might appear close. The ability of Marxism to serve for both analysis of historical structures and explanation of change had been eroded in Western scholarly circles as a result not so much of empirical research as of shifting disciplinary fashions, in particular the rise of cultural studies from the 1960s. The failure of the Marxist model as the basis for an economic system joined its political to its intellectual crisis. Yet, the fall of Communism in Eastern Europe and the Soviet Union was largely due to the specific political and economic circum-stances of the late 1980s, in particular to Mikhail Gorbachev's attempts to modernize Communism by introducing reforms. Intellectual matters were not the key issue, except in the form of the serious and debilitating failure of economic planning. Economic problems limited the funds available for social investment and consumer spending, compromising popular support for the system. The commitment of much of the population in Communist countries to Marxism as the basis for understanding themselves and their world was, anyway, limited, and debate among intellectuals was of scant relevance to them. Furthermore, the relevance of the latter was limited as the political authorities were in control of the educational process. Ironically, the crisis of Marxism as a viable theory for historical research was of relevance more for academic circles in the West that were far from the corridors of power than for Communist governments.

Not all Communist countries rejected (or, rather, were given an opportunity to reject) Communism, although the public histories of those that did not still had to confront the severe difficulties that Communism as a historical explanation and end-goal faced in the last years of the twentieth century, especially the collapse of the Communist position in Eastern Europe and the Soviet Union. In the surviving Communist states, such as Vietnam, public history became more clearly nationalist, as the brotherhood approach to public history, specifically the emphasis on fraternal relations with Soviet Communism, became less relevant. In Cuba, the Revolution of 1959 and the subsequent breakdown in relations with the USA had been followed by an aggressively anti-American presentation of national and international history. The American intervention in 1898 on behalf of Cuban rebels against Spain was presented as an occupation by imperialists, and the Cuban republic that followed it was seen as neo-colonial. Instead, history began anew in 1959. Thus, traditional Communist themes were combined with nationalist defiance of the USA, the two linked in the portrayal of the USA as an imperial power seeking economic domination. The USA was very useful to Cuban public history, and the government myth it represented, as it linked the notion of a powerful foreign challenge to that of a domestic threat.

Cuba is not alone in this, although the leadership cult in North Korea is more bizarre. The emphasis in North Korea is very much on foreign threats, and on the commemoration of the ruling Communist dynasty. In celebrating the foundation of the state of North Korea, National Day (9 September) serves as an opportunity for the reiteration of its historical myth. History and archaeology, like art and applied arts, served to justify the regime of Kim Jong-il and to legitimate its lineage.[15]

In Belarus, under Aleksandr Lukashenko, president from 1994 and, in effect, dictator from 1996, the propagation of an ideology focused on Communism and his own leadership cult also affected the teaching of recent and earlier history. As an indicator of how far he differed from the norm in the former Soviet Union, in 2004 Lukashenko unveiled a memorial focusing on a statue to one of his heroes, Felix Dzerzhinsky, the founder of the Soviet secret police, at his birthplace Dzerzhinava. That year there were reports that political decisions had played a role in the conferring of higher education qualifications by the Higher Attestation Commission. In particular, work on historical figures who had been opposed to Russia was judged unacceptable.[16] Lukashenko is pro-Russian.

The fall of right-wing regimes

A different, but comparable, process to that in Eastern Europe and the Soviet Union occurred in states which witnessed the fall of authoritarian right-wing regimes, some of which, at least in part, owed their durability to the Cold War. This was true of Greece, Portugal, Spain, Chile and South Africa. As in Eastern Europe and the Soviet Union, however, the new public histories faced serious problems in their presentation of the decades of authoritarian rule. Franco died in 1975, but Spain took a long time to address issues that had hitherto been slighted, especially the undesirable aspects of the Spanish Civil War, not least Francoist atrocities. Until very recently most people studiously avoided raking up the past at all. No attempt has ever been made to prosecute individuals for war crimes or for murders and torture committed under the Franco dictatorship. It is only now that a serious debate is taking place about the large-scale atrocities committed by Francoist forces during the Civil War, the concentration camps that were set up after the war and, in particular, about what should be done with the large number of mass graves that still litter the country. The conservative government of José María Aznar (only voted out of power in 2004) was very keen to suppress this debate. Far more rapidly after the death of Franco, however, there was a new emphasis on the regional perspective. In contrast to the views of the Franco regime, let alone the 'crusade' it waged during the Civil War (1936–9), there was a less centralized account of Spanish history, and one that was more open to Catalan, Basque and other national views. This was an instance of the relationship between political changes, government and education: in Spain, due to the role of the state in the education system, changes in the contents of textbooks provide a guide to shifts in the political system, in this case towards provincial autonomy. Political shifts also led scholars to re-examine the questions of Spanish national identity, exceptionalism and relations with the wider world.[17] In turn, in opposition to the attacks on central Spanish nationalism, came in the 1990s 'a new wave of defensive historiography' focusing on the concept of a Spanish nation.[18] At the popular level, there was also a revival in favourable treatment of Franco.

Similarly, the fall of authoritarian regimes in Portugal and Greece in 1974 was followed by a liberalism in which there was no longer an emphasis on a conservative conception of national destiny as the major theme in public history. In Portugal, the 'Carnation Revolution' of 1974 led directly in 1975 to the dismantling of the colonial empire, ending an important plank of public history: the justification of imperial destiny. This justification had been very much alive in the 1950s and 1960s, being linked, for example, to the large-scale settlement of Portuguese colonists in Angola. The *Estado Novo* in Portugal, the system created by António de Salazar, the dictatorial prime minister from 1932 until 1968, had preferred that the history taught and celebrated in Portugal focus on the Middle Ages and the Age of Discovery and had discouraged work on modern Portuguese history, which threatened to focus on divisions within the country. This changed from 1974: aside from an engagement with recent history, there was also a willingness to respond to foreign intellectual and historiographical traditions, including Marxism and the French 'Histoire Nouvelle'.

There were similar changes in Latin America after right-wing regimes fell, such as that in Nicaragua in 1979. In Chile, the role of the 1973–90 military government under General Pinochet dominated public historical attention thereafter. Indeed, human rights became the central motif of historical awareness. The post-Pinochet government established a National Commission for Truth and Reconciliation in 1990 and this demonstrated that the Pinochet administration had violated human rights. At the same time, the process of ascertaining the past was contentious, with the armed forces and police refusing to cooperate with the commission, which was itself accused of partisanship by their political allies. Subsequently, debates over the validity of the 1978 Amnesty Law for the military and a series of human rights prosecutions kept the recent past a live issue, culminating with legal moves against Pinochet from 1996 until 2001 outside, and eventually, within Chile. Reporting in 2004, the National Commission on Political Imprisonment and Torture provided clear evidence of widespread abuse of human rights including the torture of nearly 28,000 people. The army accepted 'institutional responsibility' and the president attacked the 'silence' that had covered the brutal acts of the regime. The report led to pressure for renewed legal action against Pinochet.

In South Africa, the end of White-minority rule and apartheid in 1994 was followed by a very different historiography (see p. 9). As in former Communist countries, the abrupt shift in public history recorded the impact of politics and underlined the crucial role of the latter in providing the basic dynamo of change in the public use of the past.

Notes

1   E. Zuroff, 'Whitewashing the Holocaust: Lithuania and the Rehabilitation of History', *Tikkun*, 7, 1 (1992), 43–6.

2   S. Feuchtwang, 'Reinscriptions: Commemoration, Restoration and the Interpersonal Transmission of Histories and Memories under Modern States in Asia and Europe', in S. Radstone (ed.), *Memory and Methodology* (Oxford, 2000), p. 60.

3   R.W. Davies, *Soviet History in the Yeltsin Era* (Basingstoke, 1997).

4   T. Snyder, *The Reconstruction of Nations: Poland, Ukraine, Lithuania, Belarus, 1569–1999* (New Haven, Conn., 2003), p. 248.

5   H.R. Wilkinson, *Maps and Politics: A Review of the Ethnographic Cartography of Macedonia* (Liverpool, 1951).

6   J. O'Loughlin and H. Wusten (eds), *The New Political Geography of Eastern Europe* (London, 1993).

7   M. Neuberger, *The Orient Within: Muslim Minorities and the Negotiation of Nationhood in Modern Bulgaria* (Ithaca, NY, 2004).

8   R. and B. Crampton, *Atlas of Eastern Europe in the Twentieth Century* (London, 1996), p. 156.

9   J. Marozzi, *Tamerlane* (London, 2004), pp. 169–73, 421.

10   W. Schivelbusch, *The Culture of Defeat: On National Trauma, Mourning, and Recovery* (London, 2003), p. 34.

11   C. Hoffmann, 'Introduction: One Nation – Which Past? Historiography and German Identities in the 1990s', *German Politics and Society*, 15, no. 2 (1997), 3–5; D. Prowe, 'Kohl and the German Reunification Era', *Journal of Modern History*, 28 (1995), 373–95; J.W. Müller, *Another Country: German Intellectuals, Unification and National Identity* (New Haven, Conn., 2000).

12   K. Pätzold, 'What New Start? The End of Historical Study in the GDR', *German History*, 10 (1992), 392–404; G.A. Ritter, 'The Reconstruction of History at the Humboldt University: A Reply', *German History*, 11 (1993), 339–45; A.S. Ernst, 'A Survey of Institutional Research on the GDR: Between "Investigative History" and Solid Research: The Reorganization of Historical Studies about the Former German Democratic Republic', *Central European History*, 28 (1995), 373–95.

13   R. Alter and P. Monteath (eds), *Rewriting the German Past: History and Identity in the New Germany* (Atlantic Highlands, NJ, 1997); C. Klessmann (ed.), *The Divided Past: Rewriting Post-War German History* (Oxford, 2001); A.J. McAdams, *Judging the Past in Unified Germany* (Cambridge, 2001).

14   C. Epstein, 'East Germany and Its History since 1989', *Journal of Modern History*, 75 (2003), 636–61.

15   J. Portal, *Art Under Control in North Korea* (London, 2005).

16 *Times Higher Education Supplement*, 18 Nov. 2004, 11.
17 S. Doubleday, 'English Hispanists and the Discourse of Empiricism', *Journal of the Historical Society*, 3 (2003), 205–20.
18 S.G. Payne, 'History, Nation, and Civil War in Spanish Historiography', *Journal of the Historical Society*, 4 (2004), 336.

8

The Third World

Confronting the consequences of decolonization in the Third World was an even more abrupt challenge to public history than political transformations in Europe not least because, in contrast to the former Communist states, there was also a racial component to the issues of assessing recent developments and recovering an earlier history. Thinking about history also took place in a post-colonial context in which the need for an explicit rejection of colonial traits of thought was pronounced. At the same time, as was pointed out at the 2003 meeting of the African Studies Association, serious conceptual and methodological problems were posed for scholarly historical work in the Third World by the dominance of theories, methodological categories and analytical conventions and languages, all taken directly from scholars working in the West, or, in reaction, overly uncritically from the Communist world. This situation makes the task of 'decentring' world history (abandoning a Western focus) difficult, although it does not mean that there are not indigenous traditions of history.[1]

There was also the related problem that geographical and political understandings and units derived from the colonial world. This was most obviously true of states and state boundaries, which indeed proved durable despite the end of imperial rule.[2] It was also the case with both regions, such as the Maghreb (French North Africa: Morocco, Algeria, Tunisia), and continents. For example, the Western designation of continents divided what had been zones of demographic, economic and cultural relationships. This was seen with the separation of East Africa from South-West and South Asia, and of North Africa from southern Europe. There was also, thanks to the Western pattern of continents, an emphasis on separation at a larger scale – of Africa from South America, Australia from Asia – that accorded with Western views. The creation of a particular view of the Orient is seen as a culmination of this process.[3]

The dominance of Western concepts was linked to the languages of the colonial powers, such as French in the Maghreb and West Africa, Spanish in Latin America, and English in East and South Africa and South Asia. The role of language helped direct not only academic alignments and borrowings, and educational systems, but also the wider context of popular understandings of history. The continued role of Western publishing houses, such as Longman in the former British Empire, was also important, while school examinations are still controlled in parts of Africa by British examination boards. Another inheritance from the colonial world was periodization. This was true both of the conventional thematic periodization – medieval, early modern, and late modern – and of the use of centuries based on the European calendar as the building blocks of description and analysis.

The impact of independence struggles

One aspect of decolonization was provided by discussion of the independence struggle. This was generally uncritical in public memorialization, certainly as long as the groups prominent in winning independence retained power. This was seen with the role of the Congress Party in India, of Zanu under Robert Mugabe in Zimbabwe, of the MPLA in Angola, of the FLN in Algeria, and with their many equivalents including, most recently, the PLO in Palestine. In each case, this retention of power gave a particular direction to national history. The role of the now governing party in securing independence was emphasized and efforts were made to establish an exemplary prehistory for independence. This account focused on resistance to the colonial power and on the consequent weakness of the latter. Independence, therefore, in this perspective, was won, not granted by the colonial power. In addition, rival (and unsuccessful) nationalist movements were denounced, such as in Zimbabwe that of Zapu under Joshua Nkomo, and Unita in Angola. In some countries, the creation of an exemplary history for the independence struggle was a continuation of propaganda produced during the struggle itself. An appropriate depiction of actions and actors that were portrayed by hostile critics as terrorist and terrorists was often important.

In the case of India, there was an emphasis on the Congress Party's Quit India campaign of 1942 in leading to the British withdrawal from the subcontinent five years later. There was also discussion, albeit less comfortably, of Subhas Bose and the Indian National Army in which their nationalism was emphasized and their role as a Japanese client force during the Second World War underrated. Such an emphasis was at the expense of the British success (albeit only short-term success) in overcoming the Quit India campaign, and also neglected the large numbers of Indian volunteers who came forward to fight for the King-Emperor during the Second World War, the largest volunteer force in history. This compared directly with the neglect in Ireland of its voluntary contribution as part of the British Empire to the war effort in the First World War, and, indeed, while neutral, in the Second. The presentation of Bose as a nationalist has always been contentious because he split with Congress in 1939 after his quarrel with Gandhi. He is regarded in his home province of Bengal (where Gandhi is unpopular) as a great nationalist leader (and Calcutta airport is named after him), but his status elsewhere in India is much more ambivalent. Discomfort about Bose reflects more the unwillingness after independence to discuss anti-Gandhi/Nehru forces in Congress than his status as a Japanese ally.

The rewriting of India's past also extended further back. The process by which Britain had gained and sustained power was viewed far more critically than had been the case during colonial rule. This entailed a rewriting of Indian atrocities discussed by the British in order to show their greater claim to civilization, such as the Black Hole of Calcutta, in which Siraj-ud-daula, the Nawab of Bengal, had imprisoned British captives with fatal results in 1756, and the treatment of British women and children during the 'Indian Mutiny' of 1857–9. Instead, as far as atrocities were concerned, the emphasis was now on the cruelty of the British treatment of captured sepoys blown to pieces from cannon during the suppression of the 'Mutiny', while the 'Mutiny' itself was reinterpreted, somewhat anachronistically, as India's first war of independence or nationalism (now it is widely referred to as the Rebellion). More generally, empire was presented as an economic burden to India, and a vehicle for British plunder and economic exploitation that had delayed the development of the country. Thus, instead of the British emphasis on progress towards modernity under colonial rule came a depiction of the latter as a distorting force. The nationalist historians of the 1950s and 1960s emerged in the late colonial period and at the time of India's independence in 1947 they dominated most of the major university history departments. Their major goal was the creation of a 'new' history of India free of British or Western influences. These historians placed great stress on India's past greatness and saw Western intervention as temporary. This was to be a theme taken up in many former colonies.

The presentation of an anti-colonial historiography was not only seen in opposition to Western powers. Japanese rule led to a presentation of Korean history in terms of a lesser people and power, whose weaknesses merited Japanese control. This was countered by an emphasis on past signs of Korean strength and culture and on the capacity of Korea to develop without colonial rule. Early in the century, Korean intellectuals set up a private university to train future intellectuals within the Korean tradition and to lessen the role of the public (Japanese-controlled) university in Seoul. From 1945, in both North and South Korea the impact of Japanese rule was depicted as malign. This matched the emphasis on atrocities during this period, not least enforced prostitution for Japanese troops, and also the erasure from the record of extensive Korean collaboration with Japan. In turn, the bitter and costly Korean War (1950–3) between the Communist North and the non-Communist South left a historical legacy that strengthened the already powerful divisions between the two regimes. In South Korea, the many dead were commemorated thanks to the work of the Korean War Commemoration Commission. The imposing massive façade of the War Memorial in Seoul was matched by the columns of the Gallery of the Honored Dead, with its 100 obsidian plaques listing the casualties. Memorials created their own world of ceremonies. Thus in the DMZ (De-Militarized Zone), the Liberation Bell marked where the South Korean Ninth Division had successfully resisted attack in the battle for White Horse Mountain. Kim Il-Sung, the dictator of North Korea, created an exemplary personal history, claiming a false descent from nationalists and inaccurately saying that he had been born on a sacred mountain. Kim also alleged that North Korea had descended from an ancient Korean kingdom that includes much of Manchuria and part of Russia's Pacific province. Also seeking longevity, South Korea claimed descent from a different kingdom.

A parallel to the overthrow of colonial perspectives, although not one that was welcome to the governments involved, was provided by the challenge mounted to the role of long-standing governing parties in states that had already gained independence. This was seen in both Japan and Mexico. In the latter, the Institutional Revolutionary Party, which had governed for seven decades, was ousted after elections in 2000 while, in 1993, Japan's Liberal Democrats lost overall power for the first time in nearly 40 years. In the former case, there was a definite consequence for public history and academic scholarship, with a greater degree of freedom in discussing recent history. At the same time, challenges to the governing groups that had seized the mantle of independence, for example to the FLN by the Islamic nationalists of the FIS in Algeria in the 1990s, and to Congress by Hindu nationalists in India, led to a criticism of these groups' presentations of the past. The Bharatiya Janata Party (BJP), which evolved from a nationalist Hindu body, Rashtriya Swayamsevak Sangh, drew on long-standing Hindu notions of India as a Hindu nation and civilization and on Hindu revivalism. The party was a response to the strong sense of communal identities in India, and to Hindu concern about the assertiveness of minority groups under Congress rule. Congress presented itself as deliberately non-sectarian and as concerned to give voice to minorities such as Muslims.

Thus, the volatility of Indian politics and society led, on the part of the BJP, to the reiteration of a historicist account of identity and continuity as an aspect of a concern that produced calls for national renewal as defined by and in the interests of those expressing the concern. At the political level, the tension between Congress and BJP views of India past, present and future had greater weight than the earlier challenge to Indian nationalist historiography from Communist and left-leaning historians who saw the nationalists as sharing in Western notions of elitist history and attempting to create similar obsolete lines of historical research. This theme was carried further from the 1970s by the group known as subalterns who emphasized the role in Indian history of the poor and the marginals (such as tribes), specifically in opposing the power of the colonial state. The first volume of what became a long series of *Subaltern Studies* was published in 1982.[4] In emphasizing the role of those outside the elite, for example in the Rebellion of 1857–9, a clear comment on modern India was offered:

> They were not mere adjuncts to a linear tradition that was to culminate in the appropriation of power by the elite in a post-colonial state. Nor were they mere toys manipulated by the latter in a historical project in which they played no part . . . To seek after and restore the specific subjectivity of the rebels must be a major task of the new historiography.[5]

Far from being unconcerned about Hindu revivalism, the BJP 'Saffron wave' and associated communal tensions, Indian historians sought to provide a historical perspective on the latter.[6] Under the BJP government from 1998 until 2004 historical and educational institutions, including the Indian Council for Historical Research and the National Council for Educational Research and Training, were used to support the sectarian Hindu perspective. This was seen in the replacement of school textbooks by those that matched BJP views. In turn, resistance to the adoption of textbooks was mounted by the Indian History Congress on behalf of a largely critical scholarly community that had been left out of the production of the textbooks,[7] and the government elected in 2004 sought to reverse the BJP's impact.

Over a longer timespan, there are signs in Latin America of challenges to the governing groups that seized the mantle of independence gained in the 1810s and 1820s, dominating the continent before and after independence. This challenge has come from the descendants of the indigenous population and has been particularly strong along the Andean chain in Ecuador, Peru and Bolivia, although it is also seen elsewhere, for example in Central America, where Mayan consciousness is in part an aspect of the rejection of control by the government of Mexico. Along the Andean chain, a sense of history played a role in the challenge, not only by channelling an awareness of separateness and oppression but also in terms of sites of defiance. Thus, in 2004, the mayor of Ayo Ayo in Bolivia was hanged from a lamp-post in the shadow of a large bronze statue of Tupaj Katari, who in 1781 had led an uprising of the Aymara against Spanish colonial rule.

More generally, decolonization entailed a process of rethinking pre-colonial, colonial and post-colonial history, as well as relations with the outer world. It also involved widespread renaming, as a conscious aspect of the rejection of what was seen as the imperial legacy. Whereas what had been European settlement colonies, such as Australia, Canada and New Zealand, retained imperial names, such as Sydney, Vancouver, and Wellington, these were widely rejected in newly-independent states where such settlement had been limited. The renaming of states was an important break in continuity although, as an aspect of the theme of post-apartheid reconciliation, as yet this has not happened to a major extent in South Africa. On independence in 1964 Nyasaland was renamed Malawi, while Upper Volta became Burkina Faso in 1984, and Burma became Myanmar (the name of the country in Burmese) in 1989. With the end of White-minority rule, Southern Rhodesia became Zimbabwe. Cities were also renamed. The capital of Southern Rhodesia, Salisbury, became Harare, while in India Bombay became Mumbai in 1995 and in 1996 Madras became Chennai. The rejection of colonial boundaries was a related process. Syria, which became independent in 1946, rejected the French acceptance in 1939 of Turkish claims to the Alexandretta region.

Renaming was an aspect not only of the rejection of colonialism but also of defining a new identity. While this was presented as a throwing off of the imperial yoke, it was also an aspect of the struggle for influence and control among indigenous groups, which could be seen generally in post-colonial and post-Communist societies. In Nigeria, the rejection of the colonial legacy included the movement of the capital in 1991 from Lagos to a new city, Abuja. This in part was an attempt to limit the influence of the Yoruba, who dominated the area round Lagos. Abuja is inland, in the centre of the country, and far closer to northern Nigeria which is the homeland of much of the military leadership. The army has dominated Nigeria in recent decades, and their conception of its identity is not served by a focus on Lagos.

Consideration of the pre-colonial period helped provide people with a history that had been slighted, and also directed attention to powerful civilizations and states, for example medieval Mali. Earlier attempts to explain such African civilizations as the work of Mediterranean peoples moving south, the theory advanced in Harry Johnston's *History of the Colonisation of Africa by Alien Races* (1899) and C.G. Seligman's *Races of Africa* (1930), were rejected. This was in accord with academic arguments, but also fitted the new political mood with its stress on African achievement and thus on the absence of need for European intervention. Furthermore, the historical consciousness of pre-colonial societies, to an extent, was recovered, as in work on African oral history, an approach that encourages interdisciplinarity. At times, this emphasis on African achievement was stronger on rhetoric than reality but, whether the period in question was pre-colonial, colonial, or post-colonial, the publication of books for national audiences and by native authors was central to the process of reconsidering the past.

There are important issues facing the attempt to recover the pre-colonial history of the Third World, not least the availability of information. Thus, for the millennium prior to European colonization, the information available for African history is limited and there are also specific problems with the use of oral evidence. Yet, it offers more than traditional Western historiography allowed. In the opening chapter of his *The History of England* (1754–62), David Hume reflected the values of his age when he explained why he was slighting England's pre-Roman history:

> Ingenious men, possessed of leisure, are apt to push their researches beyond the period, in which literary monuments are framed or preserved; without reflecting, that the history of past events is immediately lost or disfigured, when intrusted to memory and oral tradition, and that the adventures of barbarous nations, even if they were recorded, could afford little or no entertainment to men born in a more cultivated age.

Thus, methodological issues relating to sources were linked to a ranking of relevance reflecting the norms of fashionable Western opinion, an approach still overly influential today. Hume continued:

> The convulsions of a civilized state usually compose the most instructive and most interesting part of its history; but the sudden, violent, and unprepared revolutions, incident to Barbarians, are so much guided by caprice, and terminate so often in cruelty that they disgust us by the uniformity of their appearance; and it is rather fortunate for letters that they are buried in silence and oblivion.[8]

While modern scholars would be wary of such views, it is instructive to note how many treatments of historiography and historical method never mention Africa.

The depiction of pre-colonial Africa has greatly changed since the 1960s with research indicating that the notion of tribes advanced in works such as Samuel Johnson's *History of the Yorubas* (1921) was in large part an aspect of Western classification that was designed to aid comprehension, if not control, and, due to the pejorative connotations of tribalism, to demean African society. Instead, a more complex account of ethnogenesis was offered.[9] The extent to which the territorial scope and thus ethnic composition of many states is the work of Western conquerors, and therefore relatively recent, creates problems for the presentation of history. Western territorialization and concepts of identity and political authority have themselves been used to particular ends by African nationalists.

The post-independence rethinking of the colonial period in Africa and elsewhere has led to a greater emphasis on resistance to colonial rule, and on the historiography of resistance, although these tend to involve a misleading 'appropriation' of resistance for the cause of nationalism. Resistance was linked to later anti-colonialism. This was particularly politically useful in Guinea where the first prime minister (from 1958 to 1972) and first president (from 1961 to 1984) of the independent state, Ahmed Sékou Touré, was the grandson of Samori Touré, the leader of the Mandinke people and the 'Napoleon of the Sudan' according to his eventually successful French opponents, whom he fought in the 1870s and 1880s. Reference to him ignored the extent to which he had been a tyrant, particularly to other tribes.

Consideration of the colonial period in Africa and elsewhere was itself politically problematic, as it posed a question mark against the success of post-colonial governments in improving living standards and maintaining stability. Such consideration also directed attention to current relations with the former colonial power. Thus, in Senegal there is contention over links between the government and France, which indeed subsidizes the Ministry of Education and Culture. This contention affects the depiction of West African soldiers that served France between 1857 and independence in 1960: the government presents them as saviours of France in the two world wars and as heroes fighting for the cause of progress, the opposition as both victims and accomplices of a damaging colonialism.[10] Growing interest in former colonies in pre- and post-colonial history has ensured, however, that the colonial period can be presented as part of a longer-term process, rather than as the key episode in history. The former approach encourages interest in the continuity of issues, institutions and identities and thus displaces Europeans from the centre of attention.

Interest in pre-colonial history led to efforts to repatriate monuments and other material from that period that had been acquired by Western powers, sometimes as part of a process of post-conquest looting. The theme of apology focused not only on monetary reparations but also on the return of objects that had been seized. These had, or it is argued have, symbolic value, and their return is also designed for economic gain in the shape of reviving sites worthy of tourism. Much of the Third World has lost objects, either through seizure or purchase. Western powers became increasingly sympathetic to this pressure. In the case of Ethiopia, a state with a long history of independence, the consequences of two Western invasions are at issue. In 1868, a British force successfully sent to rescue imprisoned hostages stormed the fortress of Magdala and seized both secular and religious treasures there. The loot included crowns, shields, crosses, and manuscripts, as well as tabots, sacred carved blocks of wood or marble. The 11 tabots in the British Museum have, now, been moved aside for special treatment, and are kept in a room where only priests can visit them, but the museum insists that under its charter it is not allowed to yield to calls to return them to Ethiopia. The Italian conquest of Ethiopia in 1935–6 also led to the seizure of treasure, including a granite obelisk at Aksum. When taken in 1937 it was already broken into five parts, but the Italians shipped it to Rome and erected it at a road junction. In 1947, as part of the post-war peace settlement, Italy promised to return its wartime loot, but the obelisk was still in Rome in 2002 when another agreement was signed. At present, the obelisk is dismantled in Rome awaiting shipment.

The return of seized monuments and other material was an aspect of reversing the memorialization of colonial conquest. In addition, the statues of colonial generals were often removed and, in their place, came a recognition of the role of the resistance. In 2004, the 125th anniversary of the Zulu victory over the British at the battle of Isandlhwana led to an appropriate memorialization of the Zulu casualties. This fulfilled a goal long sought by prominent Zulu politicians, such as Chief Mangosuthu Buthelezi of the Inkatha Freedom Party, and thus underlined their role as well as serving to emphasize Zulu distinctiveness, a cause at odds with the governing African National Congress's emphasis on South African inclusiveness.

The issue of memorialization was not restricted to warfare. Under colonial rule, a life-sized bronze statue of the British explorer David Livingstone was erected overlooking Victoria Falls. Less welcome in Zimbabwe after its independence in 1980, indeed seen as a symbol of

British imperialism, the statue was defaced in 2002. In contrast, Zambia, on the other side of the Falls, in 2004 expressed interest in acquiring the statue. Siloka Mukuni, the chief of the Leya people, the major ethnic group around the town of Livingstone, stated: 'The Zambians have a great deal of affection for Livingstone's memory, unlike the Zimbabweans. We have changed a great many of our colonial place names since independence, but we have kept the name of Livingstone out of a deep respect.' Nomenclature was also an issue with the Falls. They still record the name of the ruler of Britain from 1837 until 1901, when, in European eyes, they were 'discovered' by Livingstone in 1855, not their native name when Livingstone became the first European to see Mosi-oa-Tunya, 'the smoke that thunders'.

Albeit through the very partial spectrum of the August–September 2004 issue of the London-based magazine *New African*, it was possible to probe the distinctiveness of African perspectives on historical importance. Asked to nominate the top 100 influential Africans or people of African descent, the voters emphasized heroes from independence movements. The leading figures were, first, Nelson Mandela and, second, Kwame Nkrumah, the key figure in winning Ghanaian independence in 1957 and in producing the 1961 Charter of African States. Patrice Lumumba, the founder of the Congolese National Movement and, in 1960, its first prime minister, also figured prominently. American Civil Rights leaders played a role, with Martin Luther King placed sixth and Malcolm X ninth, suggesting a historical consciousness that linked the struggle for independence in Africa and that for African-American civil rights.

The African-American quest for apparent African antecedents, especially the notion that the civilization of ancient Egypt was in fact a black African one, was probably responsible for the inclusion of Queen Nefertiti, a fourteenth-century BCE queen consort at 81st. Ironically, she is supposed by some commentators to have been an Asian princess from Motanni. The debate on origins was focused and encouraged by Martin Bernal's *Black Athena: The Afroasiatic Roots of Classical Civilization: The Archaeological and Documentary Evidence* (1992), which argued that Greek culture derived largely from Egypt which, in turn, was a black African culture. Furthermore, Bernal claimed that this had been deliberately suppressed by white Western historians who instead sought, in what he termed the 'Aryan Model', to argue that European culture derived from non-black, specifically Indo-European sources. This approach was heavily challenged by specialists, such as Mary Lefkowitz in her *Not Out of Africa* (1996) and in the collection *Black Athena Revisited* (1996) edited by Lefkowitz and Guy Rogers. Critics of Bernal have argued that his approach is a matter of assertion rather than scholarship but, nevertheless, it clearly has had an impact, particularly in some African-American circles. The African scholar V.Y. Mudimbe presented Roman writers who came from Roman North Africa as African.[11] African and African-American scholars are also prone to treat slavery and the slave trade in terms of the European Atlantic and to ignore or underrate the Ottoman and Indian Ocean dimensions.

The shadow of colonial rule lay heavy over the public history of most states that had experienced it. It could also lead to competing drives for restitution, a theme taken up in an interview by Jean-Bertrand Aristide, the deposed president of Haiti (president 1990–1, 1994–5, 2000–4). Arguing with reference to his removal from office in 2004, 'It is important to set what happened in the wider context of Haiti's history', Aristide claimed that France had played a role in his removal partly because it was the bicentennial of Haiti's success in winning independence from France. Aristide also claimed to want to set the record straight about his period in office: 'My responsibility now is to tell the truth', as a result of which he wrote a book.[12]

Israel

A particular instance of post-colonial history is provided by the historical myth associated with Israel, with the post-biblical dispersion of the Jews apparently for some an equivalent to colonial rule, and the creation of the state of Israel in 1948, in a way a return to the biblical past, at least in the sense of national independence. The creation of Israeli identity faced serious challenges, as the different sources of Jewish immigrants had very varied experiences and cultures. Furthermore, there were important contrasts between them and longer-established Jewish communities. These variations continue to be the case today, not least as the consequence of more recent large-scale immigration from the former Soviet Union. Like the use of Gaelic in Ireland, the use of Hebrew as the language of the state (rather than Yiddish, the language of most of the refugees, but a European language) was a deliberate act of identification with the biblical past, as was the nomenclature of the state. Episodes from a distant, heroic past, such as the defence of Masada against the Romans in 73 CE, were used to provide an exemplary national history, and were considered alongside the travails of the Jews in the recent past. The theme of Jews as fighting back linked Masada with the Warsaw ghetto in 1943 and sought to counter the feeling that due to passive acquiescence not enough had been done to resist the Holocaust. The Holocaust played a central role in Israeli self-identification, not least with the establishment of Yad

Vashem as a Holocaust Memorial, museum and archive in 1953, and the seizure and trial of Adolf Eichmann, a major Nazi war criminal, in 1961–2.

The use of the Holocaust in order to justify the establishment of the state of Israel was particularly effective in winning support in the USA both from Jews and, even more significantly, from non-Jews. Binyamin Netanyahu, the Israeli prime minister, declared in 1998 that 'if the state of Israel had not been founded after the Holocaust, the Jewish future would have been imperilled', because it would have been more difficult to win American support. This emphasis on the Holocaust was accompanied by a slanted account of Israeli history that in some respects was similar to that of Arab nationalists. In the former account, the emphasis on the sufferings and endurance of the Jews was not matched by adequate consideration of the plight of the Palestinian refugees nor of the extent to which they had been forcibly driven out of their homes in what is now Israel. Furthermore, the reasons offered for Israel's stance in the West Bank and Gaza were given a questionable historical foundation.[13] As a related point, the Israeli position both in these territories and in Israel itself was defended by the association of progress with Zionism, specifically the argument that Jewish settlers had rendered fertile land that had been neglected and mishandled by the Palestinians.

Inventing nationality

The extrapolation of the Western model of the nation state had, and has, immediate value for African and other non-Western nationalists, but it may be very misleading. It is possible that the states and, especially, the political identities, particularly across much of Africa, that were first charted in any detail in the nineteenth century have had their longevity exaggerated by our own assumptions and by the agendas of ethnogenesis which lie at the heart of proximate cultural nationalism. Not simply has tradition been invented, but even possibly states, for some revisionist archaeologists have thrown doubt on the extent and even existence of certain pre-colonial states. Furthermore, modern concepts of nationality have been employed misleadingly to interpret the polities and politics of the past. Indeed, there appears to have been considerable migration for centuries in almost every sphere of human activity across what have since been constructed as national borders. There were also multiple civil and sacred identities, and it would be misleading to ignore the complexity of African thought on these matters.[14] Thus, and more generally, modern Western thinking about what we are, and what we belong to, yields something very far short of

a universal taxonomy. Similar points can be made about identities elsewhere, for example in Oceania.

Given these academic problems with issues of identity, it is scarcely
surprising that governments seeking to frame a public history have
charted paths that suit their political purpose. In this process, nationalism and ethnicity have played major roles. In so far as they can be dif-
ferentiated as factors, ideological factors have also been important in
framing public histories. This is obviously significant for recent history,
with the rejection of the colonial legacy presented in terms of a unifying and uplifting account of national liberation. At the same time, the
decision by the Organization of African Unity to support the mainte-
nance of colonial frontiers chimed with that of African states. The
threat to governments from ethnically/regionally-based opposition,
even separatism, with its own distinctive memorialization,[15] also
encourages an account of the recent past in which the emphasis is on
unity. Thus, the public history of Nigeria supports federalism and is
very hostile to separatism, and this provides the context within which
the civil war of 1967–70 that stemmed from Biafran separatism is considered. In Mauritania in 1986 three history lecturers were imprisoned
for being part of a group that had alleged discrimination by the ruling
Arab-Berber military government against the southern black population. In neighbouring Morocco, the Berber issue, a cause of anti-
authoritarian if not separatist attitudes, is presented historically in
terms of the interest of the state, which has scant sympathy for any distinctive Berber agenda. Territorial claims are also important in helping
to set the agenda. The Moroccan annexation of the former Spanish
Sahara in 1975 played a role in directing writing in Morocco.

Nationalism, ethnicity and ideological factors are not simply matters
of the content of public histories. The use of national languages for the
history of formerly discrete areas which had their own oral and often
written language is an aspect of the agglomerative character of official
history as well as of scholarly work. In Indonesia, the national language
was used for official histories of areas such as Bali. Conversely, those
seeking to resist state control are keen to publish histories in their own
languages. In Spain, Basque nationalist historiography appears in the
Basque language, Euskera, while in 1967 Croatian nationalists issued a
declaration stating that Croatian was a language distinct from the
Serbo-Croat recognized by Tito's government.

The linkage between the state and national history was demonstrated
even more clearly in countries where those who wrote the latter could
serve in senior public office. For example, Jorge Basadre (1903–80),
whose *Historia de la República del Perú* (1939, frequently revised) was the
basic work for the history of Peru from independence, was also direct-

or of the Biblioteca Nacional and Minister of Public Education. His positive, inclusive account of national history was exactly what the state required.[16]

Indonesia

The same was true of Indonesia. 'Glorious past; dark present; glittering future.' This was the view advanced by Achmail Sukarno, the prominent Indonesian nationalist who became president after independence, which had been declared in 1945, was finally won from the Dutch in 1949. Sukarno, who had spent part of his youth teaching the subject, was certain that history had a key role to play in the assertion of Indonesian identity. Indeed, since the state was the product of a brief period of Dutch imperialism, and the word Indonesia was only coined in the nineteenth century – from the Greek *Indos* (Indians) and *nesos* (island) – there was clearly a need for a unifying ideology when that imperial control was removed. In search of an exemplary national past, Muhammad Yamin, a politician as well as a historian, sought to demonstrate the longevity of the concept of Indonesia. He probed this well before the period of Dutch imperialism, discussing for example the role of the fourteenth-century Javanese empire of Majapahit.

Determining that history was to be an important aspect of this unifying ideology did not provide the content for that history but, as with India, much stemmed from the nature of the independence struggle. It was obvious that opponents to the spread of Dutch rule in the nineteenth century and earlier should be eulogized. In particular, it was important that the potential encouragement to separatism represented by their individual interests should be overlaid by an emphasis on their role as proto-Indonesians. This was more necessary for Aceh, in northern Sumatra, an Islamic state that had very much followed its own path, than for Java, the island that was the kernel of modern Indonesian nationalism.[17]

Under Sukarno, the national versus regional dimension was crucial in determining the content of public history, but other disputes also relating to the protean and contested nature of Indonesian nationhood played an important role. In particular, the extent to which the new state should have a Muslim, a Communist or a liberal identity was related to the presentation of its history. Muslims emphasized the Islamic, and not the Hindu-Buddhist, past, while Communists and liberals offered different accounts of the interests and development of the state.

This was resolved in 1965–6 when the Communists were bloodily crushed by the military. General Suharto, who became president in

1968, sought to establish a self-styled New Order designed to replace ethnic and religious divisions and to ensure economic growth, and created a party, Golkar, to rally support for his army-based regime. Anti-Communist, this regime also suppressed Islamic opposition and its public history matched the content of its nationalism. This was explicitly designed to foster support for the nation and for the nationalist Pancasila ideology. Education was carefully organized to this end. This was a matter primarily of the formal education of the young through schools and universities, not least the compulsory subject 'History of National Struggle' added to the school curriculum in 1985. An authorized national history designed for schools was published in 1977. The key figure in this work, Nugroho Notosusanto, was head of the military history section of the armed forces (and a brigadier general as a result), and became minister of education in the 1980s.

Formal education in Indonesia was not only a matter of the young. The remainder of the population was also educated, or rather indoctrinated. Officials were sent on courses in the Pancasila ideology, museums and monuments were carefully used to this end, and the celebration of Heroes' Day carried forward an exemplary view of the past. This cult developed from 1957 and was continued after Suharto replaced Sukarno. The heroes were very much drawn from those who had resisted the Dutch, either the conquest or what was presented as the occupation.[18] Given this presentation of the past, it is easy to see why separatism was opposed, irrespective of the popular backing it enjoyed. This response played a major role in the crisis over East Timor in the 1990s, and does so at present over Aceh and West Irian.

Ethiopia

Ideological accounts of the past can also look far back. The left-wing Mengistu regime that ruled Ethiopia from 1974 to 1991 emphasized the historical integrity of Ethiopia and presented it as under threat from neighbouring and rival Somalia and from Western imperialism. Thus, the threat from the Somalis was seen as a continuation of earlier Islamic invasions going back to the Sultan of Adal and the Ottoman Turks in the sixteenth century. This threat was also linked to Western pressure. British imperialists were blamed for inventing the notion of a Greater Somalia, which was seen as continued by the contemporary Somalis. Thus, the leading modern rival was allegedly following an agenda laid down by an imperialist manipulator. The Italian conquest of Ethiopia in 1935–6 was bitterly criticized. In line with this, past Western links with Ethiopia were minimized or denigrated. The

Portuguese, who had provided assistance against Adal in the sixteenth century, were referred to as pirates.

The 'defensive' tone to the presentation of Ethiopian history – the sense of a country under threat – was matched by an 'offensive' reality. Eritrea was seen as part of Ethiopia. Reference was made to the 'liberation' and reunion of Eritrea with the Motherland in September 1952, a view that made little sense of, or to, the eventually successful separatist movement launched there the following year. 'Reunion' remained a theme until the counter-insurgency conflict ended in failure for Ethiopia with the overthrow of Mengistu, although subsequent conflict between Eritrea and Ethiopia has ensured that a history emphasizing hostility appears pertinent.

Iran

A similar sense of continuity in accounts of the past was seen in Iran, with, again, historical rivalries being viewed through current ideological perspectives. Under both the Pahlavi dynasty, rulers from 1921 to 1979, and the Islamic republic that replaced it in 1978–9, there was an emphasis on territorial pretensions and, in particular, a tendency to stress control over the Persian Gulf. There was also an emphasis on long-standing rivalry with whatever state had ruled Iraq, which, from the early sixteenth to the early twentieth centuries, meant the Ottoman Turks. There was, however, also a major contrast between the presentation of history under the very different governmental systems.

Under the Pahlavi dynasty the emphasis was on the positive role of past monarchs, both in terms of domestic policies and with reference to foreign challenges. In 1971, Mohammed Reza Shah allegedly spent $100 million on celebrating 2,500 years of the Persian monarchy, drawing prestige for the relatively recently established Pahlavi dynasty from a continuity stretching back to Cyrus the Great (c. 590–529 BCE). The dramatic ruins at Persepolis became a setting for the celebrations, which included parading large numbers of troops in uniforms allegedly based on those of Cyrus's forces. The treatment of Iranian history reflected the image the Pahlavis were trying to create. The Buwayhids (932–1062), a Persian dynasty that at the time had inspired a revival of national identity, were seen as playing a major role in supporting Islamic civilization and the welfare of their subjects, and were therefore praised. A far bleaker view of the Seljuk Turks (1038–1194), the empire of the Khwarizm Shah the Mongol Il-Khanate (c. 1260–1353) and Temur (Tamerlane), who conquered Persia in 1380–94, the most prominent rulers until the early sixteenth century, was then offered. They were presented as damaging aliens who, in turn, were replaced by the Safavids (1501–1722), a dynasty that seemed an apt prefigurement of the Pahlavis, not least with their regional power. Indeed, the Pahlavis emphasized and exaggerated the territorial sway of the Safavids, particularly in the Persian Gulf, which was unwelcome to the independent states on its southern shore, such as Bahrain.

The Islamic republic offered a very different historical perspective to that of the Pahlavis although, again, with a strong emphasis on ethnic identities. The emphasis was on Iran and the Iranians, and not on royal dynasties that were presented as non-Iranian. Downplaying the role of dynasties stemmed inevitably from the foundation of the republic in the overthrow of the Pahlavis. The relationship between the fundamentalist (and thus historicist) religious consciousness of the religious leaders crucial to the new republic, and the pressures of secular change, for example rapidly rising population, created, however, a serious challenge to stability.

China

In China, the Communist regime that ruled from 1949 faced the dual problems of providing a consistent account of its own activities with that of trying to make useful sense of what was now seen as a long prehistory. Ideological considerations played a role under both heads, but nationalist interests were also reflected in the attempt to provide historical backing to Chinese claims over areas for which there were territorial disputes with neighbouring powers, such as Turkestan and the Amur valley, as well as in the clash with neighbouring Vietnam, and in maritime power-projection in neighbouring seas. The emphasis was on a far-flung China, and the extent of past Chinese empires was exaggerated, not only to lend weight to specific territorial pretensions but also to provide a general sense of potency. International tensions affected public history in the region, while the complexities of past relations with China's neighbours were ignored. In Inner Mongolia (part of China), the impact of Chinese ideological control was sharpened as a result of the rift between China and the Soviet Union from the 1960s, as neighbouring Mongolia (the People's Republic of Mongolia) was a Soviet satellite. While history emanating from the latter focused on rivalry between China and the Mongols, the Chinese encouraged a different account in Inner Mongolia.

Within China, the perspectives of non-Han Chinese peoples, in particular the Tibetans and the Uighurs, was ignored. As a result, their past resistance to Chinese governments was neglected. The Uighur historian Turgin Almas was placed under house arrest from 1989 because his book on the history of the Uighurs was accused of supporting separatism in Xinjiang. The historical consciousness of non-Han Chinese peoples was also attacked. Thus, during the Cultural Revolution religious statues and religious scroll paintings in Tibet were destroyed. At the same time, the Han Chinese Red Guards also attacked their own (Han) cultural heritage during this period. Temples and cultural relics all over China were smashed and destroyed; in this regard the 'national minorities' were not singled out for special treatment.

The Chinese treatment of the history of twentieth-century China emphasized the strength of radicalism, just as accounts of earlier periods in Chinese history stressed peasant risings, which were seen as a form of class struggle. The extent of support for the 1911 republican rising was exaggerated, as was radical and anti-imperialist sentiment in the 1920s. The role of the Communists in opposition to the Japanese conquest and occupation of 1931–45 was emphasized, while that of the rival Kuomintang Nationalists was minimized, as indeed was that of Communists who fought at a distance from Mao Zedong's zone of control. Because the focus was on continuing rivalry with the alternative (Nationalist) China still in Taiwan, there was far more emphasis on the Civil War of 1946–9 than on the Sino-Japanese conflict. The Civil War was presented as a liberation war, while the role of the Communist Party in defending China against supposed American threats was given historical resonance by stressing the earlier damage supposedly done to China in the nineteenth and early twentieth centuries by Western imperialism: the resulting contrast in effectiveness served to make the Communist Party appear more successful.[19]

At the same time, events and ideas of the past were reinterpreted by the Communist government to suit different political needs. This was particularly true of the ideas of the 4 May 1919 movement, which served both the Cultural Revolution of the 1960s and the far less radical Communism of the 2000s. In 2002, a museum of the New Culture Movement opened in Beijing, with a memorial to the patriotic students of 1919 nearby.[20] As reform gathered pace in the 1980s so it became acceptable, indeed desirable, to treat the radical aspects of the recent past, especially the Great Leap Forward and the Cultural Revolution, as mistakes. The official change of position was the product of a party conclave. The Sixth Plenum of the Eleventh Central Committee of the Chinese Communist Party met on 27–29 June 1981 and adopted a 'Resolution on Certain Questions in the History of Our Party Since the Founding of the People's Republic of China'. With regard to Chairman Mao, the resolution admitted error for the first time but also declared, 'His merit is primary and his errors are secondary.' The formula that Mao was 70 per cent right and 30 per cent wrong soon became standard, but is not found in the resolution itself.[21] The role of Mao is now largely ignored and, although Marxism is still the official line in economic history, there is now far less emphasis on peasant risings.[22]

Instead, there was an emphasis on a new nationalism designed to help counter the strains created by economic and social transformation as well as the political challenge posed by American-led pressure on human rights. Commemoration of the Sino-Japanese War, as an acute form of the imperialist pressure that was condemned, played a major role in this nationalism, not least in response to Japan's alliance with the USA and to greater conservative nationalist activism in Japan from the 1970s. This has led to greater attention to the Nanjing Massacre of 1937.[23] The wooing of Taiwan also played a role, not least in encouraging a more favourable portrayal of the Nationalist war effort. The anti-Japanese struggle looms larger than the Civil War in Chinese consciousness today.

A very different account of the twentieth century was offered by Taiwan: the rejection of Communist ideology led to a strikingly contrasting historiography, although this became more diverse from the ending of military law in 1987 and the subsequent democratization. As a result, accounts of recent Taiwanese history that do not adopt the Kuomintang Nationalist approach have developed, dealing in particular with two constituencies that had been marginalized: ethnically-Chinese native Taiwanese (i.e. descendants of immigrants centuries ago), and the indigenous aboriginal population. The former are the majority of the island's population and now dominate its democratically elected government. Since the late 1980s, they have not been marginalized. The recovery of their view has led, in response to the brutality of Kuomintang rule from 1945, to a relatively sympathetic account of Japanese rule from 1895 to 1945. In November 2004, Beijing issued an outraged statement against the declaration of the Taiwan education minister that Japan should be given credit for having modernized Taiwan's industry and education. In contrast, although the identity and history of the indigenous aboriginal population (a tiny percentage of the population) have now been noted with the establishment of a Ministry of Aboriginal Affairs, they still play only a minor role in Taiwanese history.[24]

Tibetan exiles also challenged Chinese accounts[25] while, in addition, the Chinese approach to history presented a challenge to its neighbours, not least because of the stress on Chinese hegemony and territorial interests. This led to acute sensitivity and to critical responses, as in South Korea in 2004 when China was accused of appropriating the historical legacy of ancient Korean states.

Japan

A very different ideological legacy to that of Communist China was at stake in Japan, and its public history can more fairly be located in the First World, not only because, compared to that of Communist China, there was no long-lasting legacy of foreign occupation or control but also because there was an acceptance of debate to a degree unusual in most of the Third World. Thus, Marxists, nationalists and liberals were able to define different interpretations of the Japanese national past. At the same time, there was a clear public myth, well represented in the treatment of the imperial family. This was readily apparent during the Meiji centenary celebrations of 1968, but was also clear at other times.

Japanese left-wing scholars, silenced during the war years of the 1930s and early 1940s, were very influential thereafter. Their approach was broadly Marxist in terms of seeing a conspiracy, prior to 1945, between the military and big business, supported by conservative governments and the newly created urban bourgeoisie, both to repress the masses at home and to exploit surrounding nations. The most common terms in this historiography were *gunkoku-shugi* (militarism, though taken to mean a mix of Fascism and militarism) and *tennō-sei* (the emperor system, that is, a system of repression using the symbol of the monarchy to keep the masses docile). From the late 1960s, the now dogmatic Marxist critiques were accompanied by a greater range of scholarly writing. The extent to which Japan's economy was already producing a mass middle class defined by an affluent consumerist life-style may have assisted this rethinking.

The role of states

Most Third World states lacked the longevity of Ethiopia, Iran, China and Japan and, for them, pre-colonial forms of history, such as the Burmese or Asante royal genealogies (in Myanmar and Ghana respectively), were no longer relevant when independence was regained. From whatever source, the definition of exemplary national story became the prime goal of national history.

A common fault, from the academic perspective, was the focus in national histories on states, especially powerful states. This ignores the more complex and varied political nature of much history and the extent to which powerful states had only a limited role in history. Instead, there was frequently a proliferation of localized areas of authority, often as an aspect of shared sovereignty. As these entailed multiple identities, it was not what most of the makers of public history sought: the context, and goal, of their activity were far different from that of the founders of the European Union who, as already indicated, were indeed seeking to create just such a state, and a tradition to match it. Linked to this political complexity was a lack of clarity in the past across much of the world about frontiers that does not match modern assumptions. In particular, there were border zones, rather than frontier lines. As a consequence of this, much of the modern public history with its focus on frontiers, a major theme of nationalist myths with their sense of clear sovereignty, is seriously ahistorical, while this focus is also generally a cause of international tension, if not dispute.

The attempt to ensure a favourable public history is neither new nor unexpected. The following description comes from an account of pre-modern Islamic historiography, but is also relevant today:

> states had a stake in learning in general and historiography in particular. Nearly all patronized representations of the past that legitimized their exercise of power (strong and weak states alike sought to translate the power to coerce into the ability to persuade), and large-scale learning (such as sophisticated historiography) depended on urban networks of knowledge that states cultivated and defended.[26]

A common characteristic of public history after decolonization was its nationalist character with, in particular, an emphasis on national identity, character and destiny expressed through statehood. This very much matched political developments. In 1960, the United Nations stated that all 'peoples' had the right to self-determination. Yet, the principle and practice of national self-determination confronted the inchoate and controverted nature of nationhood across much of the world, for example in Nigeria, or involved the suppression of signs of alternative nationhood. Turkey provides a good instance of the latter, as the Armenian Massacres of the 1890s and, even more, the Armenian Genocide of 1915, the latter a well-planned operation that possibly led to the slaughter of more than a million Armenians, is ignored in Turkish public history or, erroneously, treated as the consequence of treasonable Armenian separatism.

Precisely because during and after decolonization it was not clear how 'peoples' were to be defined, there was an emphasis on the national character of states and proto-states. This cut across the recent Western academic emphasis on the artificiality of nations, the extent to which they were constructs, and the importance for identity and classification of other groupings, especially class, gender and culture.[27] The artificial character of states is particularly apparent in Africa, the Middle East and South Asia. Yet, public history not only asserts the identity of states in the face of divisive, if not fissiparous, tendencies, but is also a counterpoint to international pressures, not least the intense intrusion presented by what is summed up by Westernization or globalization.

Globalization

Alongside a new public history after independence came a rethinking of the economic history of Third World countries. As an aspect of the independence struggle and of decolonization, this involved in particular a critique of capitalism which was seen as a cause of imperialism and also as a distorting consequence of colonial rule. This approach remained potent as many newly independent states, such as India and Tanzania, turned to Communist or socialist models, but became less credible as Marxist economic planning produced successive crises in the Communist and Third Worlds, especially from the 1970s. From the 1990s, however, the critique of globalization came to provide a new iteration of this approach, not least because it appeared to offer a long-term explanation of relative economic failure.

Although historiographies and historical writing are still largely structured along national lines,[28] globalization has been ably studied by academics, especially in the developing field of world history.[29] Yet, globalization lacks a popular public history, a contrast also seen with comparative history.[30] In part the lack of a popular public history for globalization is due to it being largely a matter of economic forces, but more than that is at stake. Internationalism has failed to win a mass support or define a populist ideology. This is due to the failure of the United Nations to gain widespread popular backing as a key way to organize the world, and the absence of any other institution capable of generating an international public myth.

In contrast, at the level of global regions, there have been attempts to create such a myth. This is readily apparent in the European Union with support for educational and other initiatives that can be related to federalist goals. This extends, in the European University based in Florence, to an attempt to mould a key group of future educators. History is one of the biggest programmes at the university, which focuses on the training of postgraduates.

Pan-Arabism represents not an equivalent but at least a parallel. There are, however, few others. It is striking, for example, that the academic anti-Westernism represented by the critique of Orientalism by Edward Said[31] and others is not matched by a successful public discourse other than at the national level. As a result, at the international level, anti-Westernism is shot through by the consequences of particular state interests, while the statist perspective, 'historiography powered by statehood', has marginalized other ways of looking at historical experience.[32]

Globalization is represented as a negative force from both national and regional perspectives. This is part of a widely anti-economic character to popular history, a pervasive distrust of entrepreneurs and a view of economic change as destructive, that is widely expressed. At the same time, many states publicly endorse economic development as a means to enhance national strength and well-being, and as a crucial adjunct to political independence. This, however, is compatible with popular suspicion of (national) entrepreneurs and (international) globalization, because state support for economic development generally focuses on governmental control and direction. This was definitely the case during the Cold War, as Third World states, such as India, found the model of state socialism particularly attractive.

In the 1990s this situation altered as the collapse of the Soviet Union, and the reaction against state control of the economy in parts of the West, helped lead to an abandonment of Marxist ideology and state socialism. The impact of this on public history, however, was less marked. Even in states that took a conservative direction politically, there was a lack of comparable movement in public history about economic issues. This situation is likely to continue, and poses a problem for politicians seeking to foster economic growth through the liberalization that is linked to international investment and globalization.

Notes

1   For different emphases, V.Y. Mudimbe, *The Idea of Africa* (Bloomington, Ind., 1994); R. Guha, *History at the Limit of World-History* (New York, 2002), V.N. Rao, D. Shulman and S. Subrahmanyam, *Textures of Time: Writing History in South India, 1600–1800* (London, 2003), and S. Subrahmanyam, 'Europe and the People without Historiography; or, Reflections on a Self-Inflicted Wound', *Historically Speaking*, vol. 5, no. 4 (Mar. 2004), 36–40.

2   A.I. Asiwaju (ed.), *Partitioned Africans: Ethnic Relations Across Africa's International Boundaries, 1884–1984* (London, 1985); W.S. Miles, *Hausaland Divided: Colonialism and Independence in Nigeria and Niger* (Ithaca, NY, 1994); A.I. Asiwaju and P. Nugent (eds), *African Boundaries: Barriers, Conduits and Opportunities* (London, 1996).

3   E. Said, *Orientalism* (London, 1978); R. Inden, *Imagining India* (Oxford, 1990).

4   R. Guha (ed.), *Subaltern Studies I: Writings on South Asian History and Society* (Delhi, 1982); R. O'Hanlon, 'Recovering the Subject: *Subaltern Studies* and Histories of Resistance in Colonial South Asia', *Modern Asian Studies*, 22 (1988), 189–224.

5   G. Bhadra, 'Four Rebels of Eighteen-Fifty-Seven', in R. Guha and G.C. Spivak (eds), *Selected Subaltern Studies* (Oxford, 1988), p. 175.

6   G. Pandey, *The Construction of Communalism in Colonial North India* (Delhi, 1990); K.N. Panikkar (ed.), *Communalism in India: History, Politics and Culture* (Delhi, 1991).

7   L. Menon, 'Coming to Terms with the Past: India', *History Today*, 54 no. 8 (Aug. 2004), 28–30.

8   D. Hume, *The History of England from the Invasion of Julius Caesar to The Revolution in 1688* (6 vols, Indianapolis, 1983), I, 3–4.

9   T. Ranger, 'The Invention of Tradition in Colonial Africa', in E. Hobsbawm and T. Ranger (eds), *The Invention of Tradition* (Cambridge, 1983), pp. 211–62; L. Vail, *The Creation of Tribalism in Southern Africa* (London, 1989); P. Yeros (ed.), *Ethnicity and Nationalism in Africa: Constructive Reflections and Contemporary Politics* (Basingstoke, 1999); C. Lentz and P. Nugent (eds), *Ethnicity in Ghana: The Limits of Invention* (Basingstoke, 2000); J.D.Y. Peel, *Religious Encounter and the Making of the Yoruba* (Bloomington, Ind., 2000).

10   I have benefited from listening to a paper on this subject by Ruth Ginio.

11   V.Y. Mudimbe, *Idea of Africa* (Bloomington, Ind., 1994); A. Mazrui, *The Africans: A Triple Heritage* (London, 1986): C.A. Di'op, *Civilization and Barbarism: An Authentic Anthropology* (Westport, Conn., 1990).

12   *Times*, 8 Oct. 2004.

13   T. Seqev, *The Seventh Million: The Israelis and the Holocaust* (New York, 1993); R. Wistrich and D. Ohana (eds), *The Shaping of Israeli Identity: Myth, Memory and Trauma* (London, 1995); N. Lochery, 'Scholarship or Propaganda: Works on Israel and the Arab-Israeli Conflict, 2001', *Middle East Studies*, 37 (2001), 219–36; R. Ovendale, *The Origins of the Arab-Israeli Wars* (4th edn, London, 2004), p. 277.

14   B. Jewsiewicki and D. Newbury (eds), *African Historiographies: What History for Which Africa?* (Beverly Hills, CA, 1986); B. Davidson, *The Black Man's Burden: Africa and the Curse of the Nation State* (London, 1992); T. Falola, *African Historiography: Essays in Honour of J.F. Ade Ajayi* (London, 1993).

15   J. Alexander, J. McGregor and T. Ranger, *Violence and Memory: One Hundred Years in the 'Dark Forests' of Matabeleland* (Portsmouth, NH, 2000).

16   T.M. Davies, 'Jorge Basadre, 1903–1980', *Hispanic American Historical Review*, 61 (1981), 84–6.

17   For an attempt to place Java in a wider context, D. Lombard, *Le Carrefour javanais: Essai d'histoire globale* (3 vols, Paris, 1990).

18   A. Reid and D. Marr (eds), *Perceptions of the Past in Southeast Asia* (Singapore, 1979).

19   A. Feuerwerker (ed.), *History in Communist China* (Cambridge, 1968).

20   R. Mitter, *A Bitter Revolution: China's Struggle with the Modern World* (Oxford, 2004), especially pp. 230–3, 309–11, 44.

21   An English translation of the full text can be found in *Beijing Review*, 6 July 1981, 10–39.

22   J. Unger (ed.), *Using the Past to Serve the Present: Historiography and Politics in Contemporary China* (Armonk, NY, 1993).

23   Y. Daqing, 'Convergence or Divergence?: Recent Historical Writings on the Rape of Nanjing', *American Historical Review*, 104 (1999), 842–65.

24   R. Mitter, 'Old Ghosts, New Memories: China's Changing War History in the Era of Post-Mao Politics', *Journal of Contemporary History*, 38 (2003), 117–31.

25   J. Powers, *History As Propaganda: Tibetan Exiles Versus the People's Republic of China* (Oxford, 2004).

26   C.F. Robinson, *Islamic Historiography* (Cambridge, 2003), p. 189.

27   R. Samuel (ed.), *Patriotism: The Making and Unmaking of British National Identity* (London, 1989); E.J. Hobsbawm, *Nations and Nationalism since 1780: Programme, Myth, Reality* (Cambridge, 1990); B. Anderson, *Imagined Communities: Reflections on the Origins and Spread of Nationalism* (2nd edn, London, 1991); R. Porter (ed.), *Myths of the English* (Cambridge, 1992); J. Breuilly (ed.), *The State of Germany: The National Idea in the Making, Unmaking and Remaking of a Modern Nation-State* (London, 1992).

28   S. Berger, 'Representations of the Past. The Writing of National Histories in Europe', *Debate: A Review of Contemporary German Affairs*, 12 (2004), 91.

29   E.g. W.H. McNeill, *The Rise of the West: A History of Human Community* (Chicago, 1963); J.H. Bentley, *Shapes of World History in Twentieth-Century Scholarship* (Washington, DC, 1996).

30   On academic developments, see S. Berger, 'Comparative History', in S. Berger, H. Feldner and K. Passmore (eds), *Writing History: Theory and Practice* (London, 2003), 161–79.

31   E. Said, *Orientalism* (London, 1978).

32   Guha, *History at the Limit of World-History*, quote, p. 73.

9

Conclusions

The search for a past with which to attempt to control the future is inseparable from human nature: it's what we mean when we say we learn from experience.
John Lewis Gaddis, *The Landscape of History. How Historians Map the Past* (Oxford, 2003), p. 143.

It may be asked where academic activity plays a role in this story of history as a focal point for cultural conflict, and how academic historians can, and should, relate to public history, in the sense of the public use of history, and also indeed to the public. An often self-referencing fascination by some historians with the technical aspects of research and, even more, epistemologies of history may appear to offer little to the latter. In practice, however, academic history has often been very reflective of public concerns, whether official or unofficial in origin. A recent example is provided by the development of environmental history as a subject in the West. This has provided a historical context to current concerns, not least the development of environmental ideas, and also carefully integrates it with global history.[1] Many modern anxieties, such as global warming, take on meaning in chronological terms, and the environmental approach also works at a supranational level.[2] Similarly, the impact of globalization has been studied, not least with the question of its threat to cultural identities.

Despite such welcome signs, a widespread interest in many scholarly circles with what passes for theory in practice accentuates the divide between the academic pursuit of the subject and public interest, and does so without reflecting much credit on the former. This is particularly so with postmodernism, one of the leading historiographical tendencies and languages in the West in the past two decades.[3] Far from historians reflecting wider cultural currents, however, popular lack of interest, incomprehension, if not dislike of postmodernism,[4] and the accompanying popular rejection of the scholarly ethos and practice of relativism, arise from a sense that postmodernism is at best opaque and possibly meaningless. Furthermore, many academics feel challenged, if not angered, by the theorists' claim that the truth cannot be ascertained,[5] and reject 'the endless deferral of meaning' they see in postmodernism.[6]

The embrace of theory can also be very off-putting. For example, an able recent attempt to take a scientific approach to historical knowledge closes a fascinating discussion of counterfactuals with the argument that the evaluation of our degrees of belief in them is similar to the 'normal Bayesian likelihood of the evidence given the hypothesis multiplied by the prior probability of the hypothesis:

$$Pr\ (H_{cf}/E') - Pr\ (E'/H_{cf}) \times Pr(H_{cf}/Bt)'.^{7}$$

Similarly, to take another area of scholarly theoretical discussion, there is scant public interest in the non-linear consequences of the application of chaos theory to history. Such approaches, and the language in which they are expressed, have little to offer public discussion of history. In contrast, aside from scholarly work, there is an extensive and commercially successful popular literature on the related and far more accessible counterfactual – 'what if' – history, and this extends to fiction, as with Len Deighton's novel *SS-GB* (1978) and Robert Harris's comparable account of Nazi success, *Fatherland* (1992), and also to television, for example *The Other Man* (1964), and film, such as *It Happened Here* (1964).[8]

More generally, there is a tension between popular and academic approaches over the role of free will, which *tends* to be emphasized more in popular than in scholarly accounts. Drawing on the social sciences, the latter usually emphasize necessity, in the form of responding to structural aspects of situations, at the expense of choice and contingency. This emphasis, however, is unwelcome to popular interests in men and moments of destiny. Instead, in the case of many official and popular accounts of history, there is a stress on the collective will, although necessity is provided by linking this to a powerful teleology of allegedly inevitable development. The contrast between academic and popular perceptions was seen with the difference between the major impact of the French *Annales* school on the academic community elsewhere, especially in Britain and the USA, and its limited impact on popular views.[9]

The discarding of Whiggish, progressive, consensual accounts of national history by scholars across the West, and the presentation of more fractured, complex discussions, are not usually welcome to the community at large. Instead, in the West, works by academics that enjoyed a widespread and favourable public response were generally those that presented an attractive, in the sense of both positive and readable, account of the national past, such as Daniel Boorstin's *The Americans: The National Experience* (1965) and *The Americans: The Democratic Experience* (1973). Boorstin himself had trained as a lawyer and became librarian of Congress, a role in which he sought to make the world of books widely accessible.[10] Attractive accounts of national history, particularly national exceptionalism, were in turn, however, attacked from the 1960s in academic circles, themselves increasingly specialized, as complacent. Later, in response to this criticism of progressive, consensual accounts in the USA and elsewhere, there has come a more positive probing of the national perspective on the part of some scholars, although its relationship with academic fashion is often distant.[11]

Interpretations of particular issues have also reflected political circumstances and changes. This can be seen with American work on the origins of the Cold War, a key issue as far as the legitimacy of American foreign policy was concerned. Scholarship in the 1950s stressed Soviet aggression as the cause of the Cold War but, in the 1960s, there was a revisionist reaction that emphasized American responsibility, the expansion of American capital (finance) being linked to that of American power. This was a reaction to the perception of the USA as an imperial state, and was linked to bitter criticism of America's participation in the Vietnam War. In turn, in the 1980s, the post-revisionists returned to the themes of the 1950s, although this time with the added benefit of archival research. This shift was related to the renewed concern about current Soviet policies seen from the aggressive Soviet intervention in Afghanistan in December 1979 and associated with the Reagan presidency (1981–9).[12]

In the early 2000s, America's role in the Cold War remained contentious, not least with disputes over the reputation of traitors.[13] Academic debates over responsibility for the Cold War and over its consequences continued, although in public policy terms the conservative interpretation of the Cold War as a necessary and successful struggle was taken for granted by the Bush government. A defence of the Cold War and a view of American participation in it as successful helped vindicate government policy.[14] On the left, however, critics remained unconvinced, as with the remark that the Cold War 'was provoked amid a 1940s battle by U.S. capital and the U.S. government for global economic access to labor and commodity markets'.[15] The perception of the USA in the early 2000s as an imperial state also controversially affected accounts of earlier American history.[16]

177

A major divide between public interest and academic fashion relates to objectivity. The possibility of objectivity is assumed in popular history and in accounts by, and on behalf of, states but, within the scholarly community, has been widely criticized in the 'linguistic turn' in historiography. Drawing on notions of 'deconstruction', this 'turn' has put the nature of language foremost, arguing that documents and texts do not provide an accurate representation of reality and that the objective search for truth is an impossibility. An academic fascination with the past in terms of texts that need deciphering, and with both historian and reader as constrained by language and the values it encodes, leads to the conclusion that the past is constructed and history but a shifting account of this construction, which encourages partly fictionalized accounts of the past or 'faction'. Objective narrative becomes impossible, as the past cannot be shaped accurately and as causality can only be a suggestion.[17]

Such a conviction does not make for attractive, in the sense of readily accessible, accounts. The distinction between fluent accounts written for popular markets and more dense, scholarly accounts for academic counterparts was, however, at least in theory, in part subverted as in the New Historicism, some of the latter presented history as a form of literary study,[18] although rarely, if ever, in a clearly written or accessible manner. Unsurprisingly, these are arguments and treatments that find few echoes outside the academic community, and indeed are not invariably accepted within it.

At the same time as these arguments were, and are, advanced, much academic history continues to focus on empirically grounded scholarship. This offers the objectivity sought in popular history but, frequently, this scholarship also reveals a complexity and an understanding of past values that does not match modern popular concerns, nor the presentist habit of seeing the past like the present, and the related pressure for a new public history that wears its heart clearly on its sleeve. A good example is provided by military executions during the First World War. These were far less common than is generally appreciated (and than was the case overall in the Second World War), but they have been frequently discussed, and portrayed in the media, as outrages, and there has been pressure in Britain for government apologies for the 361 British military executions during the First World War, while a successful French film of 2004 dealt with their French counterparts. The scholarly point that these executions were primarily motivated by considerations of discipline is of scant interest to those calling for apologies,[19] and, more generally, the lack of interest in context is a feature of the call for apologies, most of which is seriously ahistorical, as with German pressure for British apologies for the Second World War bombing.

Public history is indeed important to the standard accounts of historiography, but academics usually devote far more weight to intellectual movements. This is part of a more widespread problem of ranking in importance, one that also places the focus on these movements at the expense of other considerations such as the formative role of the economics of publishing on what is published. In short, there is an idealist approach to historiography, and this is one that can regard consideration of philosophical issues focusing on the recovery of truth or the creation of 'truths' as more significant than the hard work of actually considering what is taught in classrooms or published in popular works. Linked to this is a structuring of relations within the historical profession, with those who focus on historiography sometimes claiming what is akin to a higher purpose when compared to colleagues working on empirical topics.

Aside from this scholarly stance, there is the more general question of the reputation of academic historians outside the profession. The decline of the academic in British public culture[20] may well prefigure similar developments in the position of public intellectuals elsewhere in the West, and a crisis in higher education was discerned in other states in the early 2000s, for example Germany. As a result of the extent of governmental indebtedness at the level of individual states and possible future crises in public finances, trouble may follow for the public sector in the USA. In recent decades, the idea of the intellectual and the institutional autonomy of universities gave academic historians a measure of independence, but this is declining. Irrespective of this, in contrast to the modern Western academic self-image, with its emphasis on freedom of thought,[21] the role of the academic as the servant of the state is more important across much of the world. It is likely that this role will become more significant in the future, especially if economic and political power increasingly focus in East and South Asia, particularly in China where academics depend on public funding and operate under the threat of censorship within a context in which the goal and content of most historical research and teaching are very sensitive.

This raises anew the question of the wider typicality of the relationship between academic and public histories in the West, and thus of the possibility of global criteria for historiography. This issue can be clearly seen in debates over the relationship between nationalism and objectivity. Whereas scholars in the West divide over the possibility of the latter, specifically of recovering the past (frequently debating the issue in a fashion that means little to the general public), they generally subscribe to a desire to avoid nationalistic partisanship that, however, means little in many states across the world. There, such partisanship is seen as an aspect of a necessary and welcome commitment to national identity.

The shift of public history on the global scale will in part be driven by global demographics. Ninety-five per cent of the world's population increase is taking place in the developing world, while the indigenous (non-immigrant) population of most of Europe is declining in numbers, with consequences in the long term for the relative import-ance of education. It is in the developing world that the pressures to provide a public history will seem most acute. Indeed, the volatility of these societies, with the relatively large percentage of the population under 25, the impact of urbanization and industrialization, the break-down of patterns of deference and social control, and pressures on established networks, identities and systems of explanation, are such that there will appear to be particular need for the development and exposition of unifying national myths. It is to this that we should devote most attention. It will be both interesting and important to see how dynamic societies come to grips with their recent and more distant past, and this will probably be the most significant aspect of historiog-raphy over the next century.

It is not likely, however, that this will be at the forefront of Western concerns for, alongside greater interest in globalization and in other world historical interpretations,[22] there is also a considerable resistance to such interest. This can be seen in the varied academic strategies rep-resented by student syllabi, academic research plans and university hirings. Indeed, the decline in foreign language skills across much of the West, especially in both the USA and Britain, is possibly responsible for a focus on postgraduate research on national history, and this emphasis is also true of France, Germany and Spain. Cost also plays a role, as the emphasis on empirical research as the core skill in post-graduate training helps encourage anew a focus on national history. Aside from the strength of native historiographical traditions, collec-tive memorialization and other aspects of the public perception of, and interest in, the past tend to lack a global dimension. Instead, the strength of both nation state and ethnic consciousness are readily apparent at this level.

Globalization, nevertheless, will play a greater role in Western histor-ical teaching and research but, within Western institutions, will largely be, as it is at present, globalization understood as links between the West and other parts of the world. Other aspects of the question will be harder to recover and will not receive comparable attention, although one source of possible change is the hiring of scholars of non-Western origins, especially Indians, to teach in American universities, while interest in East Asian history is stronger there than it was 50 years ago.

At the global level, public history in the West will be expected to provide answers to current and likely challenges. The most important current challenges that are the subject of such history are terrorism and Muslim-Christian relations. Neither of them can be readily explained in terms of the hierarchical assumptions voiced a century ago, because the religious and ethnic constructions that were aspects of Western public history are contested and are no longer regarded across much of the political spectrum as appropriate. This creates major problems as Western states struggle to come to terms with new definitions of citizenship and with new international issues.

Radical Islamists themselves offer an account of past and present that focuses not on the state, which can be regarded as decadent, but on a vanguard of true believers willing to wage holy war against non-Muslims, just as their predecessors have allegedly done. The resulting history collapses time in order to put past jihads alongside the present one.[23] This can be regarded as ahistorical, but such ahistoricism helps account for the energy of commitment and comparison. Furthermore, relations between the West and Islam are historicized in an ongoing process in which new events, such as the invasion of Iraq in 2003, at once become key historical locators for debate. This is not the perspective of all Muslims. An indication of the attempt by moderate elements to provide an account of cooperation was the guide *Muslims in Britain* published in 2004 by the Moslem Council of Britain and the Foreign and Commonwealth Office. This suggested that Muslims had been in Britain in some form since the eighth century, providing an instance of the degree to which longevity is held to support acceptability.

From a very different perspective, the role of historical scholarship, but also the slant placed upon it, was indicated in April 2004 when Paul Wolfowitz, the deputy secretary in the American Department of Defence and a key architect of American foreign policy in the Middle East, specifically the war with Iraq, made a presentation to the annual conference of the Society of Military History, held that year in Bethesda, near Washington. Asked what was the history book that had influenced him most, Wolfowitz replied Bernard Lewis's *The Emergence of Modern Turkey* (1961), with its account of the successful introduction of modernization in a Muslim country. The use by Wolfowitz of one instance in order to draw a lesson for another context, Iraq in 2003–4, was seriously misleading because in Turkey change was driven through by an internal force – the government of Kemal Atatürk – and the latter's legitimacy in part rested on defying the intervention of foreign powers, which helped provide the foundation myth of modern Turkey.

In turn, the invasion of Iraq indicated the variety of historical analogies that could be employed. Paul Bremer, who, as head of the Coalition Provisional Authority, served as American viceroy in Iraq in 2003–4, a historian by training, used the post-1945 American occupation of part of Germany as his model. His briefing book included a chart 'Milestones: Iraq and Germany' that laid out the handover of institutions during the 1945–52 occupation with corresponding plans for Iraq so that, as Bremer declared in January 2004, he could 'keep track of where we are versus Germany'. Indeed, documents from the earlier period were used as templates, on one occasion failing to change Reichsmark to dinar. The analogy with Germany was frequently cited by officials in the Bush administration.[24] In April 2002, Condoleeza Rice, the national security advisor, declared that the USA had entered 'a period akin to 1945 to 47, when American leadership expanded the number of free and democratic states, Japan and Germany among them, to create a new balance of power that favored freedom'. All comparisons invite criticism, but this was scarcely an apposite model: the Nazi and Imperial Japanese regimes formally surrendered in 1945, bringing resistance to a close, and the societies and public cultures of Germany and Japan were very different to those in Iraq in 2003. Meanwhile, critics of the Iraq invasion and occupation of Iraq referred to America's unsuccessful involvement in Vietnam as the appropriate model, again without sufficiently considering contrasts.

Foreign relations will not be the sole topic of future public history. Instead, it is most likely that the emphasis will continue to be on the assertion of national identities within states: by, or against, their governments. This will continue to be the key issue in memorialization and will also be central in education. The tension between support for, and opposition to, existing states will probably grow in importance as the fissiparous character of human society is accentuated by the consequences of democratization. A parallel can be found with consumerism, one of the great driving forces of history over the last half-century. It has grown in importance as state socialism has been discredited, and can also be related to globalization, especially in encouraging a willingness to purchase foreign or foreign-type products. If consumerism encourages a political individualism in which people choose their own allegiances and identities, and also change their choices, then this poses grave difficulties for all governments.

An obvious response, especially in authoritarian systems, will be increased quantities of the attempted indoctrination that is a key aspect of public history. This option will also be seen in democratic societies, although it will be presented as public education. Indeed, education in citizenship, a theme pushed hard in the 2000s, for example in Britain and Australia, is in part a response to the belief that the public sense of history and identity is insecure, and that this provides an opportunity for divisive, indeed fissiparous, tendencies: a breakdown of collective consciousness apparently leading to sectionalism and sectarianism.

The issue is also bound up with anxieties over immigration and Muslim separatism and the challenges these pose to practices of citizenship. Public history thus becomes an aspect of acculturation.

This is also an issue in the USA. On 20 June 2003, the American History and Civics Education Bill passed the Senate by a vote of 90 to zero. The bill created a National Alliance of Teachers of American History and Civics and founded summer residential academies for students and teachers. Its prime sponsor, Senator Lamar Alexander, declared

> This legislation will help put the teaching of American history and civics back in its rightful place in our schools, so our children can grow up learning what it means to be an American . . . When our values are under attack we need to understand clearly what those values are. And second, we should understand what unites us as Americans.

Education was linked to values, the legislation being intended 'to inspire better teaching and more learning of the key events, documents, persons and ideas that shaped the institutions and democratic heritage of the United States'. Those who received grants should plan programmes stressing the theme of 'unity amidst variety and diversity'. Alexander, a Republican, was open about his support for what he termed 'the traditional kind' of history: 'the study of the key persons, the key events, the key ideas, and the key documents that shape the institutions and democratic heritage' of the United States. History and 'civics' were therefore to be linked. This was not the sole proposal or programme seeking to develop and frame the teaching of American history in order to support civic awareness and national identity. Such ideas were also important in the National Endowment for the Humanities' 'We the People' programme and the Department of Education's 'Teaching American History' equivalent. Thus, in July 2003, hosting a conference on teaching American history, Rod Paige, the Secretary of Education, repeated the dictum that teachers were 'creators of democracy'.

Public access to the past had in fact been greatly enhanced by technological developments. The miniaturization of electronic components made it possible to create complete electronic circuits on a small slice of silicon. The Intel 4004, the first microprocessor chip, was created in the USA in 1971. Gordon Moore, the co-founder of the company responsible, predicted a dramatic revolution in capability as the result of the doubling of the computing power on chips every eighteen months. Initially, in the absence of miniaturization, computers were an industrial product, of great scale and cost, but from the late

1970s they became widely available as office and then household tools. Improvements in capability ensured that computing power became cheaper and thus more accessible. In the 1970s, fibre-optic cables increased the capacity of cable systems and the volume of telephone and computer messages they could carry. The growing number of personal computers facilitated access to the Internet, and the number of people with Internet access in the world rose to about 130 million in 1998, with nearly half in the USA. As the pace of change accelerated, so the consequences included a partial democratization of scholarship. The ability of academics to act as priests of Clio (the muse of history), or as intercessors with past wisdom, never in fact very strong, was further lessened. Academics complained about the degree to which students preferred to take information (and often plagiarize material) from the Internet, rather than use books or lectures, while many who were not students created historical opinion and fostered pseudo-histories through Internet sites. The coming of the digital archive will accentuate this process.

The questions raised by such issues challenge the established patterns, or at least power structures, of Western historical scholarship. Furthermore, from another direction, there is a scholarly challenge because other academic specialisms also seek to offer answers to, and from, the past. Historical sociology is one such. It requires historical data, not least for the comparative methodology it frequently adopts,[25] but there is an important contrast between a sociological use of the past as a data set and the academic historical attempt to understand contingent specificities and the impact of time.

These are not simply abstract issues. Instead, an awareness of the impact of historical loyalties and interests has become more important since the end of the Cold War. The issue of Muslim-Christian relations has been especially salutary in directing attention to the presentation of the past, because most Western academic and public histories have devoted far too little attention to the communal role of religion, regarding it as a product of other structures and pressures, especially social ones, and indeed as something from the past. Acceptance now of the importance of religious identity has encouraged a focus far more on the present and future legacy of the past than would have been anticipated 20 years ago. In short, in place of the putative Death of the Past or the alleged End of History,[26] both of which were mistakenly discerned and asserted in the 1980s and 1990s, there has come a revival of the past as a crucial definition for current identities and issues.

Where the past is rejected that itself is because of its connotations, and thus is an aspect of the influence of history. For example, in Chile's presidential election campaign in 1999, the conservative candidate,

Joaquin Lavin, stated that General Pinochet, the conservative military dictator from 1973 to 1990, 'belongs to the past and we have to look to the future'. In short, in his view individuals (and policies) were to be defined with reference to how they stood on a historical continuum, and only the present and future was of relevance. The particular circumstances of Chile, particularly of the Chilean right, keen to distance itself from a brutal dictatorship, explained Lavin's remarks, but around the world there is a similar emphasis on the future as progress and modernity are generally (although not invariably) seen as praiseworthy, although they are also usually located by reference to a presentation of the past.

Many politicians also claim that they will be vindicated by history, by which they mean future views of the present world. This was Hitler's conviction,[27] and was also argued, in a very different context, by both Tony Blair and George W. Bush in justifying their Iraq policy of 2003–4. Visiting London in November 2004, their most vocal high-ranking critic, President Chirac of France, declared 'History will judge whether France was right to oppose the war in Iraq or not.' Conversely, there is also anxiety on the part of some politicians that history will condemn them. In 1944, as Britain responded to Soviet demands on Poland's frontiers, Anthony Eden, the Foreign Secretary, asked 'If I give way over Lviv, shall I go down in the history books as an appeaser?' Soviet strength, in the shape of the advancing Red Army, helped ensure that Lviv indeed became part of the Soviet Union, but as part of what is now the independent state of Ukraine. As a result, its official place in history has changed considerably.[28] Reputations, both individual and collective, positive and negative, play a major role in public history. Partly neglected, this is a subject that richly repays attention.

Notes

1   A. Crosby, *The Columbian Exchange: Biological and Cultural Consequences of 1492* (Westport, Conn., 1972).

2   I.G. Simmons, *Environmental History: A Concise Introduction* (Oxford, 1993).

3   B. Southgate, *Postmodernism in History: Fear or Freedom?* (London, 2003).

4   A. Munslow, *The New History* (London, 2003). The extensive literature includes K. Jenkins, *The Postmodern History Reader* (London, 1997).

5   P. Novick, *That Noble Dream: The 'Objectivity Question' and the American Historical Profession* (Cambridge, 1988).

6   P.C. Perdue, 'Culture, History, and Imperial Chinese Strategy: Legacies of the Qing Conquests', in H. van de Ven (ed.), *Warfare in Chinese History* (Leiden, 2000), p. 286.

7   A. Tucker, *Our Knowledge of the Past: A Philosophy of Historiography* (Cambridge, 2004), p. 231.

8   P.E. Tetlock and A. Belkin (eds), *Counterfactual Thought Experiments in World Politics: Logical, Methodological, and Psychological Perspectives* (Princeton, NJ, 1996); N. Ferguson (ed.), *Virtual History: Alternatives and Counterfactuals* (London, 1997); A. Roberts (ed.), *What Might Have Been* (London, 2004); G. Rosenfeld, *The World Hitler Never Made: Alternative History and the Memory of Nazism* (Cambridge, 2005).

9   P. Burke, *The French Historical Revolution: The 'Annales' School, 1929–1989* (Stanford, CA, 1990); J.A. Marino, 'The Exile and His Kingdom: The Reception of Braudel's *Mediterranean*', *Journal of Modern History*, 76 (2004), 622–52.

10 D. Boorstin, *The Daniel Boorstin Reader* (New York, 1996).

11 J.P. Diggins, *The Liberal Persuasion: Arthur Schlesinger, Jr., and the Challenge of the American Past* (Princeton, NJ, 1997).

12 A.M. Schlesinger, Jr., 'Origins of the Cold War', *Foreign Affairs*, 46 (1967), 22–52; R.J. Maddox, *The New Left and the Origins of the Cold War* (Princeton, 1973); J.L. Gaddis, *We Now Know: Rethinking Cold War History* (Oxford, 1997).

13 For an example of pointed criticism, R.M. Platt review of R.B. Craig's *Treasonable Doubt: The Harry Dexter White Spy Case* (Lawrence, Kan., 2004), in *History. Reviews of New Books*, 33 no. 1 (Autumn 2004), 7.

14 C. Eisenberg, 'The Old Cold War', *Diplomatic History*, 28 (2004), 799.

15 N. Smith, *American Empire: Roosevelt's Geography and the Prelude to Globalization* (Berkeley, CA, 2003), p. 21.

16 A.J. Bacevich, *American Empire: The Realities and Consequences of U.S. Diplomacy* (Cambridge, Mass., 2002); D. Harvey, *The New Imperialism* (New York, 2003); N. Ferguson, *Colossus: The Price of America's Empire* (New York, 2004); A. Johnson, *Blowback: The Costs and Consequences of American Empire* (2nd edn, New York, 2004).

17 H. White, *The Content of the Form: Narrative Form and Historical Representation* (Baltimore, 1987); K. Jenkins, *Re-Thinking History* (London, 1991) and *On 'What Is History?': From Carr and Elton to Rorty and White* (London, 1995).

18 T. Brook, *The New Historicism and Other Old-Fashioned Topics* (Princeton, NJ, 1991).

19 G. Oram, *Military Executions During World War I* (London, 2003).

20 A.H. Halsey, *Decline of Donnish Dominion* (Oxford, 1992).

21 B. Bailyn, *On the Teaching and Writing of History* (Hanover, NH, 1994), p. 12.

22 P. Manning, *Navigating World History: Historians Create a Global Past* (London, 2003).

23 J. Calvert, 'The Mythic Foundations of Radical Islam', *Orbis*, 48 (2004), 38–40.

24 M. Hirsh, 'How Will We Know When We Can Finally Leave?', *Washington Post*, 26 Sept. 2004.

25 B. Roehner and T. Syme, *Pattern and Repertoire in History* (Cambridge, Mass., 2002), e.g. p. 367.

26 F. Fukuyama, *The End of History and the Last Man* (London, 1992).

27 I. Kershaw, *Hitler, 1936–1945: Nemesis* (London, 2000), pp. 821–2.

28 T. Snyder, *The Reconstruction of Nations: Poland, Ukraine, Lithuania, Belarus, 1569–1999* (New Haven, Conn., 2003). For the gazetteer of variant spellings, p. xi.

Selected further reading

B. Anderson, *Imagined Communities: Reflections on the Origins and Spread of Nationalism* (2nd edn, London, 1991).

J. Appleby, L. Hunt and M. Jacob, *Telling the Truth about History* (New York, 1994).

J. Armstrong, *Nations before Nationalism* (Chapel Hill, NC, 1982).

J. Arnold, *History: A Very Short Introduction* (Oxford, 2000).

W. Arnstein (ed.), *Recent Historians of Great Britain: Essays on the Post-1945 Generation* (Ames, Ia., 1990).

T. Bender, P.M. Katz, C. Palmer and the AHA Committee on Graduate Education, *The Education of Historians for the Twenty-first Century* (Urbana, Ill., 2004).

C. Berger, *The Writing of Canadian History: Aspects of English-Canadian Historical Writing since 1900* (2nd edn, Toronto, 1986).

S. Berger, *The Search for Normality: National Identity and Historical Consciousness in Germany since 1800* (Oxford, 1997).

S. Berger, M. Donovan and K. Passmore (eds), *Writing National Histories: Western Europe since 1800* (London, 1999).

J. Blatti (ed.), *Past Meets Present: Essays about Historic Interpretation and Public Audiences* (Washington, DC, 1987).

R.J.B. Bosworth, *Exploring Auschwitz and Hiroshima: History Writing and the Second World War, 1945–1990* (London, 1993).

K. Boyd (ed.), *Encyclopedia of Historians and Historical Writing* (London, 1999).

C. Brady (ed.), *Interpreting Irish History: The Debate on Historical Revisionism* (Dublin, 1994).

P. Burke, *The French Historical Revolution: The 'Annales' School, 1929–1989* (Stanford, Calif., 1990).

N. Cantor, *Inventing the Middle Ages: The Lives, Works, and Ideas of the Great Medievalists of the Twentieth Century* (New York, 1991).

E.H. Carr, *What is History?* (2nd edn, Basingstoke, 2001).

S. Collini, *English Pasts: Essays in History and Culture* (Oxford, 1999).

J. Collins, *Understanding Tolowa Histories: Western Hegemonies and Native American Responses* (London, 1998).

P. Costello, *World Historians and Their Goals: Twentieth-Century Answers to Modernism* (Dekalb, Ill., 1993).

A. De Baets, *Censorship of History Thought: A World Guide, 1945–2000* (Westport, Conn., 2002).

D. Deletant and H. Hanak (eds), *Historians as Nation-Builders: Central and South-East Europe* (London, 1988).

C. Diaran (ed.), *Interpreting Irish History: The Debate on Historical Revisionism, 1938–94* (Dublin, 1994).

M. Diaz-Andreu and T. Champion (eds), *Nationalism and Archaeology in Europe* (London, 1976).

G.R. Elton, *The Future of the Past* (Cambridge, 1984).

L. Eriksonas, *National Heroes and National Identities: Scotland, Norway and Lithuania* (Brussels, 2004).

R.J. Evans, *In Defence of History* (2nd edn, London, 2004).

J. Fogel (ed.), *The Nanjing Massacre in History and Historiography* (Berkeley, CA 2000).

E. Fox-Genovese and E. Lasch-Quinn (eds), *Reconstructing History: The Emergence of a New Historical Society* (London, 1999).

M. Frisch, *A Shared Authority: Essays on the Craft and Meaning of Oral and Public History* (Albany, NY, 1990).

E. Fuchs and B. Stuchtey (eds), *Across Cultural Borders: Historiography in Global Perspective* (Lanham, Md., 2002).

F. Furet, *Interpreting the French Revolution* (Cambridge, 1981).

J.L. Gaddis, *The Landscape of History: How Historians Map the Past* (Oxford, 2003).

J.B. Gardner and P.S. LaPaglia (eds), *Public History: Essays from the Field* (Malabar, Fla., 1999).

P. Gatahercole and D. Lowenthal (eds), *The Politics of the Past* (London, 1976).

R. Gildea, *The Past in French History* (New Haven, Conn., 1994).

P. Grimsted, *Trophies of War and Empire: The Archival Heritage of Ukraine, World War II, and the International Politics of Restitution* (Cambridge, Mass., 2001).

G. Himmelfarb, *The New History and the Old: Critical Essays and Reappraisals* (2nd edn, Cambridge, Mass., 1987).

History and Theory (1961–)

E. Hobsbawm, *On History* (London, 2002).

E. Hobsbawm and T. Ranger (eds), *The Invention of Tradition* (Cambridge, 1983).

R. Hofstadter, *The Progressive Historians: Turner, Beard, Parrington* (New York, 1968).

B.J. Howe and E.L. Kent, *Public History: An Introduction* (Malabar, Fla., 1986).

H.S. Hughes, *History as Art and as Science: Twin Vistas of the Past* (Chicago, 1975).

G.G. Iggers, *The German Conception of History: The National Tradition of Historical Thought from Herder to the Present* (2nd edn, Middleton, Conn., 1983).

G.G. Iggers, *Historiography in the Twentieth Century: From Scientific Objectivity to the Postmodern Challenge* (Middleton, Conn., 1997).

M. Ignatieff, *Blood and Belonging: Journeys into the New Nationalism* (New York, 1993).

K. Jenkins, *Re-Thinking History* (London, 1991).

L. Jordanova, *History in Practice* (London, 2000).

R.D. Kaplan, *Balkan Ghosts: A Journey Through History* (New York, 1996).

H. Kean, *London Stories: Personal Lives, Public Histories* (London, 2004).

H. Kean, P. Martin and S. Morgan (eds), *Seeing History: Public History in Britain Now* (London, 2000).

J.P. Kenyon, *The History Men: The Historical Profession in England since the Renaissance* (2nd edn, London, 1993).

P. Lambert and P. Schofield (eds), *Making History: An Introduction to the History and Practices of a Discipline* (London, 2004).

W. Lamont (ed.), *Historical Controversies and Historians* (London, 1998).

W. Laqueur and G.L. Mosse (eds), *Historians in Politics* (London, 1974).

P.K. Leffler and S. Brent (eds), *Public History Readings* (Malabar, Fla., 1992).

H. Lehman and J. Van Horn Melton (eds), *Paths of Continuity: Central European Historiography from the 1930s to the 1950s* (Cambridge, 1994).

B. Lewis, *History Remembered, Recovered, Invented* (Princeton, NJ, 1975).

D. Lowenthal, *The Past is a Foreign Country* (Cambridge, 1985).

J. Lukacs, *Historical Consciousness or the Remembered Past* (New York, 1968).

P. Mandler, *History and National Life* (London, 2002).

G. Marsden, *The Outrageous Idea of Christian Scholarship* (Oxford, 1997).

C. Martin (ed.), *The American Indian and the Problem of History* (Oxford, 1987).

S. Mellon, *The Political Uses of History* (Palo Alto, CA, 1958).

F. Meyer and J.E. Myhre (eds), *Nordic Historiography in the Twentieth Century* (Oslo, 2000).

A. Molho and G.S. Wood (eds), *Imagined Histories: American Historians Interpret their Past* (Princeton, NJ, 1998).

P. Novick, *That Noble Dream: The 'Objective Question' and the American Historical Profession* (Cambridge, 1988).

J. Powers, *History As Propaganda: Tibetan Exiles versus the People's Republic of China* (Oxford, 2004).

R. Preiswerk and D. Perrot, *Ethnocentricism and History: Africa, Asia and Indian America in Western Textbooks* (New York, 1978).

V.N. Rao, D. Shulman and S. Subrahmanyam, *Textures of Time: Writing History in South India, 1600–1800* (London, 2003).

A. Reid and D. Marr (eds), *Perceptions of the Past in Southeast Asia* (Singapore, 1979)

M. Restall, *Seven Myths of the Spanish Conquest* (Oxford, 2003).

J. Revel and G. Levi (eds), *Political Uses of the Past: The Recent Mediterranean Experience* (London, 2002).

J. Rüsen (ed.), *Western Historical Thinking: An Intercultural Debate* (Oxford, 2002).

R. Samuel (ed.), *History Workshop: A Collectanea, 1967–1991* (London, 1991).

R. Samuel, *Theatres of Memory* (London, 1994).

R. Samuel, *Island Stories: Unravelling Britain* (London, 1998).

W. Schivelbusch, *The Culture of Defeat: On National Trauma, Mourning, and Recovery* (London, 2003).

J.W. Scott, *Gender and the Politics of History* (2nd edn, New York, 1999).

C. Shaw and M. Chase (eds), *The Imagined Past: History and Nostalgia* (Manchester, 1989).

A.D. Smith, *The Ethnic Origins of Nations* (Oxford, 1986).

B. Smith, *The Gender of History: Men, Women, and Historical Practice* (Cambridge, Mass., 1996).

T. Snyder, *The Reconstruction of Nations: Poland, Ukraine, Lithuania, Belarus, 1569–1999* (New Haven, 2003).

B. Stuchtey and E. Fuchs (eds), *Writing World History 1800–2000* (Oxford, 2003).

B. Stuchtey and P. Wende (eds), *British and German Historiography 1750–1950* (Oxford, 2000).

R. Thorstendahl (ed.), *An Assessment of Twentieth-Century Historiography: Professionalism, Methodologies, Writings* (Stockholm, 2000).

J. Tosh (ed.), *Historians on History* (3rd edn, Harlow, 2000).

D. Tyler (ed.), *Red Men and Hat-Wearers: Viewpoints in Indian [Native American] History* (Fort Collins, Col., 1976).

I. Tyrell, *The Absent Marx: Class Analysis and Liberal History in Twentieth-Century America* (Westport, Conn., 1980).

J. Unger (ed.), *Using the Past to Serve the Present: Historiography and Politics in Contemporary China* (Armonk, NY, 1993).

J. Vansina, *Oral Traditions As History* (London, 1985).

A. Walls, *The Cross-Cultural Process in Christian History: Studies in the Transmission and Appropriation of Faith* (London, 2002).

H. White, *Metahistory: The Historical Imagination in Nineteenth-Century Europe* (Baltimore, MD, 1973).

G. Wise, *American Historical Explanations: A Strategy for Grounded Inquiry* (Homewood, Ill., 1973).

D.R. Woolf (ed.), *A Global Encyclopedia of Historical Writing* (2 vols, London, 1998).

Index